The Phraseology of Administrative French

LANGUAGE AND COMPUTERS: STUDIES IN PRACTICAL LINGUISTICS

No 57

edited by
Christian Mair
Charles F. Meyer
Nelleke Oostdijk

The Phraseology of Administrative French

A Corpus-based Study

Wendy J. Anderson

Rodopi

Amsterdam - New York, NY 2006

Cover design: Pier Post

Online access is included in print subscriptions:
see www.rodopi.nl

The paper on which this book is printed meets the requirements of "ISO 9706:1994, Information and documentation - Paper for documents - Requirements for permanence".

ISBN-10: 90-420-2022-9
ISBN-13: 978-90-420-2022-1

Printed in The Netherlands

Contents

List of Tables and Figures

Acknowledgements

In the summer of 1997, over the time of the Amsterdam meeting of the European Council which agreed the Treaty of Amsterdam, I completed a three-month *stage* in the English Translation Division of the General Secretariat of the Council of Ministers, carrying out translation and terminology work. Over the course of that summer, in working daily with EU French, English and Spanish, the linguistic idiosyncrasies of EU language and the complexity of linguistic issues in the EU became increasingly clear to me. I should like to thank everyone in the English Translation Division, especially St Clair Stewart, for making that experience possible.

I carried out the research described in this book between 1998 and 2002 for my PhD at the University of St Andrews in Scotland. Many people and organisations contributed in different ways to this work, and I am grateful to all of them. My biggest debt is to my supervisors, Dr Christopher Gledhill, who first introduced me to corpus linguistics, and Dr Clive Sneddon. The book has subsequently benefited from advice from the two examiners, Professor Anthony Lodge (University of St Andrews) and Professor Raphael Salkie (University of Brighton). A number of other researchers, among them subscribers to the Corpora, Baalmail, Francofil, and LinguistList mailing lists, also helped me by generously taking the time to reply to various queries over the years.

My PhD research was carried out with the financial aid of a Caledonian Research Foundation Studentship and a Rubric Translation Award for Postgraduate Students. I am extremely grateful to both organisations, and also to the French and Spanish departments of the University of St Andrews for giving me the opportunity to teach a variety of courses throughout my time as a doctoral student, several of them on subjects related to this research.

Midway through my research, I was delighted to find that corpus linguistics features in a work of fiction. The quotations at the beginning of each chapter are taken from *Small World* by David Lodge, published by Secker & Warburg. These are reprinted by permission of the Random House Group Ltd. (excluding USA), and reproduced with permission of Curtis Brown Group Ltd, London on behalf of David Lodge © David Lodge 1984 (USA).

I would also like to thank Nelleke Oostdijk, one of the series editors, for her many helpful comments on the manuscript, and Eric van Broekhuizen at Rodopi for dealing so efficiently with my naïve queries.

My final expression of gratitude here must go to my parents and friends, and, for his love and encouragement throughout the process of writing both the thesis and the book, to Kenneth Austin.

Preface

'I'd like to take you over to our Computer Centre this afternoon', he said. 'We've got something set up for you that I think you'll find interesting.' He was sort of twitching in his seat with excitement as he said it, like a kid who can't wait to unwrap his Christmas presents.

DAVID LODGE, SMALL WORLD: AN ACADEMIC ROMANCE

Sociolinguistics assumes that a change in context implies changes in the language produced, indeed a co-variation of linguistic and social phenomena (see Trudgill 1995, p. 13). This is true for code-switching between languages, such as in diglossic situations, and variation within a single language, owing to differences in the surrounding context. At its most fundamental level, the research described here puts this assumption to the test with relation to a particular context, and a particular level of language: the phraseology of the register of European Union administrative French.

The European Union's predecessor, the European Economic Community, was established in 1957 by the Treaty of Rome. It is therefore now nearly fifty years old. This is an appropriate time to consider the discourse of the EU from a descriptive linguistic perspective. Neither the EEC nor its associated language varieties, however, were created ex nihilo: rather France, and French, had an important part to play in its genesis, and continue to, despite the EU's increasingly complex linguistic make-up. Only six member states signed the original Treaty of Rome, and this required only four working languages.[1] The texts drawn on for this research date from the late 1990s, a time when the number of members states was fifteen, and there were eleven working languages.[2] Today there are twenty-five member states, and a total of twenty official languages.[3] This is not the first time that the register of administrative language has found itself in a situation of language contact: in thirteenth-century England, for

---

1 The original Six were Belgium, France, Germany, Italy, Luxembourg and the Netherlands, and the original languages Dutch, French, German and Italian.

2 In addition to the Six, these were Denmark, Ireland, the United Kingdom (accession 1973), Greece (1981), Spain and Portugal (1986), Austria, Finland and Sweden (1995). These enlargements entailed the adoption of Danish, English, Greek, Spanish, Portuguese, Finnish and Swedish as working and official languages and Irish as an official language only.

3 In 2004, Cyprus, the Czech Republic, Estonia, Hungary, Latvia, Lithuania, Malta, Poland, Slovakia and Slovenia joined the Union. All new accessions except Cyprus brought with them one new official language.

example, there was a trilingual contact situation of Anglo-Norman French, English and Latin. The complexity of the current EU situation, however, is unique, continually in flux, and as a result linguistically fascinating.

The ways in which, and the extent to which, the new discourse of European Union French has come to diverge from its national counterpart are the main interests of this study. This should not be understood to imply that all change will necessarily have been on the part of the EU discourse alone: rather we must also allow for the French national administrative discourse to have adapted to reflect the deepening role of the EU. Institutional change, reflecting political change, has resulted in modifications to both varieties of administrative discourse. In other words, the EU discourse can be said to have a level of autonomy sufficient for it to have a reciprocal effect on its primary source discourse. This research necessarily also highlights similarities between the two discourses, features which might be seen to be common to the administrative register as a whole, regardless of national context. This in turn implies some comparison with the "general language" – an inherently vague concept – or at least other registers of French. This study is therefore primarily a contribution to the description of the register of administration.

The language of administration, along with the language of business, the regional dialects of French, colloquial language and slang, is often the target of French prescriptive attitudes: to take just one example here, it has been affected by legislation against the use of anglicisms. Hand in hand with prescriptivism has gone a belief that the standard, literary, language is superior to other dialects and registers. Although the balance in this respect has now started to change, this view is still perpetuated even today and can be seen in the composition of many large French text corpora with their bias towards literary language. While administrative language is generally considered to be a prestige variety, indeed one which has a notable influence on the general language, it has been criticised on many other fronts: it is often perceived as obscure, excessively conservative and representative of undesirable bureaucratic red-tape. This is also true for the French of the European Union, as French and British newspapers repeatedly make clear. Despite this, both Paris and Brussels continue to carry out their administrative roles effectively. This paradoxical situation suggests that we do not fully understand how these two administrative discourses function, or to what extent they are indeed two distinct discourses.

In order to compare the EU and national French administrative discourses in terms of their typical phraseology, we need to consider the different contexts in which documents are produced in the EU and in France. This is the focus of Chapter 1. The theoretical and methodological issues raised by this study are then discussed in Chapters 2 and 3. Much of the linguistic investigation of administrative French has concentrated on its shortcomings and offered suggestions for improvement, usually targeting individual words and grammatical constructions which are perceived to be typical of the register. Understandably, terminological accuracy is crucial in translation carried out in the EU institutions, and many of the sources of information available to translators are designed to ensure this: these include electronic and online terminology databases, glossaries, and in-house terminologists. However, from the point of view of linguistic description, lexical and grammatical studies alone create a rather static and one-sided picture of the register. A more dynamic picture, and one which shows how language actually functions and how meaning is created and evolves, can be achieved by taking as a starting point the notion of phraseology, roughly defined by Gledhill (2000, p. 1) as "the preferred way of saying things in a particular discourse". Defined in this way, phraseology is a wide concept which extends to take in aspects of both lexis and grammar, and entails a marrying of quantitative and qualitative analysis. The present study approaches the phraseology of European Union and national French administrative language from the angle of collocation, that is, the typical co-occurrences of words. The collocational patterning typical of a register is less intuitively obvious than its prominent individual lexical items or grammatical constructions, but it can be readily discerned by corpus methods, and its contribution to the identity of the register, as of any register, is far-reaching. The corpus researcher Michael Stubbs has recently highlighted the importance of such co-occurrences:

> In terms of communicative competence, all words, even the most frequent in the language, contract such collocational relations, and fluent language use means internalising such phrases. In terms of cultural competence, culture is encoded not just in words which are obviously ideologically loaded, but also in combinations of very frequent words. (Stubbs 2001a, p. 313)

A phraseological approach, drawing on analysis of collocation, allows for a fuller picture of a language or register to be drawn than can a purely lexical or grammatical approach. It is a more subtle method of investigation, and its findings are of great value, as they tell us more about the ways in which language is being used, and the concepts, assumptions and ideologies which lie behind it.

Corpus linguistics is an ideal methodology for such analysis. Robin Dempsey in David Lodge's *Small World*, speaking in the quotation at the head of this preface, had a childlike enthusiasm for the potential, or perhaps just the novelty, of the methodology of corpus linguistics in literary stylistics, and created a corpus of the author Ronald Frobisher's complete writings. Over the last twenty years, corpus linguistics has become more and more practicable for such small-scale research, not just stylistic studies of individual authors, but also focused linguistic analyses of whole languages, and particular registers or text-types of a language.

Collocational patterning is often counter-intuitive, as empirical linguists such as John Sinclair (e.g. Sinclair 1991) have repeatedly shown. The use of the linguist's own intuition, or such elicitation techniques as are commonly used in sociolinguistics, are therefore not appropriate for its study. The most reliable way to investigate collocation is through the study of large quantities of real text, the actual size of the corpus of texts being determined by the nature of the analysis and the selection of language varieties under study, but ranging from tens of thousands to hundreds of millions of words. This allows a more nuanced, and more accurate picture to be established: a picture which is faithful to the subtleties of language, and one which does not ignore the infrequent or uncommon, while still highlighting what is typical. The impression built up is less clear-cut than one based on a small number of representative texts might be, but is ultimately more accurate. This research therefore draws its validity from the fact that the methodology of corpus linguistics has reached the stage where individual researchers with nothing more than a computer, a corpus compiled to their own specifications, and some user-friendly analysis tools, can now carry out a revealing linguistic investigation of a language, register or genre.

It is in the nature of corpus research to be comparative, especially while it is still a fairly new methodology and there is relatively little in the way of existing research on a particular language or register. In terms of collocational patterning, I am interested both in the extent to which the EU discourse differs phraseologically from French national administrative language, and the phraseological patterning of this register compared with the general language. In other words, what makes it recognisable as a register? The design of the corpus (see Chapter 3) makes possible the comparison of one discourse with another, and also of individual textual genres and sets of genres with others. In addition, a small comparator corpus made up of a number of different registers of French enables (limited) comparison with the general language.

Collocation and phraseology are areas fraught with terminological problems: owing to the disparate disciplinary backgrounds of researchers there has not always been agreement between the various schools of thought over the defining characteristics of different types of collocation. This has often resulted in different terms for what is arguably the same concept, or conversely, an umbrella term where different concepts may be distinguished. As a result, it is not possible to retrieve all types of collocation automatically from an electronic corpus, at least without a large amount of 'noise' or irrelevant information. No single approach, however, can give insight into all of the types of collocation which contribute to the production of meaning in a register and which enable a register to be recognised as such. While a study of this scope cannot therefore be comprehensive, to attempt to describe patterning in a register by restricting oneself to a single definition of collocation requires one to disregard many potentially fruitful areas from the outset. For this reason, I prefer here to take a number of definitions into consideration.

We might distinguish two main approaches to collocational patterning in a corpus of texts: we can take as the starting point either the words which form part of collocations - units of language - or the corpus itself. The first approach I call here a 'micro' approach, and the latter, a 'macro' approach. The former has the advantage of offering a high level of precision, and allowing the analysis to be oriented in a particular direction while highlighting infrequent, but still potentially typical, collocations. On the other hand, this approach offers only a low level of recall, and may miss quantitatively important collocations and phraseological patterning. The second, data-driven, approach, on the other hand, has the advantage of a high level of recall, while focusing attention on high frequency collocations and patterns, but at the same time can offer only low precision, that is to say that a great deal of manual analysis is needed once the computer has retrieved potential collocations. The analysis carried out here exploits both approaches. Chapter 4 takes a 'macro' approach, taking the corpus as its starting point, and deriving frequent word sequences directly from the data. Chapter 5 may be described as a 'micro' approach, beginning as it does with units of language, in this case, 'locutions' of French. Chapter 6, finally, combines the two approaches. Although it takes a 'micro' approach, to the extent that the investigation of collocational and phraseological patterning begins from individual 'keywords', these keywords, at least according to one definition, are derived from the corpus. In addition, Chapters 4 and 5 have in common the fact that they both concentrate on collocations considered as *products* of language, while Chapter 6 brings to the fore instead the *process* of collocation. In this way, the aim is gradually to build up a picture of the collocational and phraseological patterning in the discourses of EU and national administrative French.

A further point is appropriate at this stage: this relates to the issue of layout, particularly in the later chapters which set out the analysis. Rebecca Posner, in her study of linguistic change in French, draws attention to a potential problem in studies of lexis, which can be applied equally to studies of collocation and phraseology:

> [...] on the whole, discussion of change in the lexicon soon descends to citation of individual examples and a general picture of how a lexicon changes rarely emerges. (Posner 1997, p. 143)

It can be readily understood how an investigation of collocational patterns could quite easily fall into the same trap, and fail to go beyond the 'citation of individual examples'. Since my aim here is to arrive at a general picture of the workings of the phraseology of administrative French, I attempt throughout to draw generalisations, in order to highlight patterns and tendencies rather than merely to assemble lists of individual examples. On the other hand, there is also a danger to be found in excessive generalisation, and failing to keep the corpus texts themselves in the foreground. Clearly, a sensitive and carefully nuanced balance must be struck.

Chapter 1

The Register of Administrative French

'It means', he said, holding up a flat metal canister rather like the sort you keep film spools in, 'It means that every word you've ever published is in here.'

DAVID LODGE, SMALL WORLD: AN ACADEMIC ROMANCE

1. Introduction and objectives

> All the language of public administration and government may be said to be the language of planning and regulation, the language of public guidance. (Firth 1935, p. 30)

The influential British linguist, J. R. Firth here highlights the overriding function of language in administration. When one considers the number and range of areas in our lives which are regulated in some way, and the number of levels - local, regional, national and, increasingly, supranational - from which this regulation stems, it is clear that the language of public administration has a critical role to play, and the sheer mass of administrative documents is quite staggering. Even in today's electronic age, it would be impossible to cram every word ever published into Robin Dempsey's flat metal canister, as featured in the quotation at the head of this chapter. Administrative language has been described as prestige language, and in France this is arguably more the case than in other countries. Historically, it has had an important role to play in both disseminating and determining the standard language. Centralised administration both explicitly, as the propagator of linguistic policy (through such organisations as the *Délégation générale à la langue française et aux langues de France*) and implicitly, through its own use of language, increases the influence of standard French. The register, in its various states, has clearly had historical, cultural and social prestige and relevance.

The European Union over the last fifty years has played an increasingly important part in citizens' lives, as it both widens to include new member states, and deepens the scope of its influence and power. The EU is a unique organisation, although others, such as the United Nations and NATO, might be likened to it in different respects. Linguistically, too, the EU is a unique contact situation: this is set out in Section 2.1. In order to appreciate the specificity of the EU in this regard, it is useful to consider, as Section 2.2 does, the French national context and attitudes to language in Paris. The EU was not created from a void, however. Rather, France had a major role in its genesis and continues to play a large part in its subsequent development. Section 3 discusses this early and continuing influence and extends the discussion to issues of linguistic influence on the emerging discourse of EU administrative language.

Just as 'Eurospeak' has its origins in an earlier form of administrative language, so also the French administrative language of the middle of the twentieth century can be traced further back. This chapter therefore continues its reverse chronology, stepping briefly back in Section 4 to the earliest examples of the register, and working back up to the present day, highlighting some of the major external influences on the register, including earlier situations of multilingualism and language contact. While the development of the French administrative register over the centuries has been punctuated by bursts of change, this only serves to underline its adaptability and ultimately its functional effectiveness. After all, if the post-war growth of France from an agricultural to an industrial society is due to the efficiency of the bureaucracy, as Campbell et al. (1995, p. 278) suggest, then the 'obscurity' of the language cannot have been entirely counter-productive. The popular perception of administrative language, however, stands in contrast to this. Administrative language frequently excites negative public interest, as its particular linguistic characteristics and its great quantity are seen to be indicative of a lack of transparency, and consequently too great a metaphorical distance established between the administration and the citizens of Europe, or between Paris and 'la province'. Like a jargon, it can exclude the uninitiated, and in this sense one can draw parallels with John Swales' (1990a) notion of discourse communities, which tend to separate people into occupational or special interest groups. The result is that, as Rodney Ball, for example, claims, administrative language is "still frowned upon by many today" (Ball 1997, p. 182). Section 5 outlines this popular view of the register, and some measures taken to 'improve' French and Eurospeak.

The final section takes a linguistic perspective on the administrative register. Little work has been carried out on EU French in particular, but this section surveys existing research in this area, and also on related registers, such as political and legal language, and administrative registers of other languages. The aim of this section is to provide a background for a study of phraseology in the register, by reviewing research on its lexical and grammatical characteristics.

A note on terminology is necessary at this point. The object of study here is the language of public administration, that is, the language used to transmit government policy and practice to the public. This public is, of course, heterogeneous and seeks the information for many different purposes, and the various textual genres, both oral and written, must adapt to fit requirements. The interest here does not lie in the so-called 'grey literature', or 'administrative' texts defined by C. P. Auger (1994) as "publications with little or no general distribution", and often a non-professional layout, including such texts as reports, theses and meetings papers. Similarly, the boundary between administrative language and political language, in the sense of party political language, is not clear-cut, because the work of the administration and that of a party in power are inextricably intertwined. This is vividly the case in France: Knapp and Wright (2001, p. 277) point out that until 1991 and then again from 1993 to 2001 (and indeed until mid-2002), all prime ministers of the Fifth Republic had spent part of their careers in the Civil Service.

Christina Schäffner (1997, p. 119) calls political language an 'umbrella term', and the same can be seen to be true of administrative language. In the particular contexts dealt with here it is impossible completely to separate the administrative from the political and the legislative, as the quotation from Firth above suggests, especially at the level of the European Union. The European Commission, for example, is unique among international bureaucracies, combining as it does administrative, legislative and executive functions. Moreover, the President of the Commission can be viewed as either an official or a political leader. It should be borne in mind therefore that 'administrative' is to be understood here as shorthand for 'politico-administrative'. Various names have been used for this register: bureaucratic language (e.g. Charrow 1982); officialese (Longe 1985); the language of public administration (Longe 1985); Civil Service language (Crystal and Davy 1969). While the focus of each of these is subtly different, public administrative language by any name has the central function of "mediat[ing] between government and the governed" (Longe 1985, p. 307). This definition lies behind the design of the corpus used here (cf. Chapter 3).

2. The context of the register of administrative French

The European Union is a unique organisation, in terms of its changing aims, institutional make-up, and scope of activity. The French language is famously the language of diplomacy. It is necessary therefore to consider how the two interact, by looking at such issues as the degree of influence of French on so-called 'Eurospeak', and the place of the French language in the EU context, where the issue of translation is of vital importance, as compared to its use in the national context. Moving from the abstract level of a language to the more concrete question of individual texts and types of text, we need also to consider briefly the context of production of the genres and texts which play a part in the construction and day-to-day workings of the two administrations, in addition to the various constraints on text production resulting from these contexts. Gledhill (1997, p. 87) claims that a specialised corpus, whether defined in terms of its communicative register or its thematic area, must be related to the community from which it emanates. The aim of this section is to do just that.

2.1 The linguistic situation in the European Union

> [...] les langues sont au cœur des échanges, surtout dans le monde moderne, où elles sont par exemple la matière première des industries

> de service, des industries culturelles. ("La place des langues dans les institutions européennes", DGLFLF website, http://www.culture.fr /culture/dglf/garde.htm)

In few situations is it more evident that language is a raw material than in the European Union. Language issues have a high profile in the EU, and attract a lot of public attention in all of the member states of the Union. The principle of the equality of official and working languages is as old as the Union itself,[4] dating back to Council Regulation No. 1 of 15 April 1958, which is concerned with the linguistic plurality and the equality of the original French, Dutch, German and Italian, so that all citizens have equal access to Community law. At the time when the corpus used here was compiled, the Union had eleven working languages and twelve Treaty (or official) languages, Irish Gaelic having the status of Treaty language only. The Amsterdam Treaty adds that:

> Every citizen of the Union may write to any of the institutions or bodies referred to in this Article or in Article 4 in one of the languages mentioned in Article 248 and have an answer in the same language.[5] (Treaty of Amsterdam, Article 8D)

Thierry Fontenelle remarks that multilingualism is key, noting that: "Democracy, transparency and equality are superior principles which can only be achieved if multilingualism is implemented and preserved." (Fontenelle 1999, p. 123). Language is probably the most visible mark of diversity (cf. Coulmas 1991b, p. 1). Only the Court of Justice is exempt from the language requirement, adopting as it does a language for each case, although French is dominant.[6]

As the EU expands, the language issue is exacerbated, and the number of official languages can be impractical in the day-to-day workings of the institutions. Jean Quatremer, the Brussels correspondent of *Libération* claimed, in the Sunday Times on 19 August 2001 that EU officials want English to be the language of the EU, and national languages to be relegated to the status of local dialects.[7] The

---

4 Indeed even older, for the EEC followed the precedent of the ECSC, which by 1953 published its Official Journal in Dutch, French, German and Italian (cf. Judge and Judge 1998, p. 292).

5 Article 248 adds Danish, English, Finnish, Greek, Irish, Portuguese, Spanish and Swedish to the original four languages.

6 For detailed information on the language practices of the main EU institutions, see Judge and Judge (1998, p. 293ff). For a more recent treatment, see also Phillipson 2003, and Wagner et al. 2002.

7 This was certainly not the impression I got from speaking to colleagues in the English Translation Division of the Council of Ministers during a

proposal at the beginning of July 2001 to simplify the administration by moving from a system of three predominant working languages (English, French and German) to the language of choice of officials, he claims, would result in English taking over. A Frenchman himself, he says that "it is as if the French are resigned to this arrogant domination of English, upgraded to the rank of Europe's lingua franca" (*ibid.*). He goes on to suggest that dispensing with French in Brussels could turn the French against Europe. The French linguist, Claude Hagège, however, does not agree with this pessimistic view, and believes that European unity does not toll a bell for Europe's cultural minorities (see Hagège 1994, p. 271).

As France was one of the original six member states, along with part-Francophone Luxembourg and Belgium, the French language has played a part in European issues from the outset. Understandably, as French fell from being a national language of half of the member states and one language in four, to the language of a fifth of the members, and only one language in twelve (and now of course the language of three out of 25 members, one language in twenty), its relative role has diminished. In practice, however, English, French and German are the most used languages in day-to-day affairs, with French and English more or less equal in internal oral communication, and the commonest languages of document drafting. Judge and Judge give the following figures, based on research carried out in 1996 by the University of Gerhard-Mercator in Duisberg in Germany:

- internal written communications: French in 75% of cases
- oral communication with Member States: French in 54% of cases
- written communication with Member States: French in 56% of cases
- oral communication in a world-wide context: English in 69% of cases
- written communication in a world-wide context: English in 71% of cases (Judge and Judge 1998, p. 296)

According to the DGLFLF, English has quite recently overtaken French as the most popular language of drafting in the Commission (cf. Fontenelle 1999, p.125). English also currently has a slight advantage in some sectors. The recent widening of the Union towards the East, the 1995 accession of Nordic countries, both shifting the geographical centre of Europe eastwards, and the fact that English is by far the most commonly-taught second language in the European Union,[8] mean that English may already have gained the upper hand.[9]

---

three-month training period in the summer of 1997: however, it is understandable that translation professionals should be in favour of a multilingual policy.

8 Flesch (1998) claims that 90% of young people in the EU are taught English as a second language.

A natural result of the multilingual, multicultural climate of the EU is the existence of 'hybrid texts'. While French national administrative documents are strongly culture-bound, this is not the case for European Union documents. Anna Trosborg introduces the concept of hybrid texts, or "documents produced in a supranational multicultural discourse community where there is no linguistically neutral ground" (1997c, p. 145), but where documents fulfil identical functions. She goes on to suggest that hybrid texts have specific textual features, of vocabulary, syntax and style:

> In the process of establishing political unity within the Union, linguistic expressions are levelled to a common, (low) denominator. EU documents have developed a specific language involving coinage of new concepts as well as new terms for the drafting of documents and for use in Community negotiations. (Trosborg 1997c, p. 151)

In such an environment, translation necessarily plays a crucial role in communication. The languages of the member states come into contact through bilinguals, translators and interpreters. Translation is needed both within the institutions, for purposes of information, and for the public, who have a right to documents in their own language. The procedures of translation, however, vary according to the type of document and its purpose. Different genres have very different communicative aims and this has implications for the process of translation. At a basic level, while the translation of working papers can be fairly flexible, legislative texts must be strictly equivalent, even to the extent of an "équivalence numérique" (Seleskovitch and Lederer 1984, p. 28), which implies that the number of sentences and paragraphs must be identical in the source and target texts. Trosborg (1997c, p. 151) calls this the "full-stop rule": that is to say that punctuation must fall at the same place in the source text and the target text, in order that parallel versions may be easily referred to.

The translation process is consequently a massive operation, and one which draws heavily on the Community budget. As new member states join the Union, the language pairs increase exponentially: currently, with twenty working languages, there are a staggering three hundred and eighty translation pairs,[10] and measures have had to be introduced to allow the translation and interpreting processes to continue as efficiently as possible. Recent measures have included improvements

---

9 See also Phillipson (2003, pp. 64-65) for factors contributing to the increased use of English in Europe.

10 The formula for calculating the number of language pairs is n x (n-1), where n is the number of languages. Therefore, when there were four languages (Dutch, French, German and Italian), there were only twelve language pairs.

to online and computer-based terminology databases and document archives, which speed up the translation process by eliminating the need for the re-translation of passages,[11] and thereby increase linguistic consistency. Other measures include the practice of relay interpreting, or pivot interpreting, at meetings, where an intermediary language allows a two-stage translation process between uncommon pairs, such as Greek and Finnish, and the practice at summits and European Councils of having half of the translators in situ and the others working from Brussels, as happened for example at the Amsterdam Council in June 1997. Emma Wagner (2005) makes further suggestions for coping with the increased translation demand, including a more systematic editing process, and the abandonment of the principle whereby translators translate only into their native tongue.

The European Commission, in particular, also makes use of machine translation. European officials can now use the Systran system, via both an email and a web interface (cf. Fontenelle 1999, p. 124-5 and Judge and Judge 1998). While machine translation is useful for gist translations, or for aiding a decision as to whether or not to have a document properly translated, it can only replace human translators in limited situations.

In addition to a possible levelling of linguistic expressions to a low common denominator because of the number of languages involved, there is also the factor of multiple authorship of documents. As Georgin (1973, p. 234-5) says:

> Enfin la maladresse du style officiel vient souvent de ce qu'un texte de loi, par exemple, loin d'être l'œuvre d'un seul, est le résultat d'une collaboration. Chacun y a apporté ses retouches, ses additions, quelque incidente nouvelle. Et les phrases s'allongent dangereusement (Georgin 1973, p. 234-5)

---

11 The process of translating a very formulaic text by cutting and pasting sentences from very similar previously translated documents is reminiscent of the production of the formulaic style of Old French narrative verse in the oral tradition (cf. J. J. Duggan 1969 and 1973 on the *Chanson de Roland*).

Even when language contact is not an issue in the drafting of a particular document, the EU context of document production is complex. This, however, is something it shares with administrative documents at the French national level.

2.2 French national administration and language policy

The interaction between the French administration and the standard language is close and two-way. The standard language, especially its written genres, enables effective administration, and the administration implicitly promotes, and indeed often explicitly imposes, the standard language (cf. Offord 1990). The controversial 'Loi Toubon' of 4 August 1994 proclaims that the French language is "un élément fondamental de la personnalité et du patrimoine de la France. Elle est la langue de l'enseignement, du travail, des échanges et des services publics." (Article 1er). In some respects, attitudes have changed little since the Revolution.

Over the last thirty years, many bodies have been founded to deal with language issues (cf. Section 5.1). The first administrative organisation dedicated to the French language was created in 1966, and has developed into the *Délégation générale à la langue française et aux langues de France* (henceforth DGLFLF) which is part of the Ministry for Culture and Communication. The DGLFLF oversees two organisations: the *Commission générale de terminologie et de néologie*, which coordinates the work of the various terminology bodies, and the *Conseil supérieur de la langue française*, which is an 'organe de consultation', composed of language experts, including writers, scientists and linguists. This latter organisation is concerned with the French language in social cohesion, teaching, 'l'enrichissement' (including neologisms to combat the encroachment of Anglicisms), technology and the Internet, and its relation with other languages. Even today, the French government strongly favours the national language over regional languages. De Witte explains the extent of this policy:

> France has an active policy of favouring the use of the national language, which takes not only the form of restrictions against the use of other languages [...] but also that of positive incentives to French language expression. The government subsidises the translation of French publications into foreign languages; it subsidises French libraries abroad and French publications for distribution abroad; it offers special aid to theater or film productions using the French language; French language 'world' radio and the French language song also receive official financial support. It should be added that this policy is not fundamentally different from that pursued by most other European states, only perhaps more systematic. (de Witte 1991, p. 173)

The French national administration as it exists today of course has a much longer history than the European Union. Although the administration has been modified over the five Republics, it has its roots in the pre-Revolutionary ancien régime and much of its structure in the Napoleonic administration (see for example Stevens 1996 and Knapp and Wright 2001), although Robert Catherine (1985) singles out the end of the nineteenth century as the source of the specificity of the register. Knapp and Wright go further and state that "since the Revolution, changes of régime have left the apparatus of the State, as well as a significant body of legislation, largely intact" (Knapp and Wright 2001, p. 15). It was built on the principles of a meritocracy, with entry through competitive exams, and has always enjoyed the respect of the majority of French people as a strong, independent force, according to Campbell et al. "for reasons of precedent, economic history, and political necessity" (1995, p. 284).

The Fifth Republic was initially dedicated to reinforcing the role of the administration and has been called 'la République des fonctionnaires', for three main reasons: firstly, the powerful economic role of the State; secondly, the backing given by the régime's founders to the extension of the administration's activities; and thirdly the capacity of civil servants to colonise powerful positions well outside the administration itself, for example on the boards of nationalised industries.

Knapp and Wright summarise the recent changes:

> The French State is smaller, thanks to privatisations; it is less able to intervene at will; it is more fragmented, both territorially (thanks to decentralisation) and functionally (thanks to independent agencies); it is more subject to controls, both national (slightly) and European (considerably). The transformation was less radical on the other hand, within the administration itself, whether within the élite or at rank-and-file level. (Knapp and Wright 2001, p. 290)

The current relationship between State and administration is the result of a process of change, much of which is related to the widening role of the EU, which, combined with other factors such as the development of international relations, and the linguistic unification brought about by the Francophonie movement, have shaped the administrative register as it exists currently (see Catherine 1985, p. 13).

3. France and the European Union - interactions and influences

Given the assertion of sociolinguistics that language varies according to context, one would expect the language produced by the two contexts outlined in Section 2 to differ, even although the documents share a similar range of overall purposes. This section develops these ideas further by examining the nature and extent of interaction and mutual influence between the EU and national contexts.

Larsen (1997, p. 24), a political scientist, claims that the political discourses in the domains he investigates, which include European policy, are national in nature. International texts, moreover, are made up of fragments of different national discourses, that is to say that they are not truly international. Furthermore, the British political scientist, John Gaffney, has suggested that "the legitimacy of the European Union depends upon the emergence of a European-level political discourse" (Gaffney 1999, p. 199). Both of these authors suggest therefore that the European Union discourse does not as yet have a total coherence of its own. The EU discourse lacks strong central institutions (comparable to those on the national level), and mass-allegiance to its objectives. It also, at least as yet, lacks the mythology and symbols which lie behind national discourses, and it is often the case that issues at the supranational level only impinge on the general public if they contradict or are tied up with national approaches. What is more, the EU represents a different type of leadership from national political and administrative frameworks. Thus the national and EU contexts have a different foundation and draw upon different resources for their discourses.

While it is true that the EU is a unique organisation, even among treaty-based organisations, at the same time it would not be surprising if it shared many features with the national politico-administrative context. As Gaffney (*ibid.*) also points out, EU styles and registers have correspondences in the member states and, increasingly, Europe represents a shared experience and perspective for its members. There are also EU-wide correspondences at the party-political level.

If we consider France specifically:

> Dans l'Union plus encore que dans les autres organisations, le français, langue latine porteuse de concepts, d'un système socio-économique et d'une conception du droit, partagés par un grand nombre de pays (pays latins, mais aussi pays d'Europe centrale et orientale) joue un rôle privilégié qui nous donne une responsabilité particulière. ("La place des langues dans les institutions européennes", DGLFLF website, http://www.culture.fr/culture/dglf/francais-aime/1998/europe.htm)

This quotation, from the DGLFLF, shows that the French are proud of their place at the heart of Europe. There are grounds for expecting that the French administrative discourse, more than that of any other member state, will have a degree of overlap with the EU administrative discourse. France has always had a particular interest in the development of Europe-wide agreements, from the outset when it was concerned by the United States' desire to re-arm Germany as protection against the East. A supranational framework made responsibility necessary on the part of all the nations involved. As Anne Stevens puts it "the structures that were set up then [for the European Coal and Steel Community], and those which followed for the European Economic Community and Euratom, were strongly influenced by French models and patterns of administration, and tended initially to provide a milieu into which French administrative assumptions meshed rather easily" (Stevens 1996, p. 311; see also Phillipson 2003, p. 125 on this topic). De Gaulle was of the opinion that Europe could act as a 'lever of Archimedes', which could allow France to "regain the status she lost at the battle of Waterloo, as the first among nations" (quoted in Knapp and Wright 2001, p. 29). As regards France's role in institutional development, one thinks immediately of Jean Monnet and the Schuman Plan. Monnet (the Commissaire français au Plan from 1945) was convinced that gradual and pragmatic progress towards a united Europe was the way forward, and he prepared a declaration which Robert Schuman, the French foreign minister of the time, made public on 9 May 1950. The following year, this became the ECSC. France also had important roles in the development of the Treaty of Rome, and the Common Agricultural Policy and its price support mechanisms.[12]

French efforts were not always an unqualified success, however. Guyomarch et al. believe that:

> [...] if French governments have been key actors in building the EU, their record is less than consistently positive. Some French leaders have initiated key institutional and policy developments, while others have been responsible for some of the major problems and set-backs in the integration process. (Guyomarch et al. 1998, p. 17)

Various events in the history of the European Union support this view: early attempts to coordinate foreign and defence policy (such as the Pleven and Fouchet Plans), the destruction of the European Defence Community, and the

---

12 C. Flesch (1998) gives a revealing first-hand account of working within the area of agricultural policy: "As a young official, in the Agricultural Division of the Council Secretariat, I first had a German boss. We were dealing with the market organisation for cereals and pretty soon my German vocabulary as far as wheat or rye, levies and restitutions were concerned was much improved but the legal framework, the intellectual approach and the economic tools remained largely French-inspired." She goes on to say that in the years following the first enlargement (to include Britain, Ireland and Denmark) the situation did not change fundamentally for three reasons: firstly because everyone referred to the *acquis communautaire* in French, because key posts were occupied by French speakers, and finally because the British made a serious effort to use French.

empty chair crisis of 1965.[13] The French voice, or rather French voices, as it has been argued that there was never a single vision (Guyomarch et al. 1998, p. 242), were always to be heard loud and clear.

In addition, the institutions and heartland of the EU have always been in Francophone territory - Strasbourg, Brussels and Luxembourg - so even where the French system might not have had an influence, the French language might still have. This influence was two-way, and naturally the French system has also adapted as a result of power in certain domains, such as monetary policy, foreign and defence issues, and increasingly, justice and home affairs, being transferred to a supranational institution (cf. Guyomarch et al. 1998, and Knapp and Wright 2001). Especially since the Single European Act of 1986, the European question has become the concern of the whole French administration. The EU is, however, still very much a developing organism. Indeed, as its expansion continues, it becomes more and more difficult for the French government, as indeed any other national government, to mould policy development to suit its own needs and desires.

There is also of course some overlap of personnel between the national administration and the EU. These include French *fonctionnaires* working on European questions in France, for example transposing EU directives into national legislation (according to Guyomarch et al. 1998, p. 53, this accounts for several thousand civil servants), officials on secondment to the Commission, Council of Ministers, or Permanent Representation, and experts participating in European working parties.

Turning to language, a glance at any EU document shows that French has had an influence on the development of so-called Eurospeak. Especially before the arrival of English, French fed many technical expressions into Eurospeak.[14]

---

13 The 'empty chair crisis' is the name given to the period in 1965 when Charles de Gaulle instructed French ministers not to take part in Council meetings. De Gaulle was opposed to financial arrangements for the Common Agricultural Policy, and the proposed practice of majority voting in the Council of Ministers, among other issues.

14 Goffin (1997, p. 66) is an interesting study of the new words introduced by each of the Treaties of the Union. Some examples include: (Treaty of Rome) *prélèvements (agricoles), systèmes de préférences généralisées, prix de seuil, mesures d'effet équivalent, montants compensatoires monétaires, prélèvement de coresponsabilité, ressources propres.* (Maastricht Treaty) *Banque centrale européenne, citoyenneté de l'Union, Conseil des Gouverneurs, fonds à finalité structurelle, fonds de cohésion, gouvernement général, acquis communautaire.*

Timothy Bainbridge identifies three types of French influence in these expressions:

> Some of them have remained French (*acquis communautaire*), some have been at least partially assimilated into English (rapporteur), and some - perhaps the most confusing - have acquired a spurious Englishness in translation in spite of few people being entirely sure of their meaning (comitology, subsidiarity). Irritating though such expressions may be, it must be said that many of them genuinely lack an English equivalent: they are perhaps best regarded as a compact and convenient mental shorthand which, once learnt, is undeniably useful. (Bainbridge 1998, p. xi)

The following table gives examples of expressions in each of these categories, with an explanation of their meaning in the context of the European Union:

Table 1.1: French influence on Eurospeak. Information adapted from Bainbridge (1998)

Term	**Meaning**
Acquis communautaire	'Community patrimony' (The set of decisions and laws agreed to date and accepted by new member states). First named in writing in the Maastricht Treaty.
Cabinet	French term. The small group of officials who make up the private offices of senior ministers in European Commission, president of the Parliament etc.
Comitology	Term not yet fully assimilated into English. Translation of French 'comitologie'. First used in 1962, and defined as the study of committees and how they operate.
Empty Chair Crisis	'Chaise vide'. Crisis (July-Dec 1965), when French ministers (on de Gaulle's instructions) refused to take part in Council meetings and the French Permanent Representative was withdrawn from Brussels.
Engrenage	Literally 'meshing in'. Describes the practice of involving national civil servants with the work of the European institutions, esp. the Commission.
Espace judiciaire européen	'European legal area'. Proposal put forward by Giscard d'Estaing in 1977.
Europe à la carte	Model of integration in which member states decide whether or not to participate in activities on a case-by-case basis.

Europe des patries	A 'Europe of nation-states'. Phrase associated with Charles de Gaulle. Describes a model of integration in which states are the essential building blocks.
Fiche d'impact	The written assessment of impact of a legislative proposal.
Finalités politiques	The ultimate goals of the EU, part of the 'acquis communautaire', but not necessarily in the Treaties.
Hierarchy of acts	Translation of 'hierarchie des actes'. Relates to the reordering of the different types of EU legislation, modelled on French constitutional reforms of 1958.
Juste retour	Became current especially in 1979-85. Briefly, that a member state should receive a 'fair return' from the budget, relative to its contribution.
Rapporteur	Member of a committee responsible for drawing up a report on a matter referred to that committee.
Social partners	Originally a French expression ('partenaires sociaux'). Employers and employees.
Subsidiarity	The principle that decisions should be taken at the lowest level consistent with effective action within a political system. First reference in an official document in the Commission's submission to the Tindemans Report on European Union (June 1975).
Two-speed Europe	Translation of the French 'Europe à deux vitesses'. First set out in Tindemans Report (1975). Member states can proceed towards integration at different paces.

From a more terminological perspective, the French-English European Communities Glossary (1990), compiled by the English and Irish Division of the Council of Ministers translation service, is another source of examples of the use of French terms in English. The following table lists those terms in the glossary for which there is no English equivalent, or for which the accepted English translation is in fact a French word:

Table 1.2: French terminological items in English, from the European Communities Glossary (1990)

French term	English translation	Comment
Acquis communautaire	'acquis communautaire'	Also glossed as 'accession negotiations'

Acquit-à-caution	'acquit-à-caution'	Administrative document used in France in connection with the control of movement of alcohol.
Acte-clair	'acte-clair'	A provision not requiring interpretation by the Court of Justice.
Aide-mémoire	'aide-mémoire'	In reference to certain oral-diplomatic communications. Also translated 'memorandum' in other contexts.
Signer 'en blanc'	to sign 'en blanc'	To sign in blank (e.g. a cheque)
Produits dit 'brais résineux'	'brais résineux'	In relation to the Common Customs Tariff
Carte d'identité d'étranger commerçant	'carte d'identité d'étranger commerçant'	Only used in French context.
Carte professionnelle	'carte professionnelle'	In Belgian context only.
En cas de force majeure	In cases of 'force majeure'	In legal texts only. Otherwise translated 'in circumstances outside one's own control', or 'where unavoidable'.
Chef de cabinet	'Chef de cabinet'	Standard usage in the European Commission.
Société en nom collectif	'société en nom collectif'	Also translated 'private company'
Collectivité territoriale de la République française	'collectivité territoriale' of the French Republic	The official status of Mayotte
Comité interministériel pour les questions de coopération économique européenne	'Comité interministériel pour les questions de coopération économique européenne'	French committee
Contrat-cadre	'contrat-cadre'	Also translated, in different contexts, 'framework contract', 'master contract', 'skeleton contract'
Vin de coupage	'coupage' wine	In the context of wine-making
Cour des Comptes	'Cour des Comptes'	The administrative body

		which oversees public accounts in France.
Cuvée	'cuvée'	In the context of wine-making.
Liqueur d'expédition	'liqueur d'expédition'	Glossed as 'sparkling wines'
Grains mitadinés	'mitadiné' grains	In the context of durum wheat.
Laissez-passer	'laissez-passer'	Also translated 'pass'
Liqueur de tirage	'liqueur de tirage'	In the context of wine-making. Also may be translated ''tirage' liqueur'
Location vente	'location vente'	A leasing contract with obligation to buy.
Société de / à participation financière	'Société de / à participation financière'	Investment company (Luxembourg).
rapporteur	rapporteur	In the context of the Economic and Social Committee
À six	'à six'	Decisions taken in the early days of the EEC, when there were only six members.

These terms represent only a tiny proportion of the 30,000 or so items in the Glossary. It is notable, however, that other languages hardly show their influence at all.[15] As can be seen from the table above, often the French term is the only accepted form to use in English in a specific context. Often also, the term refers to an institution or a body which is particular to France or a Francophone country: this explains its lack of an English equivalent. A third category of term is those which are used in particular domains, especially in wine-making, which have their own specialised terminology in French. More interesting from the point of view of the role of French in the development of the European Union are those terms which stem from the French administrative framework, or appear to have only an arbitrary connection to France, such as 'acquis communautaire', 'acte-clair', 'signer en blanc', 'en cas de force majeure', 'rapporteur' and 'à six'.

15 One exception to this is the term 'Butterkäse' from German, which appears in this form in both French and English.

4. The historical context

While an appreciation of the present-day situation in the EU and in France is essential for a study of their administrative discourses, it is also valuable to look at the register diachronically, to gain insight into some of the constraints and demands that have contributed to the form of the administrative French from which the EU discourse drew so much in the latter half of the twentieth century.

The development of the administrative register of French is closely linked to the development of the French language itself, as it gradually took over various functions from Latin.[16] A study of French-Latin language contact in the context of administrative writing is beyond the scope of this work, but would certainly be a revealing area of study in itself. Some of the earliest surviving French texts are administrative documents, although Latin remained the usual language of administration for several more centuries (cf. Ayres-Bennett 1996, p. 21). The very earliest extant text which is accepted to be French, the *Serments de Strasbourg*, or Strasbourg Oaths, which dates from 842 A.D., is a legal-political document, and sealed the alliance between Charles le Chauve and his brother Louis le Germanique.[17]

Anthony Lodge, whose interest lies primarily in the history of spoken and colloquial French, points to the charters of Tournai (1197) and Douai (1204) as the first surviving non-literary texts in the *langue d'oïl*, and to eleventh-century legal texts and administrative documents as their equivalent in the *langue d'oc* (Lodge 1993, p. 107, p. 113). He goes on to discuss the replacement of Latin by French in various functions, noting that:

> [...] between the thirteenth and sixteenth centuries French acquired a wide range of official and public functions, not only as the language

---

16 From an early twenty-first century perspective, it is easy to view the situation simplistically, and not appreciate its multilingual nature, and the fact that Latin was far from uniform in the Middle Ages. In a fascinating study, Julia Smith (1992) discusses the development of Brittany as a territorial principality in the ninth and tenth centuries, and shows the variety in the Latinity of ninth-century Breton hagiographers: she finds that the Latin of Eastern Brittany shows the influence of Carolingian hagiography, and differs noticeably from that of Western Brittany which is closer to the Latin of late antiquity.

17 The text of the *Serments de Strasbourg* and a discussion can be found in Brunot (1905, pp. 142ff).

> of government and the law but also as a language of learning. (*ibid.*, p. 120)

This process, which began in the south of France in the late eleventh century and reached the north by the thirteenth (*ibid.*, p. 120),[18] happened in two stages:

> [...] in the first instance each of the regions introduced its own vernacular writing system into the administrative and legal domains; in the second instance the writing system of Paris gradually spread throughout the kingdom (and beyond), eliminating not only Latin but also regional vernaculars, notably the *langue d'oc*. (*ibid.*, p. 120)

This second stage paralleled the increase in the dominance of Paris in the fourteenth century (*ibid.*, p. 122). By 1539, François I's famous *Ordonnances* signed in Villers-Cotterêts recommended that the "langaige maternel françois" was to be used in preference to Latin for administrative and judicial purposes (*ibid.*, p. 126; cf. also Battye et al. 2000; Brunot 1906).[19] As France grew to take in new provinces, the edict extended the boundaries of the French language in the administration (see Brunot 1917, p 89ff.). A single language of administration would make for more efficient control, a view shared by some with regard to the linguistic situation in the European Union today.

With the French Revolution two and a half centuries later, the state changed in nature from feudal to bureaucratic, and the French language took on a new role in symbolising that state. The Revolution also influenced the development of the French lexicon (Ayres-Bennett 1996, p. 229). The new bureaucratic state, with control over every aspect of people's lives, "required that all its members speak the same language. Language became the essential symbol of the nation: "République une, langue une: la langue doit être une comme la République" (Lodge 1993, p. 213).

Since the Revolution, even more so than under the ancien régime, public administration and language have gone hand in hand in France. Malcolm Offord

---

18 See also Brunot (1905) on the early history of the French language. In particular, he states that "à partir de la deuxième moitié du XIIIe siècle [...] le français devient la langue administrative de la plus grande partie du royaume. D'où vulgarisation d'une foule de termes d'administration et de droit empruntés au latin pour la plupart."

19 Rebecca Posner (1997, p. 83) explains: "What the Article [Article 111 of the *Ordonnances*] actually said was that to avoid ambiguity in edicts, in which Latin words could be misinterpreted, all sorts of legal instruments should henceforth be 'prononcez, enregistrez et delivrez aux parties en langage maternel françois et non autrement'."

(1990, p. 16) shows that both the protection and promotion of the standard language "ha[ve] been achieved by means of policies aimed at centralising and unifying the country administratively and socially, and thus linguistically" (cf. also Section 2.2 above, and Battye et al. 2000 for a century by century examination of French attitudes to the standard language). Rebecca Posner puts forward a possible motivation for having a standard language:

> The standard can be a means of control. Legitimate language is used in legislation and administration. It can serve an authoritarian regime, by distancing the prestige code from the language of the populace. It can also have a democratic purpose - by encouraging the populace to adopt the same code, in which opinions can be cogently expressed in free discussion, or by tolerating variation within the code, without stigmatising some variants as socially unprestigious. (Posner 1997, p. 46)

Today, there is an increasing number of governmental and private organisations which aim to protect and promote the language (cf. Brulard 1997; Judge 1993; Lodge 1993, p. 236ff; Offord 1994), even if some of these organisations apparently do very little in practice (Offord 1994).

Linguistic as well as historical analyses have been carried out on early administrative documents. Dees (1980) carried out a computer-based corpus study of several thousand charters, comprising almost a million words, from the *langue d'oïl* area, including Belgium, from the thirteenth century. Charters are particularly useful for linguistic purposes in that they tend to have been consistently preserved, and cover the area in question fairly evenly; this is essential for a study like Dees' in which the geographical distribution of phonological, morphological and syntactic features is important.

Lodge (1985) presents analysis of a different genre of document from the same period. The language of his thirteenth-century 'livres de comptes', or account books, from Montferrand "est plus variée que celle des terriers et des chartes, laquelle est plus soumise aux formules conventionnelles" (Lodge 1985, p. 49). There is little evidence to allow any conclusions or generalisations to be drawn with regard to the syntax of the Auvergnat dialect, however, as the syntactic structure of the sentences is restricted, and as a result Lodge concentrates instead on morphology, lexis and orthography.

Thus far, this chapter has briefly surveyed the French language and its internal development, and some sociolinguistic influences on its development. More could certainly be said on the genesis of administrative French itself, and the situation of language contact between administrative Latin and the vernacular in France. A further issue is that of the contact in Britain between French and English within areas related to public administration. This all adds up to a situation of trilingual language contact in the Anglo-Norman culture of the thirteenth century. Its extent should not be overemphasised, however. Wardhaugh explains that although there is evidence of bilingualism, from the late eleventh century most people apparently remained unilingually anglophone (Wardhaugh 1987, p. 68). Rather, "Bilingual ability was necessary for both anglophones and francophones only in those areas in which the two groups came into contact." (*ibid.*, p. 68).

As Section 6.2 discusses, there is considerable overlap between the language of administration and the language of the law. After the Norman Conquest, English finally triumphed in Britain, but the French influence was extensive (cf. Lehmann 1992), because of the "official grip of the Norman government, church, legal system, and various aspects of social and economic life" (Anttila 1989, p. 162). Borrowing is a common outcome in such situations, if both languages are to survive.[20]

The influence of French on English in these areas is perhaps most evident in the hundreds of Romance loanwords dating from this time and the following centuries right up to the time of the Revolution (cf. Crystal and Davy 1969; Anttila 1989; Lehmann 1992; Galonnier 1997; Wise 1997;[21] Iglesias-Rábade 2000). The influence was not, however, limited to single words. As Thomason points out, "all aspects of language structure are subject to transfer from one language to another, given the right mix of social and linguistic circumstances" (Thomason 2001, p. 11), despite the fact that some researchers claim that certain kinds of feature cannot be borrowed (*ibid.*, p. 63; and cf. also Anttila 1989, p. 169). Roger Lass (1997), for example, proposes a hierarchy of diffusability,

---

20 For a more extreme example, see Dorian (1978) on the influence of English on East Sutherland Gaelic in the Scottish Highlands. While Gaelic was the original language of the area, English became associated with the ruling class and the machinery of government, and its influence spread from the centres of secular and ecclesiastical administration, gradually taking over the functions of East Sutherland Gaelic.

21 Hilary Wise (1997, p. 82) gives some specific examples of French political terminology acquired around the time of the Revolution which originated in English: "Although the Revolution interrupted such activities, political terminology continued to flow across the Channel in both directions, producing Anglicisms like *ultimatum, pétition, opposition, constitutionnel, majorité, motion*." "We should however remember that influence was reciprocal during the eighteenth and nineteenth centuries. French was not only the diplomatic language of Europe; it acted as a kind of lingua franca for the ruling élite [...] From the failed diplomacy in the nineteenth century English imported 'détente', 'rapprochement', 'fait accompli', 'entente cordiale', 'communiqué', 'attaché', 'protocol' and many more."

according to which lexis (in a suggested descending order of nouns, adjectives, verbs, adverbs and prepositions) is more readily borrowed than morphology, which is in turn more readily borrowed than word order, and so on. Uriel Weinreich, in his seminal work on language contact (1953), however, would presumably have objected to such a hierarchy (he cites similar orderings by Whitney, Pritzwald and Dauzat), claiming that opinions on relative amounts of borrowing are superficial, and indeed may lack any real meaning.

Language contact between French and English has certainly gone beyond isolated lexical items. Crystal and Davy highlight instances of French loanwords co-existing alongside their English counterparts and indeed sometimes forming pairs of terms, such as ‘breaking and entering’ and ‘goods and chattels’ where, they suggest, there was doubt as to whether the words were true synonyms, and the need for inclusiveness, given the function of the legal register, led to the coupling (Crystal and Davy 1969, p. 208; see also Stubbs 1996 and 2001b). Also borrowed, although perhaps less salient, were idioms (according to Lehmann 1992, this was made possible because of the extended period of borrowing); syntactic phrases (such as the noun and adjective combinations ‘attorney general’ and ‘malice aforethought’, cf. Lehmann 1992, p. 268), although these non-native patterns were not usually generalised beyond the collocation in question; and syntactic patterns into which native words were substituted for foreign (Anttila 1989). Luis Iglesias-Rábade also highlights the influence of French on phraseology (Iglesias-Rábade 2000), suggesting that phrasal structures made their way into English by way of literature and translation rather than directly through bilingualism in society.

Within the administrative register therefore, the situation of language contact in the EU is not brand new. Indeed, D. A. Trotter (2000, p. 2), discussing late Medieval Britain says that: “Outside literary texts, documents in two or more languages, and language-mixing within the same text, were widespread, and this phenomenon, an oddity to modern eyes, patently created no obstacle to effective communication.” In the context of the EU, this is not an oddity to modern eyes. Laura Wright points out that bills, accounts and inventories are a text type in which a mixing of two or more languages is the norm. She claims that this variation is rule-governed and concludes that “an appreciation of the multilingual content of business records leads to the perception of Britain not as a monolingual island, but as a multilingual part of the European trading area” (Wright 2000, p. 149). Reminiscent of the ‘équivalence numérique’ of EU documents, accounts conventionally had “a close visual affinity with both languages” (*ibid.*), in this case medieval Latin and English. William Rothwell confirms this, saying that: “The evidence from the *York Memorandum Book* [records detailing administrative and commercial life of York between 1376 and 1492] shows that a wide range of differing combinations of Latin, French and English may be identified in the drafting of administrative documents around the turn of the fourteenth century.” (Rothwell 2000, p. 230).

While the particular configuration of the EU is new and politically uncharted territory, therefore, the contact situation in which the administrative register of French has found itself is not linguistically brand new. It has previously come into contact with both Latin and English. Similarly, while the complex system of translation in the EU is unique, it is certainly not new for individual administrative documents to reveal in themselves the multilingual environment in which they originate. The EU is however particularly fascinating for the very complexity of its linguistic situation, and its novelty: we are able to glimpse change and language contact actually in progress.

5. Popular perceptions of administrative language

The current language of public administration is often derided, both in popular opinion and even in the view of the public figures who use it, for obscurity and an inability to innovate (Crystal and Davy 1969, p. 242). It is often felt that it is inaccessible to a large number of those affected in some way by it (see for example Fairclough 1989, p. 218); that is to say, like the language of a discourse community, the administrative register can shut out the uninitiated, as the connotations of its partial synonym 'bureaucracy' make clear.[22] Raymond Williams in his study of keywords in society notes that Thomas Carlyle as early as 1850 referred to bureaucracy as a "Continental nuisance" (Williams 1976, p. 40).

The notion of the modern bureaucracy is generally considered to have been developed by Max Weber. From his essay on bureaucracy (Gerth and Mills 1948, Chapter 8), one can extract a number of characteristics of such a structure. Firstly, the bureaucratic structure is based upon written documents.[23] This allows for continuity of function, beyond the lives of the individuals who determine policy. Secondly, matters are regulated abstractly - that is, there is a "principled rejection of doing business 'from case to case' " (*ibid.*, p. 224), which involves frequently reinventing the wheel. Thirdly, "modern loyalty is devoted to impersonal and functional purposes" (*ibid.*, p. 199). Finally, secrecy increases the power of the informed. It is therefore not surprising that the language which emanates from such organisations should be criticised as being excessive, abstract, authoritarian, impersonal and inclined towards obscurity. Like the community of science writers, the community of administrators (and translators) is also "highly aware of

---

22 Cf. the Concise Oxford Dictionary's second definition (9th Edition): "the officials of such a government, esp. regarded as oppressive and inflexible".

23 According to Giddens, documents serve a dual function as "records of the past and prescriptions for the future" (1984, p. 152).

the power and pitfalls of terminology and written expression" (cf. Gledhill 1999, p. 231). Knapp and Wright suggest that the French, Napoleonic, model of administration "resembled a Weberian bureaucracy before Weber: hierarchical, impartial, rational, predictable, self-contained" (Knapp and Wright 2001, p. 271). The practice, however, they claim, never matched the model. The EU model, similarly, may be seen to fill these criteria of a Weberian bureaucracy.

Rodney Ball, who discusses a related type of language under the name "the administrative / technocratic style", a wider concept but one which appears to encompass the notion of the administrative register used here, traces its emergence in France back to the 1930s, and claims that commentators have been criticising it for half a century (Ball 1997, p. 182) and continue to do so today. He identifies the root of negative popular opinion when he notes that the language variety originated in specialist circles but "is found more and more often in material intended for the general reader" (*ibid.*, p. 182).

Opinions are similar, it appears, on both sides of the Channel. The success of a book such as Sir Ernest Gowers' *The Complete Plain Words*, whose stated purpose is "to help officials in their use of English as a tool of their trade" (Gowers 1973 (1954), p. 1), attests to the popular belief that Civil Service writing is unclear. Gowers is careful to point out, however, that "The fact is not that officials do uniquely badly but that they are uniquely vulnerable. Making fun of them has always been one of the diversions of the British public." (*ibid.*, p. 227). One only has to think here of the success of the 1980s television series *Yes Minister* and *Yes Prime Minister*.

René Georgin's 1973 work, *Le code du bon langage. Le langage de l'administration et des affaires*, is a prescriptive discussion of administrative and commercial French, written for officials in public and private administrations as "un manuel pratique du langage, qui traite à la fois de la grammaire et du vocabulaire" (1973, p. 11), and as such is very similar in content and purpose to Gowers' work. Georgin believes that: "on constate de plus en plus, de tous côtés et à tous les échelons de la hiérarchie sociale et bureaucratique, un emploi moins pur et moins sûr de notre langue" (*ibid.*, p. 227). He points to such 'faults' as inappropriate words, neologisms, some of which, such as *actualisation, environnement, globalisation, parution* and *utilisateur*, originate in the administrative context, clichés (*procéder à un échange de vues, faire un tour d'horizon, une chute verticale*), Anglicisms, slang and abbreviations, and truncated words. With specific reference to administrative language, he says:

> On peut lui reprocher (...) le manque de simplicité, un excès de pompe et de formalisme, l'emploi de formules-clichés routinières et démodées, des recherches littéraires et une affectation hors de propos, des néologismes barbares, des pléonasmes qui alourdissent

> inutilement la rédaction, la longueur embarrassée de ses phrases. (Georgin 1973, p. 234)

Attitudes to the register had not changed by the late 1980s. The researcher Claude Labarrère, following the defence of his thesis on French in legislation in 1989, was overwhelmed by media attention, and realised that he had struck a chord with the French public:

> Même son de cloche partout: "On ne comprend plus rien aux textes émanant de l'Administration. C'est un charabia. Les textes qui intéressent la vie de chacun d'entre nous (législation fiscale, législation sur les loyers, etc.) sont de plus en plus difficiles à comprendre". (Labarrère 1990)

He goes on to show that it is not only those who are affected by the policy and regulations transmitted or 'explained' by such language who would like it to change, but also many of those who use it. These include such influential figures as Georges Pompidou, who hated jargon, Valéry Giscard d'Estaing, who strove for clarity in his administrative documents, and François Mitterrand.

Of course, a lot can change in thirty years in an organisation as young as the EU. Perhaps what Georgin was referring to in 1973 were merely teething troubles? Apparently not, however. The linguist Thierry Fontenelle, who has worked in the EU, noted in 1999 that:

> Some criticism is constantly being levelled at the obscure nature of European texts and the 'distance' which separates those who produce these texts and the target audience, i.e. the European citizen, is repeatedly emphasised. It should be borne in mind that this is also partly due to the nature of the texts in question, however, and the somewhat sceptical attitude towards official texts is not really different when these texts are produced by a national administration for its citizens. (Fontenelle 1999, p. 122, note 2)

If criticism is due to the nature of the texts then it is unlikely to abate. For the same reason, measures to change administrative language are unlikely to be wholly successful.

Within the context of French in the European Union also, then, there are continuing attacks, by the public, politicians, the press and linguists within the administration themselves, on what has been called, in different languages, 'Eurospeak', *eurobabillage, le brouillard linguistique européen*, 'Eurofog' (cf. Goffin 1997, p. 63 and also Phillipson 2003, p. 3), all of which labels encapsulate the register's perceived obscurity. If anything, the register should be less foreign and obscure for a French speaker than for an English speaker, since a large number of the terms peculiar to the EU construction are, as we have seen, direct translations from French, or are effectively still French words.

In Georgin's work and that of other researchers, the obscurity of the register is blamed particularly on individual vocabulary items and grammatical constructions and for this reason these are the focus of his work (cf. Section 6.3). Bilingual glossaries and databases, compiled in the EU, similarly, contain terminological items, proper names and abbreviations (cf. *European Communities Glossary*, 1990). As Chapter 2 will discuss, the linguist Michael Halliday was one of the first to point out that "often it is not the lexical item alone but the collocation of two or more lexical items that is specific to one register" (Halliday, McIntosh and Strevens 1964, p. 88). Gledhill, through his work on scientific papers, has also shown that phraseology and the collocational patterns of, especially, grammatical items, vary according to genre and register (see Gledhill 1995). There has been little work on these features of administrative language, although Goffin (1997, p. 64) points out that the criticism has been extended to phraseology among other areas, and even to the concepts which lie behind such linguistic manifestations. The popular view is that the language cannot hope to be clear and precise if the concepts are vague and perceived to be designed to conceal the truth.

5.1 Attempts to 'improve' administrative language

Claude Labarrère (1990) makes the point that "l'Administration [...] est le premier écrivain de France", and that consequently, administrators, along with teachers, play an important part in the future of the French language. For social reasons too, it is important that the reader should be readily able to understand administrative documents. As Gowers points out:

> The need for the official to take pains is even greater, for if what the professional writer has written is wearisome and obscure the reader can toss the book aside and read no more, but only at his peril can he so treat what the official has tried to tell him. (Gowers 1973, p. 2)

As such, the administrative register has been the target of purist and prescriptive attitudes and measures which aim to make it more accessible. This obscurity is only partly due to unfamiliar technical terms. With reference to English, Crystal and Davy suggest that a distinction can be made between such irreplaceable technical terms and merely confusing terms which could, without detriment to the meaning of the text and the context from which they issue, be worded more clearly (cf. Crystal and Davy 1969, p. 242).

The French nation is well known for its attempts to standardise, promote and improve its national language (cf. Lodge 1993 and Wise 1997), and the administrative register has not been excluded from such measures, despite being considered a prestige variety. A number of ministerial terminology commissions have been formed to target vocabulary items, writing courses have been organised in ministries and the *Conseil supérieur de la langue française*, since its foundation in 1989, has created various working groups (Labarrère 1990). For a time, there even existed an *Association pour le bon usage du français dans l'Administration*: this was set up in 1967, under Georges Pompidou (cf. Georgin 1973, p. 341, Caput 1975, p. 237, Catherine 1985, p. 9, and Labarrère 1990), but was dissolved in 1982, because of a lack of both funds and influence. Such attitudes are not restricted to Paris, either: in Belgium, the Walloon *Conseil supérieur de la langue française* has issued recommendations on the "lisibilité des textes administratifs" (see http://www.cfwb.be/franca/publicat/pg019.htm).

In July 2001, a *Comité d'Orientation pour la Simplification du Langage Administratif* (COSLA) held its first meeting. This committee was formed under Michel Sapin, the Ministre de la fonction publique et de la réforme de l'Etat, and was composed of a number of experts, linguists, language users and administrative representatives, including, among other famous names, Alain Rey, Henriette Walter and Julia Kristeva. Its aim was to make administrative forms, letters and reports more comprehensible: in the short term this involved the rewriting of administrative forms, and in the longer term a process of language simplification, taking the form of a guide to administrative drafting, a glossary of terms, and related computer software. *Le Petit Décodeur,* a collection of 3000 words and expressions translated into clear language, was published in February 2005. *The Scotsman* (7 August 2001) explained that: "its task is to sweep out the mounds of circumlocution, archaic legalese and pompous obscurity that make any encounter between the citizen and the apparatus of the state an exercise of sheer mental endurance".

Within the European context, clear language has the additional advantage of accelerating and improving the translation process, and thereby lowering costs. To give just one example of the manner in which the EU is attempting to put into practice its official policy of using clear, simple language, the Commission Translation Service, the world's largest translation service, which accounts for approximately one third of the institution's staff,[24] has run a light-hearted campaign, called 'Fight the FOG',[25] to encourage the use of plain language by

---

24 Thierry Fontenelle (1999, p. 122) puts the total of Commission translation staff at 1800, of which 1400 are translators and the others are terminologists, documentalists, computer support staff and secretaries. In addition, 25% of translations are farmed out to freelance translators.

25 The website address of the 'Fight the FOG' campaign is http://europa.eu.int/comm/translation/en/ftfog/index.htm. The 'Fight the FOG' booklet is available here, along with the text of various lectures presented during the campaign.

authors and translators. Its booklet, which defines FOG as "that vague grey pall that descends on EU documents, obscuring meanings and messages, causing delays and irritation", makes an important distinction between 'Eurojargon', which is not readily understood by outsiders, and 'Eurospeak', which is seen as valuable, and indeed essential, for discussing EU-specific concepts which have no national counterpart.

The view that the perceived verbosity of administrative language serves a certain purpose is shared by the systemic functional linguist, Rick Iedema, who points out:

> If administrative texts are sometimes (or often!) seen as unnecessarily formal, imposing or verbose, we may be forgetting that their linguistic subtlety and complexity serves two purposes at once: the organization of human activity (shouldness) and institutional positioning (interpersonal distance). To want to make administrative/bureaucratic discursive practices more 'user-friendly' may either encourage the kind of 'synthetic' democratization Fairclough talks about, or it may favour reductive kinds of linguistic 'simplicity', which end up signalling greater differences in power than the original bureaucratese. (Iedema 1997, pp. 95-6)

In other words, the very function of administrative documents necessitates a level of complexity.

6. Linguistic characteristics of administrative French

The previous section discussed the popular perceptions of the administrative register. It was noted that administrative language is generally considered to be obscure, unintelligible, and excessive, both quantitatively and qualitatively. This section sets out some expectations of the register from a linguistic perspective, which serves to balance the picture created above.

While the interest here lies in administrative language, it is clear that the administrative register overlaps considerably with other registers, notably political and legal language. This is inevitable, given the interrelation of the roles of politicians, who decide policy, lawyers, who translate policy into legislation, and administrators, who implement policy, apply it to concrete cases and transmit the legislation to the public. In France, there is an especially close link between the administrative and the political structures: Knapp and Wright comment that in the Fifth Republic "it became hard, in short, to know where the civil service ended and the government began" (2001, p. 277). With this in mind, Sections 6.1 and 6.2 highlight salient features of political and legal language respectively, before moving on to the administrative register itself. None of these sections aims to be comprehensive, but rather to concentrate on features which are revealing for the present study.

6.1 Administrative language and political language

There is a large degree of overlap between political and administrative language, compounded by their reciprocal influence. To simplify greatly, the function of the administration is to implement policy (made by politicians), and to act as a bridge between legislation and the public. Not unlike politicians' speeches, although with different aims and motivations, administrators popularise political decisions and legislation. Like administrative language, the boundaries of political language cannot be easily delimited, and the register covers a wide range of subject matter, or fields.

A large part of the work on political language is qualitative and interpretative in focus (cf. Seidel 1985 for a survey of approaches to French political discourse). This is hardly surprising, if one agrees with Musolff, Schäffner and Townson that "politics is constituted in discourse, both in written texts and oral debates, which in turn shape and modify material political developments" (1996, p. 4). George Orwell's famous essay on political language is just one such example. He says of political writing:

> As soon as certain topics are raised, the concrete melts into the abstract and no one seems able to think of turns of speech that are not hackneyed: prose consists less and less of *words* chosen for the sake of their meaning, and more and more of *phrases* tacked together like the sections of a prefabricated hen-house. (Orwell 1946, p. 355)

Of course, this is far from objective: Orwell goes on to say that political writing is generally "lifeless, imitative" (*ibid.*, p. 362) bad writing, and that clichés are frequent, regardless of text type.

For John Gaffney too, "politics is essentially a question of language" (1993, p. 185), not only for politicians themselves, but also for others dealing with political language, including civil servants, and diplomats. For Gaffney, the exploitation of language variety has the potential to maximise effectiveness, not to exclude the uninitiated. Accordingly, much work has been done on the language and discourse of individual politicians, through the analysis of single texts, or collections of texts.[26] However, the study of individuals' language is not as narrow as it might at first appear:

---

26 See Gaffney's (1993) analysis of de Gaulle's 'Vive Montréal' speech and Mitterrand's 'Lettre à tous les Français', and the papers on individual politicians in Drake and Gaffney (1996).

> By studying the discourse of contemporary French leaders, we can expect to learn not only about the individual leader's discursive styles, but the political leadership role itself and, most significantly, the political process within which it operates, and the political culture in which it is embedded and from which it draws its effectiveness. (Drake and Gaffney (eds.) 1996, p. 12)

Political culture and processes can also be approached at a more detailed level. In politics, "potentially significant changes can occur not simply at the level of 'ideology' or 'political tradition', but at the level of the sentence, the word, or the spaces between words" (*ibid*., p. 4). Thus, the analysis of individual words can be enlightening too.[27] Susan Hockey (2000, p. 91) discusses work by Olsen and Harvey (1988) which carries out analysis of the collocations of keywords in French-Canadian political texts more or less contemporaneous with French revolutionary documents. Keywords such as *droits, patrie, pays* and *peuple* differ greatly between the two discourses.

In one of the few French introductory volumes on corpus linguistics, Habert, Nazarenko and Salem draw attention to the fact that corpus studies have shown that one form of a word can differ significantly in its usage from another form of the same word:

> On peut dire que de grandes oppositions idéologiques se sont souvent exprimées à travers l'emploi du singulier ou du pluriel d'une même forme de vocabulaire. Les classes *ouvrières*, proclamait le pouvoir monarchique sous Louis Philippe (1830-1848); *la classe ouvrière* contestaient les organisations ouvrières. De même, les années 1970 ont vu s'opposer les défenseurs *des libertés républicaines* (la gauche et les syndicats) aux défenseurs de *la liberté*, avec, bien entendu, des contenus partiellement différents. (Habert et al. 1997, p. 211)

It can sometimes be most useful therefore to treat word forms separately: this was one reason behind the decision not to lemmatise the corpus compiled for this research (cf. Chapter 3).

Research has also been carried out on metaphor in political discourse. In this regard, Christina Schäffner's (1999) work on the metaphors of construction and movement in European discourse on unity and integration gives clear insights into the ways in which politics is conceptualised - in particular that metaphor variation in different countries reflects different attitudes within the particular

27 See, for example, Trew (in Fowler et al. 1979) and Musolff (1996, p. 16) on 'internationalisms' or etymologically-related expressions which carry different connotations in different languages.

country, or even within political parties, rather than intercultural differences. Although one might expect administrative language to exploit metaphor much less systematically, it would not be surprising for its presence to be noted in speech genres in particular, genres which can be seen to straddle the divide between politics and administration. Straehle et al.'s study (1999) of the item 'unemployment' in two genres of EU language (Commissioners' speeches and Presidency Conclusions) is also in this vein, and links the study of individual words with the study of metaphor; Straehle et al. find differences between genres, connected to their respective purposes and audiences, whether external or internal, and similarities stemming from a broader metaphor of 'struggle' which is linked to economic discourses in general.

Finally, the well-known translation scholar, Peter Newmark has discussed English political language from the point of view of collocation and translation:

> One characteristic of political language is that it tends to collocations that are repeated so often that they become clichés, therefore weaker in force, giving them the same dull thud as many abstractions. (Newmark 1991, p. 159)

He mentions such collocations as 'loudly applaud', 'stick firmly' and 'overriding priority', which he claims "don't usually bear one-to-one translation, but [...] have to be translated in all their banality (not difficult)" (*ibid.*, p. 159).

Political language, then, has tended to be studied from the point of view of rhetorical structure and the centrality of key concepts. This will be particularly relevant to this study where the focus is on the speech texts contained in the corpus, and in Chapter 6, where the analysis looks at the collocational patterning of keywords.

6.2 Administrative language and legal language

As was noted above, administrative language borders not only on political language, but also on the language of the law. A great deal of work has been carried out on this highly distinctive register, and it is not the aim here to do more than summarise briefly some of the most significant linguistic characteristics of the register, with reference to the particular constraints on legal draughtsmen.

Gowers notes that "legal drafting must [...] be unambiguous, precise, comprehensive and largely conventional" (1973, p. 8). While intelligibility is important, the need for an appropriate degree of accuracy outweighs this. The many and easily-recognised peculiarities of legal style are due in large part to the need for caution, balancing precision and vagueness where necessary, and conveying a particular meaning while simultaneously excluding alternatives. Crystal and Davy present an excellent discussion of the characteristics of legal

English. They point out that legal language is one of the least communicative registers in function, as it is not designed to "enlighten language-users at large" (1969, p. 193), but rather to present information for scrutiny by experts. The job of administrators is partly to translate expert-to-expert language in a huge variety of fields into language which is intelligible to the lay-person. In doing so they encounter strong linguistic conservatism, manifested in archaisms and a dearth of punctuation, among other features, owing to a reliance on language which has proven its effectiveness. Legal language is also characterised, according to Crystal and Davy, by long sentences with a relatively high proportion of dependent clauses, most notably in recitals, and subordinating devices, lexical repetition rather than pronouns for precision of reference, adverbial clauses, a highly nominalised style, a lack of adjectives and intensifying adverbs, and technical vocabulary, whether items specific to the register, or items with specific meanings in the legal context. English legal language has the additional feature of a large French and Latin element, dating back beyond the Norman Conquest, and while some of the terms effectively became English words, even if only seldom breaking the boundaries of legal language, many are still considered foreign terms.

Although the constraints and many of the linguistic characteristics of legal English are shared by French, one cannot presume that the context of production will manifest itself in the same ways. Indeed, there are also divergences, for historical and linguistic reasons. In his discussion of convergences between legal language in French and English, Bernard Galonnier (1997) notes the presence of specific jargon, including Latinisms, set formulae and obsolete terms, an elevated tone, owing to the use of certain prepositions, nominalisation, and elaborate syntax, and the presence of terms from the general language which have a particular, narrower, meaning in the law. The two specific registers are further brought together by the presence of French terms in both. The differences, too, are notable. For example, in the specific context of pronouncements:

> [...] dans leurs jugements les magistrats anglais, loin d'être concis et synthétiques comme leurs confrères français, se montrent fort prolixes et ne craignent pas de faire preuve d'humour et de recourir à une langue imagée. (Galonnier 1997, p. 428)

Spoken legal English can be differentiated from French in its specific concepts, prolixity, for example in its use of litotes and hedging, metaphorical language, and anti-intellectualism. Galonnier shows that the differences are more fundamental than terminology, rooted rather in "l'émanation de l'âme d'un pays et de ses particularismes culturels" (*ibid.*, p. 437).

In a similar way to administrative language, attempts have been made to simplify legal French. Hilary Wise points to the *Journal Officiel* of 24 September 1977 which aimed to "faciliter la compréhension par les justiciables du langage employé par les practiciens du droit" (Wise 1997, p. 193). It was proposed, among other measures, that twenty-nine Latin expressions should be rendered in French, and many excessively long formulae be shortened.

On the basis of the work briefly surveyed in this section and the previous one, we can expect the administrative corpus used here to contain a wide variety of linguistic styles, bordering as it does on both political and legal language.

6.3 Administrative French

Atkinson and Biber have pointed out that research into bureaucratic language is more often carried out for prescriptive purposes than descriptive ones (1994, p. 356). It would not therefore be surprising for such work to be strongly biased. Not all work, however, has been prescriptive, although this work does tend to go into more detail: the administrative register is often passed over quickly in descriptive, stylistic, work. In his introduction textbook on French and the French-speaking world, Rodney Ball notes that in administrative French, which he terms the administrative-technocratic style, as in colloquial French (and also as in legal French as has been seen), "newly coined and traditional items [are] to be found side by side" (Ball 1997, p. 181). The examples he gives also indicate that administrative language is characterised by nominalisation, complex syntax and technical vocabulary which originates in specialist circles.

The Italian linguist, Gaetano Berruto has carried out detailed descriptive research into the administrative register of Italian (Berruto 1987, 1997). He discusses what he calls "italiano burocratico", which is "la varietà (scritta ma anche parlata) usata negli ambiti amministrativi, ufficiali"[28] (Berruto et al. 1997, p. 14). Some of the most salient characteristics of this register, which covers a large number of conceptual fields, are: officialness and uniformity, an appearance of solemnity, archaisms and Latinisms but at the same time also neologisms, richness in set phrases, and repetition. In the area of morphosyntax, Berruto draws attention to the highly nominal style, and textually, the variety's well-defined text structures. One of the reasons for these characteristics, according to Berruto, is the prestige and power accorded to the bureaucrats by a special language.

Linguistic analysis of the French administrative register is not new. Robert Catherine's study of *Le style administratif*, originally published in 1947 (fifth edition 1985), aims to "expliquer l'écriture de l'Administration, en vue d'en tirer un enseignement pratique d'ordre professionnel et, si possible, d'en améliorer la qualité et l'audience" (Catherine 1985, p. 7). Catherine therefore states his aim to be prescriptive. While remaining aware of the internal variation within what he

---

28 "the variety (written but also spoken) used in administrative or official domains." (my translation)

defines as administrative language, variation caused by factors such as the age of the department or service in question and its level of contact with the public or business, Catherine looks in detail at the vocabulary typical of the administration, elements of its sentence structure and types of document. As regards vocabulary, he points out that:

> L'originalité du vocabulaire administratif est beaucoup moins constituée par l'existence d'une terminologie propre à l'Administration que par le goût de cette dernière pour un certain nombre de mots et de tournures qui se retrouvent dans la plupart de ses manifestations littéraires. (Catherine 1985, p. 27)

That is to say, that administrative language is recognisable less by its terminological items than by the way it draws on non-specialised words and phrases, such as *mettre en œuvre* and *communiquer*. These, through constant usage, "transforme en autant d'idiotismes plus ou moins justifiés" (*ibid*., p. 27). However, it is not just the words and phrases which define the register, but their arrangement. Even back in the 1940s, Catherine touches briefly on the importance of collocation for the definition of the register of administration:

> [...] chaque mot pris en lui-même n'a pas, le plus souvent, de caractère spécifique. [...] Et puisque ce sont surtout ici l'agencement des mots et la fréquence de leur emploi qui importent. (1947, p. 24, 1985, p. 27)

Certain types of locution are also more or less likely to be used: in particular "les locutions verbales à forme imagée ou familière" are very unlikely to occur.

René Georgin's (1973) study of administrative French is also prescriptive in nature, indeed more obviously so than Catherine's. However, there is also necessarily an element of description. The features of the register which Georgin proscribes are likely to be those which appear to him more salient. Of course, there are many areas left untouched in such a study also. Georgin discusses a number of features of the register in turn, beginning with what he calls 'les mots nobles', or weighty words, which create an effect through their apparent specificity, but in fact can be paraphrased in a much simpler manner. An example is the verb *effectuer*, used often unnecessarily in a wide variety of contexts. Georgin notes: "C'est à croire que le verbe *faire* est rayé de son vocabulaire" (1973, p. 236). The second feature to elicit comment is the use of personification in administrative language, as in the example 'la décision s'inspire de ce principe'. He goes on to proscribe *impropriétés*, such as *mise en place* being used for abstract ideas and not just physical objects; clichés (*étroitement lié, à la lumière de*); the use of pleonastic expressions (*exclusivement réservé*, *un achat d'un montant de cent mille francs*); over-use of nominal constructions, the present participle, passive constructions; the inversion of the subject (*Sont prohibées...*, *Sont exempts de la taxe...*), and finally what he calls *gaucheries*, a rather fuzzy catch-all category for clumsy turns of phrase. We might deduce from this that these are some of the most salient characteristics of the register as he sees it. Georgin also identifies a number of verbs in his study of administrative French, which typically collocate with a particular noun or adverb (Georgin 1973, pp. 274-6). A list of these, with their typical environment in the administrative corpus, can be found in Appendix 7 (see also Chapter 7 for discussion).

Within corpus linguistics, very little has been said about collocations in administrative language specifically. However, this has been noted as potentially fertile ground for analysis. The corpus linguist Göran Kjellmer, for example, finds that collocations are frequent in the 'miscellaneous' category of the Brown Corpus. He explains:

> This is only natural when we realise, first that collocations are characteristically established and invariable or formulaic chunks of language, and secondly that genre H contains a large number of official reports and documents where that kind of language is generally favoured. (Kjellmer 1987, p. 136)

If this is true also of French, and there is no reason to believe that it would not be, administrative language should reveal a lot about collocation and inversely, a study of collocation should provide a useful addition to the description of administrative language.

7. Conclusion

A multilingual situation in which language contact plays a large part is not unprecedented for the administrative register. Rather, this register has been the point of contact between languages before, as in the Anglo-Norman culture of thirteenth-century England. The current linguistic situation in the European Union is, however, both unique and increasingly complex: there is a constant tension between the principle of the equality of the official languages of all of the member states, and the practical demands this puts on the translation process and the Community budget. In practice, this had led to a situation where some languages are more equal than others. French, English and German have been the major players for nearly thirty years: now, however, the balance is beginning to change with English apparently gradually taking over from French as the first among equals. It is an appropriate time, therefore, to take stock of EU French.

On the one hand, French has clearly had a major part to play in the development and evolution of Eurospeak. The origins of the EU discourse in the French language, and of the EU institutional make-up in the French administrative framework, and the continuing central role of France, have clearly had an influence at the conceptual level and on lexical items. The part which the national discourse has played in the phraseology of Eurospeak remains to be seen.

On the other hand, the increasingly complex language contact situation, although it is limited to one particular register, should, according to theories of language contact, have an effect on the discourse of EU French. Interaction between Brussels and Paris should, reciprocally, have led to variation in the national discourse. Has institutional change, from the 1950s onwards, resulted in a modified administrative discourse in both the EU and the French national contexts? A synchronic study of the state of divergence of the two discourses at the end of the twentieth century is the first step to answering this question.

A further question, and one on which we can currently only speculate, is whether the emergence of a monoglot environment is the most likely outcome. Research into languages in contact shows that this is a common outcome (e.g. Thomason 2001, p. 12), but most such work is based on languages in a national context, which often encroach on each other's territory in more than one domain. The choice of multilingualism in the EU, however, was deliberate, and fundamental to its objectives, however impracticable it might sometimes appear. A more likely scenario is a move towards a larger number of document types being made available in only one or two languages; closer to a functional diglossia. If this turns out to be the case, one might wonder whether the weight of the conceptual basis in French will be sufficient to guarantee its continued place as one of the main languages.

Chapter 2

Concepts of Phraseology and Collocation

His eyes gleamed with a kind of manic glee, like he was Frankenstein, or some kind of wizard, as if he had me locked up in that flat metal box.

DAVID LODGE, SMALL WORLD: AN ACADEMIC ROMANCE

1. Introduction

In administration, as in other specialist domains such as science and the legal profession, there are well-developed terminological resources, the function of which is, as the linguist John Sinclair has put it: "to maintain the semantic isolation of the terms and to counter the natural pressures of usage" (Sinclair 1996, p. 102). The Commission of the European Union, for example, has its own terminological database, Eurodicautom, which is constantly updated and now also available online. The Secretariat of the Council of Ministers too has its own in-house terminological database, and publishes the *European Communities Glossary*, for a number of language pairs, detailing the accepted translations of technical terms in the areas covered by the Council's work, in addition to acronyms and the names of agreements, conventions, organisations and treaties.

In order to develop such resources, the EU institutions have terminologists in the different translation services. Terms are identified in documents as they are processed: that is to say that, although terminology work is not normally based on corpora as such, it is grounded in authentic texts. The study of terminology has been quite slow to exploit the methods of corpus linguistics: Meyer and Mackintosh (1996) suggest that this is due to practical considerations of time. Since terminography deals with new words, it is impractical to design and compile corpora for the extraction of terms. However, they come to the conclusion that such problems can be overcome and that corpora will be invaluable to terminographers in the future (cf. also de Schaetzen 1996 for a similar view). This is already being proved to be correct, as work by Jennifer Pearson (1998) shows.

A terminological approach to EU administrative language is only one side of the coin, however. A focus on terms brings to the fore the conceptual domains touched on by the EU, but can provide little insight into the workings of the language itself, and how meaning is created in the register. In recent work, John Sinclair has made a fundamental distinction between the 'terminological tendency', the "tendency for a word to have a fixed meaning in reference to the world", and the 'phraseological tendency', or the tendency whereby "words tend to go together and make meanings by their combinations" (Sinclair 2000a, p. 13). These tendencies are closely related to Sinclair's earlier conceptions of the open-choice principle and the idiom principle (see Section 5.1 below). The phraseological tendency accounts for the co-occurrence of 'manic' and 'glee' in the quotation at the head of this chapter: new connotations of meaning are created by their combination.

The main issue investigated in this chapter is the ways in which words can be said to 'go together' in language. Chapters 4 to 6 then attempt to answer this question with regard to the administrative discourse of the EU, comparing this with the French national administrative discourse. The corpus linguist Alan Partington points out:

> If the *raison d'être* of the idiom-collocation principle is to save processing time and effort, then it would tend to be most typical of on-line, spontaneous discourses, that is to say, conversation. We might expect preconstructed and semi-preconstructed phrases to be less common in writing, where time constraints tend to be less rigid. (Partington 1998, p. 20)

This is not the case, however. In fact, the administrative register relies to a large extent on prefabrication, and as Partington himself goes on to note:

> [...] in very many genres of writing, pre-cooked expressions are still diagnostic, vital elements. We need only think of legal documents, scientific/medical papers, business reports and so on. There are two reasons for this. Many kinds of lexical items, including prefabs, function as powerful indicators of register, and in most circumstances it is important for a writer to signal the register to which the text belongs. Secondly, although it may be less pressing than in conversation, there is still a need in written texts to balance new information with old information, novelty with habit, (prefabs contributing to the second items of these pairs) to cut down processing effort, especially if the text is long. (*ibid.*, p. 20)

It would appear, therefore, that prefabrication in administrative writing is motivated by more than mere time constraints, although of course this is still an issue, especially given the actual context of text production and translation. Rather, prefabrication has an important part to play in defining the register and genres in question: set phrases can be seen to function as a "membership badge" (McKenny 1999). Legal issues are also crucial and, related to this, intertextuality plays a significant role in the register: in other words, existing texts are to a certain extent the 'memory' which allows for a consistent and recognisable register.

In her work on the relationship between phraseology and terminology in Language for Special Purposes, Gläser (1992) suggests that while Language for General Purposes has a fully developed system of phraseological units, in LSP phrases are uncommon, and seldom figurative (that is to say, non-compositional idioms). She claims that they function instead as terms, are stylistically neutral and are linked to particular discourse communities. Resche (1997), on the other hand, sees comparative phraseology as a useful complement to comparative terminology. For her, phraseological units add a functional dimension to terminological units, and do indeed exist in specialist genres.

2. Phraseology and collocation - problems of definition

Sinclair's definition of the phraseological tendency is by its nature very general: it covers all types of lexical co-occurrence. Within the umbrella term of the phraseological tendency there are a number of terminological problems: both 'phraseology' and 'collocation' have been used in different ways. The multiplicity of terms has been seen as proof of inconsistency: Howarth, for example, says, "the main reason for this lack of consistency lies in the way in which most of those with an interest in prefabricated language have focused on only a part of the whole spectrum of such expressions" (Howarth 1998, p. 6). It is also a consequence of the fact that collocation has been considered relevant in the context of more than many discipline, lexicography, language teaching, psycholinguistics, stylistics, among others. Indeed collocations even have a role in language change: Anttila, for example, points out that "Habitual linguistic collocation may become permanent, and if part of the collocation is lost, the remainder changes meaning, when it takes on the semantics of the earlier phrase" (1989, p. 138). The systemicist Gordon Tucker has commented (2000) that collocation is a phenomenon in search of a theory. Rather it is not short of theories, but is certainly in need of a unifying theory.

The term 'phraseology' has traditionally focused on co-occurrence in the form of set phrases, particularly with regard to the Russian and East European traditions of research in lexicology, although it has recently also been used to describe the rhetorically-motivated expression of discourse communities. Gledhill, for example, in his study of collocation in science writing, proposes a rough definition of phraseology which is a very convenient working definition for the purposes of the present research. Phraseology for him is "the preferred way of saying things in a particular discourse" (Gledhill 2000, p. 1 and p. 202). He goes on to expound this definition:

> The notion of phraseology implies much more than inventories of idioms and systems of lexical patterns. Phraseology is a dimension of language use in which patterns of wording (lexico-grammatical patterns) encode semantic views of the world, and at a higher level idioms and lexical phrases have rhetorical and textual roles within a

> specific discourse. Phraseology is at once a pragmatic dimension of linguistic analysis, and a system of organisation which encompasses more local lexical relationships, namely collocation and the lexico-grammar. (Gledhill 2000, p. 202)

As such, phraseology is a means of relating different types of collocation, the "process by which words combine into larger chunks of expression" (*ibid.*, p. 1). This is a wider definition of collocation than many researchers would accept. Geoffrey Williams agrees that collocation is a problematic term, saying that: "de par sa nature, la collocation demeure un concept difficilement formalisé, aucune définition ne satisfait tout le monde" (G. C. Williams 2001b). He suggests that it is therefore best to describe collocation in terms of prototypes, and extracts two main tendencies from research on collocation: firstly, "la tendance lexicographique qui tend à une formalisation des collocations pour les inclure dans des dictionnaires", and secondly, "la tendance contextualiste, en ligne directe avec les travaux de Firth, qui considère les collocations comme un phénomène textuel et les définit en fonction de l'apparition de cooccurrences à l'intérieur d'une fenêtre" (*ibid.*). 'Collocation' has been used in particular in the Firthian tradition to highlight lexicogrammatical aspects of co-occurrence: it too comes loaded, however, like a palimpsest, with connotations of previous uses.

Van der Wouden has drawn attention to the double meaning of 'collocation', saying that "this shift of meaning between an abstract term for a certain phenomenon and the concrete instances of this very same phenomenon is extremely common and hardly ever leads to misunderstanding" (van der Wouden 1997, p. 6). Collocations are generally seen as products, or units, in lexicographical approaches, while the process of collocation has been stressed by recent work in neo-Firthian linguistics, and is being developed into a more inclusive view of language, all the time based on actual language data, as intuition is rarely a reliable guide.

It is tempting to retain the term 'collocation' regardless of how far away from a prototypical definition we move. Michael Hoey disagrees with this solution, however:

> [...] it is not in my view helpful to allow the term 'collocation' to expand in a shapeless manner to cover any observation made about the relationship of a word with its environment. It would be better to reserve the term for the particular association a word may have with another word: when we talk of 'the company a word keeps', let us mean 'company' in the old-fashioned sense reflected in the idiom that talks of a young man and woman of good reputation 'keeping company' rather than in the more general sense used when one talks of a person mixing in 'bad company'. The first 'company' assumes a special relationship with a particular other; the other use of 'company'

> assumes a general relationship with a wide range of people with common characteristics. (Hoey 1997, p. 4)

While it might nonetheless be argued that a single term has certain advantages, since it does not introduce unnatural divisions between phrases and non-phrases, or between lexis and grammar, the term 'collocation' is reserved here for the particular relationship between one word (lexical or grammatical) with another, and 'phraseology' is used with the more general sense of 'typical linguistic environment'.

The next three sections of this chapter examine the relationship of words with their typical environments in language: the analysis in Chapters 4 to 6 puts these concepts into practice by investigating the typical patterning of items in administrative language. Clearly, semantic and pragmatic factors have an important role in word co-occurrence. So too do issues of register and genre. The three sections share a focus on the locus of creation of phraseology. Section 3 considers phraseology which is the creation of the administrators: that is to say, phraseological patterning which has developed to fulfil the needs of the EU and French national discourses. Section 4 turns to phraseology as it has generally been considered by lexicographical approaches, focusing on word patterning which has its origins in the general language: that is, phraseological items which are the cumulative creation of language users, and part of the linguistic heritage which the EU register has adopted from French. This notion emphasises the syntactic and semantic features of phraseological patterning. Section 5, finally, turns to the neo-Firthian statistical, text-based, notion of collocation, and its recent developments. This final type of patterning, therefore, is the creation of the text.

3. Phraseology as the creation of administrators - discoursal notions

Much of the patterning of language can be explained by real-world factors of semantics and pragmatics. Lexical items occur in each other's company because their concepts are related in the world. An instruction manual for a car, say, is likely to contain the lexical items 'gear-stick', 'clutch' and 'engine' because these objects are closely related in the real world. When things come together frequently in the world, or when particular actions are frequently carried out through language, then language can develop mechanisms to save processing time. Administrative language has a reputation for being formulaic, for having a high proportion of conventionalised phrases which express common events and entities in the real world.[29] We are dealing here, therefore, with lexical co-

29 Such formulae, repeated sequences of words which aid text production by expressing common ideas, are reminiscent of the use of formulae in the Old French oral tradition. For further information on this, see J. J. Duggan

occurrences created by the discourse in question. The phenomenon of intertextuality in the EU discourse, whereby sections, particularly in legal texts, are re-used in subsequent texts, heightens the appearance of its formulaic nature. In this respect and because of the habitual practice of translation, it cuts across the notion of natural language.

This kind of phraseological patterning can be highlighted by analysis of recurring sequences of words in a corpus: this is the approach taken in Chapter 4. This also necessarily emphasises frequent terminological items in the discourse.

According to the corpus linguist Göran Kjellmer, all recurring sequences of words are potential collocations: actual collocations are both lexically determined (that is, recurrent in the corpus in question)[30] and grammatically well-formed (Kjellmer 1984, p. 163 and 1991, p. 116). Within the bounds of these two constraints, however, some collocations "possess a higher and others a lower degree of lexicalisation" (*ibid.*, p. 164), where lexicalisation is the result of a number of factors, namely absolute frequency, relative frequency, length, distribution over texts and text categories, and structure. Kjellmer's definition of collocation thus includes traditional idioms. However, collocations should not be seen to constitute a well-defined category like single-word lexemes. Rather they should be placed along a continuum ranging from established collocations (which often do function as one-word lexemes, e.g. 'the Soviet Union') to sequences of doubtful cohesion. Kjellmer allows for combinations of lexical and function words too: indeed he notes that it is only when we take into consideration such phrases as 'it is obvious that', and 'a number of', that "the ubiquity and indispensability of set expressions become fully apparent" (Kjellmer 1991, p. 115). Such collocations are the concept behind his *Dictionary of English Collocations* (1994), which is based on recurrence in a corpus: the Gothenburg Corpus of Collocations, itself a sub-corpus of all of the collocations in the Brown Corpus.

According to this definition we can expect to find a high proportion of collocations in the administrative corpus: Kjellmer explains that while collocations are indispensable in all types of text, they are more characteristic of informative, formal, text types (Kjellmer 1987, p. 133). His findings support the conclusion that collocations occur most frequently in Category H of the Brown

---

(e.g. 1969, 1973), who has created a concordance of the *Chanson de Roland*, which highlights the repeated hemistiches. Formulae are "received by the singer from the tradition just as individual words are received by the literary poet from the lexicon of his language" (1969).

30 This is also a criterion for inclusion as a collocation in Sinclair's work - see Section 5 below. It is not however a requirement in a lot of work on collocation from a pedagogical perspective - cf. for example Howarth (1996).

Corpus, the miscellaneous category, made up predominantly of administrative, business and official documents and reports. In this type of writing, he claims, "clarity and communicative success are more important than originality" (*ibid.*, p. 139). Such a finding is of course wholly dependent on the corpus used, and since the Brown Corpus is fairly small and relatively heterogeneous, it is not necessarily the case that similar results would have been found with other corpora. It may simply be that this category is more cohesive, and the texts less heterogeneous than those in, say, the literature categories.

The approach taken in Chapter 4 of this research to extracting collocations from a corpus of texts follows on from Kjellmer's definition of collocation as structured patterns which recur in identical form. Similar work has been described by Altenberg (Altenberg and Eeg-Olofsson 1990; Altenberg 1993, 1998). Altenberg and Eeg-Olofsson recognise two conceptions of collocation, a broad and a strict, Firthian, sense. In its broad sense, collocation can be seen as more or less equivalent to 'recurrent word combinations', or continuous sequences of words in identical form (Altenberg and Eeg-Olofsson 1990, p. 3). The grammaticality of the sequence is therefore no longer a necessary requirement. This notion is by definition corpus-based and particular to a limited sample of language. The Firthian notion of collocation on the other hand "goes beyond this notion of textual co-occurrence and emphasizes the relationship between *lexical items in language*" (*ibid.*, p. 3, emphasis, Altenberg and Eeg-Olofsson). It is still corpus-based to the extent that a language is constituted by actual texts. It is not, however, restricted to contiguous items, nor is it specific to particular word forms. In an important sense, then, the Firthian notion of collocation can be seen as the broader of the two. Altenberg and Eeg-Olofsson's research investigates the former type of collocation. They extract recurrent word combinations from the London-Lund Corpus and analyse the resulting combinations in terms of lexicogrammar (grammatical structure and collocability) and function. Altenberg and Eeg-Olofsson claim that multiword expressions are an intermediate component in language, being partly generated by the speaker/writer and partly retrieved from memory, and therefore that research into collocation will cause the borderline between lexis and grammar to become fuzzier and more complex (Altenberg and Eeg-Olofsson 1990, p. 19).

Altenberg (1998) continues this line of enquiry, examining the phraseology of spoken English as represented by the London-Lund Corpus. He shows how an approach which might be expected to obscure any variation in recurrent word combinations can in fact prove to be of significant theoretical and practical importance in describing the phraseology of speech. Altenberg claims that spoken English has a high proportion of such combinations - he estimates that over 80 per cent of the words in the corpus form part of a recurrent word combination - although many of them have little or no phraseological interest, and relatively few are completely frozen.

The British linguist Chris Butler has carried out work in a similar vein, based on a corpus composed of five sub-corpora covering spoken and written Spanish and based predominantly on journalistic texts. His work has found that few of the frequent sequences relate to the subject matter of the texts (although this figure is higher in the written corpus than the spoken one); and also that many of the frequent sequences are of an interpersonal, rather than an ideational, nature (Butler 1997, p. 69). Butler has further determined that there is a relationship between lexical sequences and the mode of communication: namely that the written corpus has much fewer frequently-repeated sequences, but more which relate to the subject matter of the texts.

The approach taken in Chapter 4 here combines the interest of Altenberg and Butler in recurrent multiword sequences with the work of Gledhill (e.g. 2000) on the phraseology of specific registers. It aims to show how multiword sequences, involving both lexical and grammatical words, establish the fundamental phraseology of the administrative register.

4. Phraseology as the creation of language users - semantic / syntactic notions

The previous section focused on phraseology as it has been developed by administrators themselves to express frequent meanings in the register of administration. The administrative register is not, however, a self-contained part of the French language: rather it exploits lexical, grammatical and phraseological resources of the general language where these suit its purposes. This section therefore surveys the phraseological resources available.

> [...] we can mention idioms, fixed phrases, variable phrases, clichés, proverbs, and many technical terms and much jargon, as examples of recognised patterns where the independence of the word is compromised in some way (Sinclair 2000, p. 10)

Sinclair here points to a number of types of phraseological unit. Terminological items and jargon are closely related to the discourse of the language variety in question: we might turn to the general language for the other types of unit listed here, which are related by their focus on semantic and syntactic elements. Gledhill has claimed that "science writing is highly devoid of idioms of the traditional kind, but is rich in metaphor and collocational restrictions" (1999, p. 234, and cf. also 2000, pp. 1-2). Given its predominant informational function, we might expect administrative language to be similarly devoid of such units as idioms and proverbs, but whether this is restricted to particular genres or modes within the register is another matter: this is discussed further in Chapter 5.

This section begins by relating work on phraseology to research on idioms, setting out Adam Makkai's useful distinction between encoding and decoding idioms, which is crucial for an appreciation of collocations. It then widens the object of study to idiomaticity as a whole: it is important to note that in looking at idioms and phrases we are not dealing here with collocation in its narrow sense, but with lexical patterning which contributes to the phraseology of a language or register. The next sub-section glances at lexicographical approaches to collocations. With the benefit of these discussions, the final part of this section looks at work in France on 'locutions'.

Ultimately, it would seem to be impossible, and also perhaps undesirable, to lose sight of the parallels between idioms and collocations. Although collocations are usually distinguished from idioms on the grounds that they are semantically compositional (cf. van der Wouden's definition, 1997, p. 9), that is to say that the constituents all contribute to the overall meaning of a collocation, there is clearly some degree of semantic cohesion involved in a collocation, otherwise meaning could not be produced by collocation. Compositionality appears to be a 'more or less' feature of word combinations (cf. also van der Wouden 1997, p. 11), with idioms at one extreme and collocations at the other.

4.1 Encoding and decoding idioms

> Matters of wit, curiosity and love of the unusual, the absurd, etc., have a further impact on the intuition. These things are memorable, and ordinary things are not. The computer does not discriminate. (Sinclair 1997, p. 33)

Idioms, that is to say, semantically non-compositional phrases, or phrases which have a meaning which is more than the sum of their component words, such as *il pleut des cordes* ('it's raining cats and dogs'), have a tendency to stand out in language whereas other, less intuitively eye- (or ear-) catching word combinations do not. This is one explanation for the predominance of studies of traditional idioms in linguistics, especially outside corpus linguistics.[31] Their salience has the result of making them appear more common and fundamental than they are.

The linguist Adam Makkai, writing in 1972, opened his seminal study of *Idiom Structure In English* by noting that idiomaticity had been neglected in Western scholarship (1972, p. 23). Thirty years on, this is still at least partly true, although corpus methodology has enabled a focus on idiomaticity and collocation that was not previously possible. For Makkai, collocations can be subsumed under the

---

31 Among these studies, see in particular Hockett (1958) and Householder (1959), who both proposed reductionist conceptions of idioms, emphasising semantic non-compositionality above any other criterion for the recognition of idioms.

general concept of 'idiomaticity'. His work is crucial for studies of collocation, because it introduces some important distinctions. Makkai suggests a reason for the terminological confusion apparently inherent in the study of idiom:

> [...] almost every linguist, or philologist for that matter, who considered the problem, saw something else in idiomaticity. To some, it was a matter of UNUSUAL ENCODING, that is a PHRASEOLOGICAL problem, to others a matter of MISUNDERSTANDABILITY, that is AMBIGUOUS DECODABILITY; and again to others the failure to understand a form despite previous familiarity with the meanings of its constituents, and so forth. (Makkai 1972, p. 7, emphasis is Makkai's)

His own approach recognises two types of idiom, accounting for all of these conceptions of idiomaticity:

> It seems appropriate to consider these 'phraseological peculiarities'[32] as IDIOMS OF ENCODING, and lexical clusters (*hot dog, hot potato, red herring*), and tournures (*to fly off the handle, to seize the bull by the horns*, etc) as IDIOMS OF DECODING. (*ibid.*, p. 25)

It follows that idioms of decoding are necessarily also idioms of encoding, or 'phraseological peculiarities', but the reverse is not true. Idioms of decoding are traditional or semantic idioms. Idioms of encoding, however, include phraseological items and collocations. In accordance with this definition, the overriding principle can be considered to be that of 'idiomaticity', with 'idiom' and 'collocation' as subcategories. Idioms are necessarily also collocations (since idioms of decoding are simultaneously idioms of encoding), but collocations are not idioms, although they do display idiomaticity.

Although in a large part of his work Makkai limits himself to idioms of decoding, this research is concerned in the main part with idioms of encoding, or those phraseological items and collocations which are not also idioms of decoding. As van der Wouden says: "Collocations are compositional *post hoc*: once the form and meaning of a certain collocation are known, the combination is not surprising any more" (van der Wouden 1997, p. 55). Phraseological items and collocations can be seen as lexicogrammatically non-compositional. The distinction made here between idioms and collocations is crucial to an investigation of the wider principle of idiomaticity. In later work (1992b), Makkai takes this line of argument further in claiming that the essence of language is idiomaticity, because even syntax and phonemes can be subsumed under idiomatic structures. He has moved away from idioms as a counterpart to collocation, to a more fundamental

---

32 For example, the use of the preposition 'at' rather than any other in 'he drove at 70 mph'.

idea of idiomaticity as an organising principle of language, a view not dissimilar to Sinclair's current notion.

4.2 Idiomaticity

The Hallidayan linguist Chitra Fernando's conception of idioms continues the move away from the traditional notion of sequences which add up to more than their component parts. It is this broadening of the notion that allows Fernando to claim that idioms, which are sometimes but not always non-literal, are not marginal in language, but have nonetheless been neglected by linguistics. Fernando's study is an analysis of idioms from a Hallidayan perspective. She clarifies her terminology:

> Idioms and idiomaticity, while closely related, are not identical. The basis of both is the habitual and, therefore, predictable co-occurrence of specific words, but with *idioms* signifying a narrower range of word combinations than *idiomaticity*. Idioms are indivisible units whose components cannot be varied or varied only within definable limits. (*ibid.*, p. 30)

Idiomaticity on the other hand:

> is exemplified not only in idioms and conventional *ad hoc* collocations, but also in conventional lexicogrammatical sequencing most apparent in longer text fragments. (*ibid.*, p. 30)

Faithful to Halliday's three metafunctions, Fernando sets out a three-way typology of ideational, interpersonal and relational idioms (the last an adaptation of Halliday's textual metafunction). The first of these, ideational idioms (she gives as examples *bread and butter* and *red herring*), are the closest to the traditional notion of an idiom, contributing as they do to the content of a discourse. It is not surprising then that Fernando should comment that it would be unusual to find this type of idiom in administrative regulations or legal documents. Much more pervasive in language, although not as intuitively salient, are interpersonal and relational idioms (examples of which include, respectively, *bless you, go to hell* and *on the contrary, in sum*). Although Fernando does consider these to be idioms, they are also phraseological units and as such display idiomaticity.

Parallels can be drawn between Fernando's work and that of Gloria Corpas Pastor on the collocational units of Spanish. She uses *fraseología* as the overriding term for her focus of study, following, yet adapting, the definition of the *Diccionario de la lengua española* (Real Academia Española, 1992):

> Conjunto de frases hechas, locuciones figuradas, metáforas y comparaciones fijadas, modismos y refranes, existentes en una lengua, en el uso individual o en el de algún grupo. (Corpas Pastor 1996, p. 16)[33]

Corpas Pastor's definition, however, is wider than this in that it includes additional types of combination, especially to allow for internal variation in phrases, and at the same time narrower in excluding types of combination that do not belong to the general language. Corpas Pastor identifies three subgroups of phraseological unit, with a primary distinction between *enunciados fraseologías,* which are complete speech acts, and *locuciones* and *colocaciones* which are not. While *locuciones* are fixed in the system the latter are fixed, to a greater or lesser extent, in norms of usage. This distinction is adopted here (cf. in particular Chapters 5 and 6).

More recent research has found traditional idioms to be rarer than is generally perceived in language. Rosamund Moon (1998a, 1998b), for example, draws this conclusion from her study of the rhetorical function of fixed expressions and idioms (FEIs) in a corpus of 18 million words of English, made up predominantly of journalistic and literary texts, registers which might be expected to contain a relatively high proportion of idioms. It is only with the development of corpus linguistics that the actual role of idioms has been open to investigation. Chapter 5 of this study follows an approach similar to Moon's, although with an ultimate interest in the phraseology of a particular register rather than in the behaviour and patterning of a set list of expressions.

For Moon, the category of FEIs covers both collocations and idioms and has three macrocategories, each of which comprises a number of subcategories and demonstrates a different 'problem'. These are: anomalous collocations (for example, *kith and kin* - a so-called 'cranberry collocation' - *by and large* - an 'ill-formed collocation'); formulae (e.g. *I'm sorry to say* - a simple formula with a special discourse function - proverbs, sayings and similes); and finally metaphors (e.g. *on an even keel*, ranging from opaque (pure idioms) to transparent). Respectively, these three categories represent problems of lexicogrammar, pragmatics and semantics, and reveal the three factors which Moon takes into account in identifying FEIs, namely lexicogrammatical fixedness,

---

33 "A group of set phrases, figurative idioms, fixed metaphors and similes, idioms and proverbs, which exist in a language, or in the language usage of an individual or group." (My translation)

institutionalisation and non-compositionality. FEIs therefore demonstrate idiomaticity in that they are "single choices syntagmatically, restricted lexical choices paradigmatically, and motivated by discoursal considerations" (Moon 1998a, p. 19).

4.3 Lexicographical approaches

As for collocations, much of the research on phraseological units has aimed to formalise them in dictionaries.[34] This section looks briefly at the major lines of research in this vein, which stem from the Russian tradition of phraseology.

The BBI Combinatory Dictionary of English (Benson, Benson and Ilson 1986) presents a definition of collocation which is in keeping with a neo-Firthian view, in that it defines collocations as non-idiomatic (i.e. semantically compositional) phrases and constructions, which can be either lexical, composed solely of lexical words, or grammatical, that is, containing grammatical items in addition to lexical words. The BBI Dictionary is broadly speaking within the Russian tradition of phraseology. This tradition, which has spread from Eastern Europe and the former Soviet Union to Western Europe, is centred around the phraseological unit, and has been particularly influential in dictionary compilation.[35] Its principal legacy, as Cowie notes, is "a framework of descriptive categories that is comprehensive, systematic, and soundly based" (Cowie 1998, p. 4), the various researchers being united by a primary distinction between word-like units (nominations) and sentence-like units (propositions).

Igor Mel'čuk's work can certainly be considered to be within the classical Russian tradition. An important concept in Mel'čuk's work, in which collocations are a subclass of set phrases, is that of the lexical function:

> [...] a very general and abstract meaning, coupled with a D(eep) Synt(actic) role, which can be lexically expressed in a large variety of ways depending on the lexical unit to which this meaning applies. (*ibid.*, p. 32)

In other words, a lexical function relates a node word to another word in terms of meaning. An example of lexical functions in action is the pairing 'clean shave', or in Makkai's notation: 'Magn(shave$_N$) = clean', which means that the general meaning of 'very' in the context of 'shave' is realised by the accompanying

---

34 Čermák (2001) offers a good discussion of lexicographic approaches to idioms and phraseology.

35 A useful summary of the Russian tradition of collocation can be found in Cowie (1998).

adjective 'clean'. A substantial body of work has been carried out on lexical functions in various languages.[36]

4.4 Locutions

Given the focus here on phraseological items adopted by the administrative register from the general language, perhaps the obvious place to start in identifying phraseological units in the corpus is with a dictionary of such units: this is the approach employed in Chapter 5 which investigates the role of generally recognised phraseological units, with reference to Alain Rey and Sophie Chantreau's *Dictionnaire des expressions et locutions* (1993). It is useful at this stage to examine Rey and Chantreau's concept of an 'expression' or 'locution'. In their own words, their object of study is 'la phraséologie':

> [...] un système de particularités expressives liées aux conditions sociales dans lesquelles la langue est actualisée, c'est-à-dire à des *usages*. (*ibid*., p. v)

Phraseology is therefore seen here as particular expression within a social context, and not isolated from the context of use, as is often the case. The definition can therefore be compared with that of Gledhill (1995, 1999), although Rey and Chantreau still focus on expressions which are fixed to a greater or lesser extent. This phraseological system is composed of groups of words which are more or less unpredictable in form and meaning (1993, p. 6). Their wide definition thus coincides with Makkai's notion of idioms, embracing as it does both decoding idioms, which are unpredictable in their form and meaning, and encoding idioms, which are unpredictable in form.

'Locution' and 'expression' in fact describe the same reality considered from different perspectives. While a 'locution' is "une unité fonctionnelle plus longue que le mot graphique, appartenant au code de la langue (devant être apprise) en tant que forme stable et soumise aux règles syntactiques de manière à assumer la fonction d'*intégrant*"[37] (*ibid*., p. vi), that is to say, a functional form, an

36 Cf. for example Wanner (ed.) (1996), which contains papers on a number of languages, including Russian, English, German and the Mexican Uto-Aztecan language, Huichol, and also contains a paper, by Ulrich Heid (1996), on the use of lexical functions to extract collocations from corpora.

37 Rey and Chantreau (1993, p. vi, footnote) note that: "L'*intégrant* de Benveniste est une unité apte à être reprise pour être intégrée dans une unité du niveau supérieur: élément dans le mot, mot dans le syntagme, syntagme dans la phrase minimale, etc."

expression is the same reality, but seen as a rhetorical or stylistic device for expressing an idea.

The emphasis here differs from Gross's notion, in which a locution is the result of the adaptation of words to a new context, specifically the loss of what links them to their original context (Gross 1996, p. 144). Guiraud's (1961) definition of locutions also differs considerably from Rey and Chantreau's. For him, there is necessarily a certain archaism which has survived in a locution, whether it be an archaism in the form of the expression (in the syntax, for example), or in the content of the expression, in referring to something which no longer exists.

Rey and Chantreau likewise note that locutions can help older forms to survive in the French language, in including archaic words (they give the examples of 'au *fur* et à mesure' and 'avoir *maille* à partir'). There can therefore be a strange clash between modern and archaic forms in language as a result of these locutions. It would not be surprising, given Ball's remark, mentioned earlier (1997, p. 181), to find that in administrative language traditional and newly-formed items regularly collocate: whether or not this is due to the presence of locutions remains to be seen. The units in which this study is most interested, however, are not marginal, and are not necessarily metaphorical, but rather are fundamental to the administrative register.

This approach to phraseology, that of identifying units, has a tendency to produce taxonomies of types. While this has undeniable uses and advantages, for example in education, taxonomies by their very nature risk misrepresenting the nature of the phenomenon. In the course of this section a variety of types of phraseological unit have been set out, motivated by such criteria as fixedness, semantic compositionality and institutionalisation. It is possible to envisage a synthesis of these, a multidimensional space in which phraseological units could be positioned on a number of continua. However, given that phraseology and collocations are register-bound, a large part of lexical patterning and phraseology, which allows registers and genres to be recognised, would remain unaccounted for.

5. Phraseology as the creation of the text - statistical notions of collocation

The third main notion of phraseology investigated in the administrative register here has been developed from the work of the British linguist J. R. Firth. The notion has been shown to be very powerful, and has been extended far beyond lexical collocation, to a more holistic concept. The essential quality of such collocational patterning is that it is text-based: the focus is on actual instances of co-occurrence, rather than abstract relations. For this reason, corpus linguistics has been the framework within which much of this research has been undertaken.

5.1 John Sinclair and the idiom principle

As John Sinclair, paraphrasing Firth (1957a), has said, "The basis of lexical patterning is the tendency of words to occur in the vicinity of each other to an extent that is not predicted by chance" (Sinclair 1992, p. 390). Some of this patterning results from real-world considerations. Other types of patterning are tied up with register and genre considerations, which Sinclair describes as "large-scale conditioning choices" (*ibid.*, p. 110). It is easier to re-use patterns, especially where creativity is not the main goal, but this does not explain why a particular sequence of words or pattern should gain currency and others should not.

Section 1 drew attention to Sinclair's latest conception of the terminological and phraseological tendencies. These tendencies demonstrate the two types of lexicon used by speakers (Sinclair 1996). Sinclair claims that users of a language have two resources open to them: first an 'extended term bank', or set of words which have a consistent meaning; and secondly an 'empty' lexicon, or words which have no permanent set of properties attached to them. The lexicon entry in this case is built up through an examination of usage. Chapter 6 here examines the usage and environment of a selection of items.

In order to see how the holistic phraseological tendency has been developed, it is important to go back to its roots, in Sinclair's earlier work, and Firth's pioneering work, among others. While lexical collocation is at the centre of such studies, it has never been the only phenomenon at work.

Sinclair (1991) is a fundamental work in the study of collocation, especially as it relates to recent developments in corpus linguistics. His is a statistical or textual definition:

> Collocation is the occurrence of two or more words within a short space of each other in a text. (Sinclair 1991, p. 170)

The 'short space' is traditionally taken to be four words each side of the node word (cf. Sinclair and Jones 1974). Collocation is therefore not dependent on a semantic relationship between the items in question, although of course semantics plays an important role. This definition has been criticised: Howarth, for example, notes that this view "takes no account of any psychological aspects of significance, such as the role that the use of familiar expressions might have in language production and comprehension, nor the internal grammatical or lexical structure of an expression" (Howarth 1996, p. 6). Howarth's aims however are pedagogical, and here psychological considerations are clearly important. When the aim is to identify the typical or characteristic features of a genre or register, the statistical or textual notion of collocation is in fact an ideal starting point.

Collocations, being partly generated and partly retrieved, are an intermediate component of Sinclair's two interdependent organising principles: the open-choice and the idiom principle. These principles are models of interpretation which explain the way in which meaning arises from text. The open-choice principle is also known as the 'slot-and-filler' model, and is the basis of most grammars. Slots open up whenever a unit, whether it be a word, a phrase, or a clause, is completed, and the only restraint is grammaticality. The idiom principle, on the other hand, accounts for constraints that cannot be accounted for by the way the world works, or by register choices:

> The principle of idiom is that a language user has available to him or her a large number of semi-preconstructed phrases that constitute single choices, even though they might appear to be analysable into segments. To some extent, this may reflect the recurrence of similar situations in human affairs; it may illustrate a natural tendency to economy of effort; or it may be motivated in part by the exigencies of real-time conversation. (*ibid*., p. 110)

An example of the idiom principle in action is Sinclair's example of the patterning around 'naked eye', (cf. for example Sinclair 2000), where the boundaries of the phrase are indeterminate, and internal lexical or syntactic variation is possible. As Hunston and Francis point out, the idiom principle breaks down the artificial barrier between the phrase and the non-phrase (Hunston and Francis 1999, p. 231).

Collocations and idioms are both surface manifestations of the idiom principle. This definition implies that idioms and collocations overlap to a considerable extent. Idioms have a rhetorical function in text and have been seen as pragmatically marked (cf. Gledhill 1999). Sinclair explains the difference as follows:

> In principle, we call co-occurrences idioms if we interpret the co-occurrence as giving a single unit of meaning. If we interpret the occurrence as the selection of two related words, each of which keeps some meaning of its own, we call it a collocation. (Sinclair 1991, p. 172)

Diachronically, therefore, collocations may become idioms, in a process not unlike the development of Guiraud's locutions (cf. Section 4.4 above).

5.2 J. R. Firth and early neo-Firthian collocation

Sinclair's current view of the phraseological tendency of language can be traced back directly to J. R. Firth's work on collocation. Firth is generally agreed to have been the first to adopt the term 'collocation' in its present, technical sense in linguistics, in the context of a theory of meaning, although the concept and indeed the term can be traced further back. Robins (1967) notes that the Greek Stoics pointed out 2300 years ago that "word meanings do not exist in isolation, and they may differ according to the collocation in which they are used" (1967, p. 21). Kennedy (1998) points to Cruden's identification in his *Concordance*, over 250 years ago, of repeated co-occurrences of certain words in the Bible. McEnery and Wilson (2001, p. 23) identify the basic idea behind collocation as dating back to 1930s Prague School linguistics, where it is termed 'automation'. Just over a decade before Firth's influential adoption of the term, G. L. Trager (1940) used it in a technical sense in context of a technique for analysing morphological and syntactic phenomena in order to establish Russian noun categories: in his use, syntagmatic collocation stands in opposition to paradigmatic 'congruence'. More in the Firthian vein, although from a lexicographical rather than a contextualist perspective, is the work of H. E. Palmer (see Palmer 1917, and Palmer and Blandford 1976 (1924)), for whom collocation is the co-occurrence of both lexical and grammatical words.

It is only with Firth, however, that analysis and the theoretical study of collocation as a linguistic phenomenon really took off. He first drew attention to the phenomenon of collocation in his 1951 paper 'Modes of Meaning'. Collocation is introduced here as a level at which meaning can be analysed: meaning by collocation is part of lexical meaning. In the later 'Synopsis of linguistic theory' (1957c), Firth states that:

> the habitual collocations in which words under study appear are quite simply the mere word accompaniment, the other word-material in which they are most commonly or most characteristically embedded. (Firth 1957c, p. 11)

Over the following pages he develops and modifies this definition, claiming that collocation is not simply juxtaposition, but "an order of *mutual expectancy*" (*ibid.*, p. 12). According to this definition, idioms are necessarily collocations, but the converse is not true: collocation is the more general category. Slightly later again, the definition is of "actual words in habitual company" (*ibid.*, p. 14), a more general definition still in that it does not specify whether the 'habitual company' should be understood to be particular words, or words with a related meaning, or grammatical classes. This is a definition which has informed much neo-Firthian research into collocation thirty-odd years later and which is implied by Firth's famous line "You shall know a word by the company it keeps!" (Firth 1957c, p. 11).

A parallel concept to collocation in Firthian linguistics, and one which has been picked up again recently, is that of colligation. If collocation is an order of mutual expectancy of particular words, colligation operates at one remove:

> Collocations are actual words in habitual company. A word in a usual collocation stares you in the face just as it is. Colligations cannot be of words as such. Colligations of grammatical categories related in a grammatical structure do not necessarily follow word divisions or even sub-divisions of words. (Firth 1957c, p. 14)

Colligation operates at the grammatical level of meaning. The relationship between collocation and colligation can therefore be seen on a scale of generality, although the two do not necessarily work in parallel. The notion of colligation today has been extended to cover the syntactic constraints, or even just preferences, of particular words. Hoey, for example, suggests that "*colligation* can be defined as *the grammatical company a word keeps.*" (Hoey 1997, p. 8)

According to Firth, collocation should be studied from attested examples, and in this respect it is possible to draw a direct line from Firth to modern corpus linguistics with its inductive approach and reliance on complete attested texts. Firth himself recommended studying the collocational patterns of key or pivotal words, that is, sociologically important words. This is still an approach to collocation in linguistics today.

From this initial recognition of the phenomenon of collocation, there has been a concern with register theory. Firth claimed that statements of meaning at the collocational level could be made for the key words of a "restricted language", and in fact help to justify the restriction of the field. This concept has developed into that of register, and the notion of general or core language has been undermined.[38] Elena Tognini-Bonelli (1996) has suggested that Firth did not extend the usefulness of collocational meaning to the standard language as a whole only because such collocational data was unavailable. A word's most frequent meaning does not necessarily correspond to people's intuitive ideas of its primary meaning, and there are perhaps superficially surprising differences between registers. The concept of meaning by collocation can resolve these difficulties.

Although he did not develop the concept, or indeed the study of collocation as much as he might have, Firth was, characteristically, quite far-sighted in this respect. He called for collocational study of ordered series of words, such as calendrical terms, which are traditionally seen, and indeed learned, as members of a semantic set. He claimed that such study could be revealing: Hoey has recently pursued such ideas (2000), and has shown that even intuitively 'uninteresting' words, such as items in the number system, have their own distinctive collocational patterns. Indeed, words should always be regarded separately, not

---

38 However, see Gledhill (1999) for the idea that collocational shift may be the key to our understanding of core and periphery in language.

just from other members of a set, but also from other members of a paradigm. Thus the collocational patterns of the form *marcher* could differ significantly from those of *marches, marché* etc., patterns which an undifferentiated analysis of the lemma MARCHER would conceal (cf. Firth 1957c, p. 12, and also Halliday 1961, 1966b, Sinclair 1992, p. 390). The corpus used in this research is not lemmatised; therefore differences in the environments of different word forms are brought to the fore.

This notion of collocation is necessarily based on actual texts, and accounts for the success which corpus linguistics has had in elaborating the notion of collocation. It has been able, as Krishnamurthy has expressed it, "to raise the status of collocation beyond the simple definition 'the co-occurrence of two lexical items in a text within a certain proximity'" (2000, p. 34). This work was foreseen in Halliday, McIntosh and Strevens' *The Linguistic Sciences and Language Teaching*. They pointed out that linguists had started to use computers to study collocations in large volumes of text, and that "this work should yield much new information about the lexical level of language" (1964, p. 34).

5.3 Later developments

The statistical notion of collocation has subsequently been developed in various ways. The extensions to the notion discussed here, non-contiguous collocation and the collocational patterning of grammatical words, represent the widening of the notion to a holistic phraseological tendency of which collocation is at the heart.

For Sinclair in 1966, mutual prediction between lexical items depended on a number of elements: the strength of the predictions of items over each other; their distance apart; the nature of the items which separate them; grammatical organization (Sinclair 1966, p. 411). With regard to the second of these, while distance ultimately sets the boundary of collocation, there is no smooth decrease in predictability as the distance from the node word increases. Rather, some nodes are routinely separated from their collocates, or from particular collocates. Sinclair and Renouf, in a paper concerned with lexis in language learning (1988), investigated this further, drawing attention to grammatical frameworks: these are presented in more depth in Renouf and Sinclair's 1991 paper. A framework is a grouping of common grammatical words, specifically "a discontinuous sequence of two words, positioned at one word remove from each other; they are therefore not grammatically self-standing; their well-formedness is dependent on what intervenes" (Renouf and Sinclair 1991, p. 128). An example is the framework 'a [time phrase] ago', which gives the sequences 'a year ago', 'a fortnight ago', 'an age ago', among many others. Renouf and Sinclair demonstrate that such grammatical frameworks offer important insights into collocation: firstly, in that the choice of lexical word between the framework is limited; and secondly in demonstrating that grammatical words have collocates and can collocate with each other. Although Firth's best known examples of collocation demonstrate the habitual co-occurrence of lexical items, such as 'rancid butter' and 'dark night', collocational relevance for him was not restricted to lexical words. He claimed rather that the study of the collocations of such words as 'and' and 'for' raises the problem of the grammatical classification of words. Sinclair has subsequently questioned the classification of 'of' as a preposition, based on its phraseological patterning (Sinclair 1991).

Grammatical items may be used as a starting point for the phraseological characterisation of a register or discourse. Gledhill (2000), for example, looks at the patterns of collocation of the salient grammatical items in his corpus of pharmaceutical science research articles, investigating the rhetorical role of these items and also analysing phraseological differences between the rhetorical sections of research articles. Lexical collocation obviously has a role to play in the predominant phraseology of genres, but grammatical collocation "is involved in an immense portion (if not a majority) of the typical kinds of expression to be found in a particular text" (2000, p. 220). One of his major contributions is to emphasise the part played by phraseology in the genre. He suggests that even something as fundamental as tense choice is partly determined by phraseology rather than semantics (see also Hunston and Francis 1999, p. 254).

5.4 Beyond collocation

Two further approaches, which undeniably extend beyond collocation in its strict sense are, however, valuable concepts and useful to a holistic model. These are the notions of pattern grammar, and semantic (or discourse) prosody.

In recent years, British linguistics has seen an attempt to integrate all of these types of collocation, and indeed all co-selection tendencies. This attempt began with Gill Francis's 1993 paper, and has subsequently been developed by Hunston and Francis (1998, 1999) in the form of 'pattern grammar'. Pattern grammar, which can be seen as a high-level motivation for many of the co-occurrence phenomena above, follows on from, but goes beyond, Firthian collocation and colligation. While for Firth and Sinclair 'patterning' is the general patterning around a word, for Hunston and Francis 'patterning' is much more restrictive. Francis explains:

> While there is colligation at work here in the broadest sense, the most interesting aspect of this and many other structures is the blend of colligation and collocation, where the collocational possibilities involve not individual words, but semantic sets of words and phrases. (Francis 1993, p. 141)

Interest in such patterns can be traced back many years, to Hornby (cf. Hornby 1975 (1954) and Cowie 1978), who developed verb patterns for pedagogical dictionaries, thereby providing a link between grammar and meaning. Hornby, however, illustrated his dictionary with invented examples rather than examples drawn from authentic text, as corpus methodology does today. Grammatical items, by reason of their very frequency in language, are fundamental in a description of what is characteristic in a register or genre, even if they are less psychologically salient than fully lexical items. Hunston and Francis suggest that grammatical items occur in typical patterns, alongside lexical items which are often semantically restricted. Pattern grammar shows that it is possible to create a grammar which begins with the word: this is the opposite approach to that of Hasan who treats lexis as the most delicate grammar (e.g. Hasan 1987).

Pattern grammar is the result of a project to code the complementation patterns of all the verbs in the Cobuild dictionary, and is a natural development from Renouf and Sinclair's grammatical frameworks, although it takes lexical words and not the frameworks themselves as the starting point. Most importantly, theoretically speaking, pattern grammar constitutes important evidence for the interdependence of lexis and grammar. The notion of patterns can also explain semantic, or discourse, prosody and semantic clusters. The end result, as Gill Francis explains, is:

> [...] that we will be able to specify all major lexical items in terms of their semantic preferences, and all grammatical structures in terms of their key lexis and phraseology. (Francis 1993, p. 155)

Hunston and Francis define patterns as follows:

> [...] a pattern is a phraseology frequently associated with (a sense of) a word, particularly in terms of the prepositions, groups, and clauses that follow the word. (Hunston and Francis 1999, p. 3)

There can be several elements in a pattern or just one. Some patterns are very familiar, such as the simple patterns V and Vn which correspond to the traditional distinction between transitive and intransitive verbs. It can thus be seen that pattern grammar to a large extent develops traditional grammatical analysis, although it takes the idea of the habitual company of words much further in attempting to describe the whole of the language in a principled fashion.

Hunston and Francis have shown that there is an important correlation between the patterns they have identified around particular verbs, and the various senses of the verb in question, namely that the division into patterns tends to correspond to the senses of the verb. This relation can also be seen by analysing the verbs which manifest a particular pattern: intuitively recognisable sense groups can be discerned. Tightening the link further, they have identified groups of semantically-related verbs which have two, or more rarely, more than two, patterns in common.

The concept of patterning can be seen to account for some instances of collocations, in the concrete sense of fixed phrases. Highly frequent collocational units are simply extreme cases of patterning, in that the patterns allow only a restricted lexis (Hunston and Francis 1998, p. 63). At the other extreme, utterances which are apparently produced by rules are merely the instantiation of patterns which allow a wide range of lexical items. Patterns, however, can only ever indicate typical usage or typical phraseology, and never rules. They are neither fixed nor free. It can be seen therefore that co-occurrence and the idiom principle are not restricted to lexical phrases, but extend also to patterns in general (*ibid.*, p. 66). The result is the phenomenon of 'pattern flow', where utterances move from one pattern to the next, like a wave. The grammar is therefore based on the pattern and no longer on the clause, or any other unit. In this way co-occurrence and co-selection are shown to have an even more important place in language production, as they are no longer restricted to lexical phrases, but can be extended to lexical, grammatical, word-class and various other groupings.

In addition to the link between patterns and meanings, finally, pattern grammar also makes clear the interdependence of lexis and syntax. Hunston and Francis describe their grammar as "the first pedagogic grammar to integrate syntax and lexis using corpus data" (*ibid.*, p. 45). Hunston and Francis claim that the notion of pattern precisely captures the interface between lexis and grammar (*ibid.*, p. 62). The idea that lexis and grammar are ultimately inseparable is not new:

> A general and vague idea exists that the study of a given language should proceed on a double basis: lexicology, or the study of words, and grammar, or the study of their mutations and combinations. A little reflection, however, will convince us that this is far from being a true and logical conception of the problem. It will be found that the two subjects are bound up with each other and interdependent, and that they can only be differentiated by doing violence to each. The words themselves and their attendant phenomena cannot be separated except by invoking the arbitrary. (Palmer 1917, p. 32)

In a sense we have come full circle from Palmer. The study of co-selection and collocation appears now to have found the power to draw together many previously divided areas of language study.

The notion of discourse prosody, or semantic prosody, continues the gradual move away from Firth's original concept of collocation as the co-occurrence of one lexical word with another. Semantic prosody can be seen as either the collocation of a word with a particular field of meaning, or the cumulative effect of collocations, that is the meaning a word assumes by virtue of its frequent or typical collocates. Collocation is therefore taking on a pragmatic dimension.

While the node word itself is neutral, it assumes a particular colouring as a result of its collocates.

The concept of semantic prosody was introduced by Sinclair (1991),[39] and developed by Louw (1993), Stubbs (1995, 1996, 2001b), and Partington (1998), among others. Later work (e.g. Stubbs 2001b) prefers the term 'discourse prosody', which emphasises their role in discourse coherence. Sinclair shows how certain words have a tendency to occur with particular meanings. The verbs *happen* and *set in* for example, are associated with unpleasant things. As Partington puts it, semantic prosody is an aspect of expressive connotation:

> Often a favourable or unfavourable connotation is not contained in a single item, but is expressed by that item in association with others, with its collocates. (Partington 1998, p. 66)

Louw's memorable definition of semantic prosody is that it is:

> A consistent aura of meaning with which a form is imbued by its collocates. (Louw 1993, p. 157)

'Prosody' is used in a sense similar to Firth's, that is, a feature which extends over segmental boundaries. Semantic prosody is the spreading of connotational, rather than Firth's phonological, colouring beyond single word boundaries. Louw shows how established, though not consciously recognised, semantic prosodies can provide a background against which irony can be introduced, deliberately or otherwise, to a text, and also how prosodies can bifurcate into positive and negative through such grammatical principles as transitivity.[40] For example 'build up' used intransitively with things or forces as the subject has a negative semantic prosody (e.g. 'lactic acid that builds up in the muscles that causes you pain', '[hard skin] builds up'), whereas used transitively, often with a human subject, it has a positive semantic prosody ('alternative training methods, particularly for building up leg strength', 'build up the confidence of our members').[41]

---

39 Louw (1993), however, points out that the phenomenon was perceived by Bréal in 1897, who writes of 'contagion'. Sinclair (1996) also highlights the notion of 'contagion' in Darmsteter's work in 1886.

40 Formally similar words can also have completely different semantic prosodies, as Sealey (1999) shows in her discussion of the negative semantic prosody of 'childish' which can be contrasted with the positive semantic prosody associated with 'childlike'.

41 These examples are all authentic examples taken from the BNC Sampler CD (1999).

The phenomenon of semantic prosody demonstrates the interrelationship of *langue* and *parole*, as the word in question acquires particular connotations from its typical collocates. *Parole* therefore affects *langue* in the long term.

Hoey (1997) takes the notion a logical step forward in suggesting that semantic prosody need not be restricted to a positive/negative dichotomy.[42] Rather he proposes that:

> If *cause* and *happen* have semantic prosody with negative events, it follows that we should talk of *train as a* having semantic prosody with 'occupations', rather than collocating with them. Of course this semantic prosody will include many items that are also collocations but what makes the notion so useful and important is that is cannot be subsumed by its collocations. (Hoey 1997, p. 5)

In following Hoey's suggestion we need not wait until a co-occurrence becomes significant in the corpus or text in question before the relationship between node and collocate can be accounted for linguistically. By looking at the field of meaning associated with the node word, rather than the particular collocates thrown up by a corpus, it is thus possible to make more powerful generalisations (cf. *ibid*., p. 7).

A closely related notion is that of the local semantic prosody, introduced by Tribble (cf. Tribble 1998). A local semantic prosody is a connotation which a word picks up only in a particular context, and which constitutes important local knowledge for writers in a genre, although Tribble points out that this may be part of its general semantic prosody, or semantic prosody in the 'general' language.

Studies of semantic prosody have until very recently been limited to investigations of individual words (cf. Sripicharn 2000 for a survey of work up to that date). Louw (2000) suggests that semantic prosody can be a more general concept, and one with a greater theoretical role in linguistics. He proposes an updated working definition of semantic prosody:

> A semantic prosody refers to a form of meaning which is established through the proximity of a consistent series of collocates, often characterisable as positive or negative, and whose primary function is the expression of the attitude of its speaker or writer towards some pragmatic situation. A secondary, although no less important attitudinal function of semantic prosodies is the creation of irony

42 There is a close relationship between semantic prosody and van der Wouden's polarity items. 'Positive polarity items' are items which cannot felicitously appear in negative contexts (van der Wouden 1997, p. 24).

> through the deliberate injection of a form which clashes with the prosody's consistent series of collocates. (Louw 2000, p. 57)

Louw goes on to suggest the possibility of contextual prosodic theory which could provide a means of finding all of the semantic prosodies in a language by computational means. It remains to be seen whether this will be successful.

6. Conclusion

Throughout this chapter it has been quite clear that, as Fontenelle has noted, "there is no such thing as a clear, non-controversial and all-embracing definition of collocation" (1994, p. 47). Nor is the term 'phraseology' without its problems. However, in terms of the concepts lying behind these terms, neo-Firthian linguistics is already able to offer a powerful model of phraseology, which has at its core a statistical notion of collocation. It can be imagined that the turn to discourse and pragmatics which is behind the notion of discourse prosody will be the focus of much attention in phraseology and collocation studies within corpus linguistics over the next few years. This allows for a holistic model of language patterning, which in turn breaks down divisions of lexis and grammar and makes way for a subtler and more nuanced description of language.

In examining phraseological patterning, however, it is important not to dismiss more traditional notions, such as set phrases and locutions, while still taking advantage of corpus techniques which enable a thorough and all-embracing analysis of a register or a discourse. This allows us to approach phraseological patterning in administrative language from three separate but related angles: from the perspective of the discourse, through patterning which is the creation, or has been developed by, administrators themselves; from the perspective of the general language, the phraseological heritage from literary and journalistic French in particular; and from the perspective of the texts. With the description provided by each of these three approaches, we can come to a fuller understanding of the specificity of EU administrative French than is possible through more restricted analysis.

Chapter 3

Methodological Considerations and Language Variety

'What's the use of that?' I asked. 'What's the use of it?' he said, laughing hysterically. 'What's the use*? Let's show him, Josh.'*

DAVID LODGE, SMALL WORLD: AN ACADEMIC ROMANCE

1. Introduction

Given the phraseological approach to language outlined in Chapter 2, how can the methodological framework of corpus linguistics advance the description of administrative French? Before considering this question, however, it is necessary to consider administrative language in linguistic terms. Chapter 1 introduced the context of production of EU and French national administrative texts: the question is now raised as to how these texts can be characterised in terms of register and genre? Only then can we decide how a corpus should be designed in order to be a valid representation of the register.

The first section of the chapter looks at register and genre analysis, with two main aims. Firstly, at a theoretical level, it discusses some of the many ways in which the notion of a general language can be subdivided for the practical purposes of language description. The second aim, to situate administrative language in terms of register and genre, is more practical. Although administrative language is united by a common aim of communicating policy to a more general public, this does not imply that there will be no regular, systematic linguistic differences among texts of this type. Indeed work in register and genre analysis suggests that there will be patterns of difference owing to situational and functional differences: the ways in which this extends to phraseological patterning is one of the questions investigated in Chapters 4 to 6.

The second main section tackles the relatively young methodology of computer-based corpus linguistics, and aims both to justify its suitability for a study of this type, and to set out some methodological decisions which have been made in the compilation of the administrative corpus used here. The final section of the chapter then sets out the design of the corpus.

2. Register and genre

Sociolinguistics as a branch of linguistics takes as its starting point the fact that languages are not unstructured, homogeneous wholes. Rather, language varies according to considerations outside of the system itself. Sociolinguistics, therefore, can be seen as the study of the co-variation of language and society: the sociolinguist William Labov, for example, has said that "We may define a *sociolinguistic variable* as one which is correlated with some non-linguistic variable of the social context" (1972b, p. 237, the emphasis is Labov's). Sociolinguistics makes a primary distinction between user-related variation and use-related variation; that is, between language which takes the form it does because of factors related to the speaker or writer (sex, geographical factors, social class, age, generation and so on), and language which is shaped by the uses to which it is put (varying according to level of formality, mode of language, subject matter, etc). As Trudgill expresses it, "behaviour does not only have to be appropriate to the individual, it also needs to be suitable for particular occasions and situations" (1995, p. 84). Even here of course, in distinguishing between *who* someone is and *what* he or she is doing, it is impossible completely to separate the two, as there are natural correlations between user and use - in Halliday's words: "the two are interconnected - what we do is affected by who we are: in other words, the division of labour is *social* - dialects become entangled with registers" (1978, p. 2). However, the fact remains that the two are ultimately separate - any person *could* use any type of language, so the division is essential in theory, and valuable for description.

Not only does language vary according to factors external or internal to the user, but it also forms recognisable varieties. Configurations of factors lead to conventional forms of text (cf. Hudson 1996, p. 22), which can be recognised by sets of linguistic items. Recent work has also shown that it is not just sets of linguistic items as such, but also collocational and phraseological patternings, which can identify a language variety (cf. for example Partington 1998, pp. 17-19; Gledhill 2000). Although this premise is straightforward and intuitive, the situation itself is complex in practice, and this is demonstrated by the great variation in linguists' divisions of language, not to mention the often contradictory terminology used. With regard to language varieties and text typology, numerous dimensions and subdivisions have been suggested. A discussion on the Corpora electronic mailing list in summer 2000 highlights this intractable problem.[43] In response to a query about whether a corpus of written academic prose in the disciplines of commerce/economics and natural science/history should be called specific registers or genres, the four linguists who commented all proposed different solutions, involving a range of definitions of 'register', 'genre', and related notions such as 'sub-register', 'super-genre' and 'high-level genre'.

---

43 Archives can be found at http://www.hd.uib.no/corpora. The discussion in question ran from 31 August to 4 September 2000.

2.1 Register - situational variation

Coleman and Crawshaw draw attention to a fundamental distinction which can be made between studies of register:

> [...] register could be defined either as a series of points on a scale of formality (*niveau de langue*), or as a concentration of stylistic features which was conditioned by context or occupation and exemplified by particular categories of text (*registre* or *variété*). (Coleman and Crawshaw 1994, p. 8)

The notion of register is often linked to level of formality in language. This is especially true of many of the discussions of register in French language studies.[44] Sanders (1993) provides an overview of such studies in the late 1970s and 1980s, from Caput's early treatment of register, through Muller's five-point scale of variation, to Battye and Hintze's three register levels – *le français soigné, le français familier* and *le français non-standard.* Sanders concludes that much work remains to be done, especially in disentangling register variation and social class variation in French. This biased description is due to the "adherence to an artificially predetermined, largely written, standard" (*ibid.*, p. 50). Sanders also concludes that style labels do not permit a fluid representation of socio-situational variation and are therefore not satisfactory.

Sometimes, the term 'style' is also used to mean a register defined by degree of formality (cf. Trudgill 1995). 'Style', however, has been used in many other ways as we have already seen: indeed it is probably the term with the widest range of usage.[45] For this reason, I believe it is preferable to reserve style for an individual use of language, or deviation from a defined 'norm', something which is rare in administrative language, with the exception of speeches.

Situationally-defined varieties (diatypic variety), like dialects, are not discrete (cf. Hudson 1996, p. 24), however one chooses to describe them, and many terms,

---

44 Cf. Sanders (1994, p. 88), who notes that 'register' and *registre* have been used in different ways: in English generally to emphasise functional variation, and in French to emphasise situational variation, especially with regard to the formality/informality continuum.

45 Cf. for example Carter and Nash (1990), who discuss style as deviation, style as ornamentation, and style in context (in relation to a contextually-defined norm). The notion of style as ornamentation, presupposing as it does that style does not affect the meaning of language, does not accord with a Firthian or Hallidayan view.

including register, style, variety and text type, have been adopted in linguistic research. The next section discuss Halliday's very influential, thoroughly developed notion of register, which does not depend on one single feature of context.

2.2 Register - functional variation

In addition to being used for varieties defined on a scale of formality, register has also been used for occupational varieties of language, which have a partial correlation with the situational features outlined above. In his introduction to sociolinguistics, Trudgill (1995, p. 84-85) ties register to occupations, claiming that registers are usually characterised solely by vocabulary differences.

For Halliday, register is determined by the context of situation, and accounts for much more than vocabulary differences. Registers are "not marginal or special varieties of language." Rather, "Between them they cover the total range of our language activity." (Halliday, McIntosh and Strevens 1964, p. 89). The term register for variation of this sort was proposed by Reid (1956, cf. Ellis and Ure 1969; and also Halliday 1978, p. 110), and interpreted in the framework of Hill's institutional linguistics (cf Hill 1958) by Halliday, McIntosh and Strevens (1964). Interesting from the point of view of this research is that "often it is not the lexical item alone but the collocation of two or more lexical items that is specific to one register" (Halliday, McIntosh and Strevens 1964, p. 88).

There are three types of factor in the context of situation in Hallidayan linguistics which configure to define a register: these are the field (the focus of the activity); the tenor (the relationship between the participants); and the mode (the role of language, at the most basic level whether it is written or spoken) (cf. Halliday 1978, p. 31; Eggins 1994, p. 9). These are related to the ideational, interpersonal and textual metafunctions of language in the context of Systemic-Functional Grammar (cf. Halliday 1994). With knowledge of these three factors it is possible to predict linguistic features in language: that is to say, the three dimensions of variation have consequences for linguistic form. Administrative language of the sort examined here could be considered in the following way. In terms of field, what is happening in abstract terms is that information, about policy, legislation, decisions taken and so on, is being transmitted from parties in the administration to other interested parties (the public or selected groups). As regards tenor, there is a formal, social, relationship between writer/reader and speaker/listener, especially to the extent that the writer/speaker is often anonymous, depersonalised, and not necessarily representing his or her individual view. The relationship ultimately is that between those who govern and those who are governed. In terms of mode, the texts dealt with here do not all fit into a single mode. Some are written, including press releases and reports, while others are spoken, or, more accurately, written to be read aloud, as in the case of speeches. The written mode however takes priority.

2.3 Biber and the notion of text type

While some linguists reject the term 'register' because of its vagueness in practice, others consider this vagueness an advantage. Douglas Biber, for example, chooses to adopt a very broad definition of register, stating: "I use the term *register* [...] as a general cover term for all language varieties associated with different situations and purposes" (Biber 1994, p. 32). In other work he uses the terms register and genre indiscriminately for any externally-defined varieties of language, from the very specific to the very general,[46] arguing that because there is a continuous space of variation, discrete distinctions are not useful (cf. also Biber 1988, 1989, 1992, 1994, Finegan and Biber 1994, Biber, Conrad and Reppen 1994).

Biber's influential notion is that of the linguistically-defined 'text type'. The distinction between situationally- and linguistically-defined varieties is important. While Halliday defines varieties by external criteria and then identifies linguistic features, and patterns of collocation, associated with them, Biber proceeds in the opposite direction, identifying features which co-occur in texts, and then interpreting these in functional terms. His approach is macroscopic, and "sets out to define the underlying parameters of textual variation" (Biber 1985), as opposed to a microscopic analysis which would investigate individual linguistic features in detail. He uses factor analysis to group linguistic features (identified empirically on the basis of text corpora) by their co-occurrence in texts. The salient co-occurrence of these features indicates shared underlying communicative functions. He remarks:

> This approach is based on the assumption that strong co-occurrence patterns of linguistic features mark underlying functional dimensions. Features do not randomly co-occur in texts. If certain features consistently co-occur, then it is reasonable to look for an underlying functional influence that encourages their use. (Biber 1988, p. 13)

Biber's most influential work (1988) uses sixty-seven syntactic and lexical features. These fall into sixteen grammatical categories (cf. Biber 1989, p. 7), and include for example, THAT-deletion, demonstrative pronouns, word-length, third person pronouns, infinitives, BY-passives etc. From these, Biber develops seven dimensions of textual variation. These dimensions are continuous scales of variation; that is, they are not dichotomous, although they are named after the end points of these scales, for example 'informational versus involved production',

---

46 Indeed for Biber, even writing is a register "at an extremely high level of generality in that only one parameter is specified: primary channel" (1994, p. 42).

'explicit versus situation-dependent reference'. This enables Biber to challenge much previous linguistic research in showing that:

> [...] there is no linguistic or situational characterization of speech and writing that is true of all spoken and written genres. On the one hand, some spoken and written genres are very similar to one another (e.g. public speeches and written exposition). On the other hand, some spoken genres are quite different from one another (e.g. conversation and public speeches), as are some written genres (e.g. personal letter and academic exposition). (Biber 1988, p. 36)

The notion of text type has both advantages and disadvantages from the perspective of the present research. At the most basic level, it is a post-hoc notion: one cannot therefore design a corpus on the basis of a text type without a large amount of prior analysis. Rather, Elena Tognini-Bonelli states that "in corpus building the only safe first step is to base the initial selection of texts on situational parameters" (Tognini-Bonelli 2001, p. 61). Biber recognises this and warns against compiling a corpus on this basis, agreeing that register or genre distinctions take precedence when defining the total population for a corpus because "There is no a priori way to identify linguistically-defined types." (1993a, p. 245).

The second problem concerns the linguistic features on which Biber bases the dimensions. This number is necessarily limited, with around sixty-seven lexical and syntactic features, although this varies between studies. The problem is not so much the restricted number of features, as the fact that those which are included are all at a very high level of generality. The lexical features, for example, include such general categories as 'nouns', 'first person pronouns' and 'infinitives'. Biber does not take account of individual lexical items, nor does he consider collocational patterns, despite the fact that he recognises elsewhere that these can be register-specific, and can act as powerful indicators of register:

> [...] linguistic features from all levels - including lexical collocations, word frequencies, nominalizations, dependent clauses, and a full range of co-occurring features - have patterned differences across registers. (Biber, Conrad and Reppen 1998, p. 234)

More importantly, Biber's approach assumes that features have a similar function throughout language. Features vary in their relative value from register to register, but they have a register-independent function (see Finegan and Biber 1994, p. 315). This has been shown not necessarily to be true: Gledhill (1997, p. 91), for example, has shown in work on phraseology in science language that the function of even such a high-level feature as tense is determined in part by the phraseological constraints of a register.

Despite these problems, Biber's approach is valuable, beyond providing the important theoretical notion of a text type as an internally, and linguistically-defined variety. Biber himself sets out the strengths of corpus methodology, claiming that one great advantage is the use of large databases of naturally-occurring language, allowing analyses of a scope which would not otherwise be possible (Biber, Conrad and Reppen 1994, p. 169). In this way, it does not accord undue weight to individual texts or genres.

Biber's work is also important for its multi-dimensional perspective. This emphasises the fact that there are continua in language, and that registers vary along a number of dimensions, which explains in part continuing terminological and definitional problems in this area of linguistics. Register or genre groupings are never discrete. Moreover, "Genre distinctions do not adequately represent the underlying text types of English […]. Linguistically distinct texts within a genre represent different text types; linguistically similar texts from different genres represent a single text type." (Biber 1989, p. 6)

While Biber's text types are not suitable for the purposes of building a corpus, especially one which aims to demonstrate correlations between context of situation and language used, the notion is theoretically important, and serves to emphasise that genres and registers are not discrete categories.

2.4 The notion of genre

The term 'genre', like register, has been used in many contexts since the time of Aristotle who distinguished literary genres such as epic poetry and comedy as classes of texts and placed these in a hierarchy, with tragedy as the highest genre (cf. Bywater 1909). John Swales has overviewed the meaning and use of the term in such areas as literary studies, folklore, rhetoric and its more modern adoption in linguistics, where it refers to classes of text which are no longer necessarily literary (1990a, pp. 33-34). This section looks briefly at the Hallidayan notion of genre, distinguishing it from register, and then considers Swales' conception of the term, along with his related notion of discourse community.

Genre in Halliday's sense is defined in terms of "total social activity" (cf. Ventola 1984, p. 285). Genre is at a higher level of abstraction than register, beyond the ideational, interpersonal and textual metafunctions: in other words, whereas register is defined by the context of situation, genre is related to the wider context of culture, a notion which Firthian and Hallidayan linguistics has adopted from the anthropologist Bronislaw Malinowski (cf. Malinowski 1935, p. 18). In this way, genre contextualises register which in turn contextualises language.

A crucial distinction between register and genre is that genres can only be realised in complete texts, because they specify conditions for beginning, continuing and ending texts. Registers on the other hand can be realised in any stretch of text in context. The context of culture is more abstract than the context of situation, and defines the overall function of the interaction. The focus in Hallidayan genre analysis is on the stages which make up a complete text, its 'schematic structure' (cf. Eggins 1994, p. 36).

For Swales, register labels are misleading, and over-privilege similar content while ignoring communicative purpose (cf. Swales 1990a, p. 3). For this reason Swales prefers the notion of genre, often used in ethnographic approaches and also systemic linguistics. He sets out a working definition of genre, making five observations:

> - A genre is a class of communicative events.
> - The principal criterial features that turns a collection of communicative events into a genre is some shared set of communicative purposes.
> - Exemplars or instances of genres vary in their prototypicality.
> - The rationale behind a genre establishes constraints on allowable contributions in terms of their content, positioning and form.
> - A discourse community's nomenclature for genres is an important source of insight. (from Swales 1990a, pp. 45-54)

A further related notion is that of a discourse community, which is a socio-rhetorical network with a common set of goals, which 'owns' genres. Discourse communities recruit by persuasion, training or qualification (*ibid.*, p. 24), and have a number of defining characteristics, including a broadly agreed set of public goals, and mechanisms of intercommunication (*ibid.*, p.. 24-27). Swales' later book (1998) revises the notion of discourse community, adopting Killingsworth and Gilbertson's distinction (1990, quoted in Swales 1998, p. 201) between local discourse communities, in which members habitually work together, and global discourse communities, which are defined by their commitment to particular kinds of discourse. By this definition, the EU institutions house a number of related local discourse communities.

Gledhill (e.g. 1995, 1997) combines Swales' approach to genre analysis with corpus linguistics. Unlike Biber's notion of text type, the concept of genre does not presume that linguistic features are uniform in their function across different varieties of language. Rather, grammatical features can be unique to a genre: for instance, the function or meaning of the passive in one genre need not be equivalent to the meaning of the passive in another genre (cf. Gledhill 1997, p. 91 and 2000, p. 33).

The discussion of language varieties in this chapter has considered notions of register, text type and genre. Halliday's concept of register is situational, defined on the basis of features of the context of situation. Biber's multidimensional notion is unusual in being an internally or linguistically-defined notion. We have seen, however, that one cannot design a corpus on the basis of a post-hoc variety. Finally, Swales' notion of genre stresses communicative purpose, and allows differentiation between the context of situation and the actual purpose of texts.

The distinction between register and genre is theoretically significant. These varieties are alike in important respects: both are external definitions, unlike the notion of text type. However, there is a distinction to be made between features in the context of situation, and aspects of the communicative purpose. Some researchers choose not to distinguish at all between different types of variety: Stubbs (1996), for example, does not distinguish between text type and genre, arguing that:

> The important point is not knowing in some mechanical way which genre an example fits into, but knowing how the category can make a difference to the way in which it is integrated. (Stubbs 1996, p. 12)

Indeed the index to Stubbs' work cross-references genre, register and style to text type, listing such distinct varieties as authoritative texts, parliamentary debate, religious texts, spoken and written language as text types. While Stubbs' solution is perfectly justified in its own context, as is Biber's decision not to distinguish between genre and register, the question remains as to what to call the categories of text which make up the administrative corpus used here. Since the aim is to show how some phraseological patterning is related to the context of the language in the corpus, while other patterning is tied to aspects of the communicative purpose, it makes sense to make the distinction between register and genre. It can be said therefore that this research is dealing with the corpus of a register - the register of administrative language - which comprises many genres, and that the texts instantiate genres. The two halves of the corpus, European Union and French, represent separate discourses. It is not strictly true to state that this analysis investigates a corpus of a register in a Hallidayan sense because, at the most basic level, the texts display more than one mode (texts which are written and texts which are written to be spoken). The possibility of adopting another term entirely was considered - a term such as institutional domain (cf. Ellis and Ure 1982), for example - but there is no such thing as a purely neutral term and any term would have brought its own theoretical baggage. Rather, I prefer to consider the corpus as representative of the register of administrative language. It is what Hatim and Mason (1990, p. 54) would call an 'open-ended' register as opposed to a 'maximally-restricted' one.

3. The methodology of corpus linguistics

> One cannot guess how a word functions. One has to *look at* its use and learn from that. But the difficulty is to remove the prejudice which stands in the way of doing this. It is not a *stupid* prejudice. (Wittgenstein 1967, p. 109)

Expressed most simply, a corpus is any body of text. Over the last forty years, however, in parallel with developments in computer technology, the word has come to refer to a more specific concept, although according to Kennedy, the very rapidity of the increase in activity in corpus linguistics, keeping pace with these developments, means that "even the very notion of what constitutes a valid corpus can still be controversial" (Kennedy 1998, p. 2). Nevertheless, the term is now generally understood to mean a sample of naturally-occurring language, usually in machine-readable form and often designed to be representative of a language, or a language variety, such as a particular register, genre, mode and so on. Elena Tognini-Bonelli has recently provided a description of a corpus which incorporates its accepted core features and optional tendencies:

> A corpus can be defined as a collection of texts assumed to be representative of a given language put together so that it can be used for linguistic analysis. Usually the assumption is that the language stored in a corpus is naturally-occurring, that it is gathered according to explicit design criteria, with a specific purpose in mind, and with a claim to represent larger chunks of language selected according to a specific typology. (Tognini-Bonelli 2001, p. 2)

Definitions of corpus linguistics are often just as vague. McEnery and Wilson begin their introduction to corpus linguistics by reducing the methodology to its essence: "the study of language based on examples of 'real life' language use" (1996, p. 1). This definition points to the fact that corpus linguistics is "the modern face of empirical linguistics" (Teubert 1996, p. vi). As such, it stands in contrast, although not necessarily in contradiction, to the top-down approach of general or theoretical linguistics.

Corpus linguistics is a methodology: that is to say, it is a way of approaching or analysing language, and as such it has a wide range of applications. A glance down the contents pages of the *International Journal of Corpus Linguistics* which has existed since 1996, any introductory volume on corpus linguistics,[47] or any of the many edited volumes in the field[48] provides an idea of the versatility of the methodology today. Indeed it is one of the strengths of the methodology that it can be applied to a wide range of areas and questions in linguistics, lexicography, language and literature.

---

47 For example, Biber et al. (1998); Sinclair (1991); McEnery and Wilson (1996, 2001); Kennedy (1998), among others.

48 For example, Aarts and Meijs (1984, 1986, 1990); Aijmer and Altenberg (1991); Kytö, Rissanen and Wright (1994); Meijs (1987); Svartvik (1992a); Thomas and Short (1996); Wichmann, Fligelstone, McEnery and Knowles (1997), among others.

It is not a theory of language, although it can be, and often is, exploited by various linguistic theories. Similarly, it is not a branch of linguistics in the same way as, for example, sociolinguistics or historical linguistics. Nonetheless, the actual status of corpus linguistics is still debated. Graeme Kennedy takes a rather conservative view, claiming that "the use of corpora does not in itself constitute a new or separate branch of linguistics. Rather, corpus linguistics is essentially descriptive linguistics aided by new technology." (Kennedy 1998, p. 268). Gordon Tucker (2000), at the other end of the scale, however, claims that corpus linguistics is on the way to becoming a discipline in its own right, at least to the extent that such modes of communication as conferences, journals and electronic mailing lists mean that researchers working with corpora in distinct linguistic disciplines could be seen to constitute a wide discourse community.

John Sinclair, writing now over a decade ago, summed up the changing face of corpus linguistics in saying:

> Thirty years ago when this research started it was considered impossible to process texts of several million words in length. Twenty years ago it was considered marginally possible but lunatic. Ten years ago it was considered quite possible but still lunatic. Today it is very popular. (Sinclair 1991, p. 1)

This quotation indicates three things. First, it indicates that developments in corpus linguistics have gone hand in hand with development in computer technology. Increased computer memory and more refined software tools have enabled larger and larger collections of text to be analysed more and more delicately. The process of 'tagging' or annotating text with additional information such as word class, or intonation, has opened up further possibilities for research. Although the general tendency has been to compile ever-larger corpora, such as the 100 million word British National Corpus, and the Bank of English, which currently stands at 415 million words, not all progress has been made in this direction. Smaller, specific corpora (of individual genres, learner language, child language, etc.) have retained their own place in the field. Size is not everything: design and representation are also crucial, and are dictated by the aims of the research in question.

Second, the quotation points to the fact that corpus linguistics has over time improved its public face. The intellectual climate in linguistics in the 1960s and 1970s was biased towards the predominance of rationalism and the rise of Chomsky's Transformational Generative approach. As a result, empirical linguistics was experiencing a period of unpopularity. Over the decades, as the methodology has produced unexpected, and otherwise impossible findings about language, it has entered the mainstream.

Third, Sinclair's words are a reminder that computerised corpus linguistics is still a young methodology. Although it stems from a much older tradition of empirical linguistics, it is only in the last forty years or so that technological progress has enabled empirical linguists to make the move from index cards to computers for storing data, and thus achieve qualitatively as well as quantitatively distinct results. W. Nelson Francis (1992), one creator of the famous Brown corpus, surveys the extent of corpus linguistics 'B.C' (before computers), with reference in particular to three 'meta' aims: lexicographical corpora, such as the corpora of examples which lay behind such renowned dictionaries as Johnson's, the OED and Webster's,[49] the dialectological corpora popular in the late nineteenth century, and grammatical corpora, such as that of Jespersen, and the Survey of English Usage. We can also look to anthropological linguistics and such linguists as Boas and Sapir, who carried out linguistic analysis on early corpora of native American folktales (cf. Biber 1990, p. 257). Until the advent of computers, however, the impression was of a patchwork of isolated studies with no overall aim, and little coherence.

In the late 1950s, work began on huge mainframe computers, with data painstakingly entered by hand on punched cards. It was this climate which provided the background for such landmarks in corpus linguistics as the Brown corpus of one million words of written American English published in 1961 (created at Brown University), its British English counterpart, the LOB (Lancaster-Oslo-Bergen) Corpus, and the work on the Survey of English Usage at University College London in the 1960s, which led to major grammars of English (e.g. Quirk et al. 1985). Since this time, corpora have developed in two parallel ways: some have become larger, and others have become more specific. In the latter category might be considered such corpora as the CHILDES corpora of child language at Carnegie Mellon University, and the various parts of the International Corpus of Learner English (ICLE), among the many personal corpora created to answer specific research questions. Finally, there is much potential for work to be done with different types of corpus, such as multimedia corpora, incorporating images, sound and video, as discussed by McEnery and Wilson (1996 and 2001, p. 188). The Scottish Corpus Of Texts & Speech (SCOTS) at the University of Glasgow is one example of this new generation of multimedia corpora.[50]

---

49 McEnery and Wilson (2001) also draw attention to Juilland's (1956) 'mechanolinguistics', corpus work which resulted in word frequency lists for French, Spanish, Romanian and Chinese.

50 The SCOTS Project corpus can be found at www.scottishcorpus.ac.uk.

3.1 Corpora and collocation

Patterns of collocation are not easily open to the linguist's intuition (see for example Berry 1977, p. 54). On the other hand, corpus linguistics is an ideal methodology for the investigation of collocation: corpora can provide the large quantities of data which are necessary in order to discern (sometimes fairly infrequent) patterns in language, and when investigating collocation, one tends to begin at the level of the word, and the analysis tools used in corpus linguistics are ideally suited to finding surface features of language.

For this reason, corpus linguists have been criticised for paying too much attention to collocation, and indeed only investigating collocation because corpora and concordance tools are convenient for this purpose. Alan Partington accepts that this attention is partly due to novelty, but counters the criticism in the following way:

> The paradox of the observer - that we can only perceive physical reality by means of (and some would say distorted by) the tools we use to observe it - is common to all sciences which rely on data. Think, for example of how the object of study of, say, astronomy is very much defined by the tools available to it - the telescope and radio-telescope. When new tools become available in linguistics, new phenomena will be accessible to study. In the meantime we make the fullest use of what we have. (Partington 1998, p. 144)

Stubbs (1999) puts forward a similar view, drawing parallels with the use of the telescope in astronomy and the microscope in biology. Like Partington he introduces a note of caution, pointing out that we must proceed carefully since patterns may be created by this new observation technique which may mistakenly be attributed to language rather than to the technique.

The literature on collocation using corpus methodology is extensive, as Chapter 2 has already demonstrated. Research has been carried out on lexical collocation in the general language (cf. Kjellmer 1987, 1990, 1991), and on lexical and grammatical collocation in specific registers (cf. Gledhill 1995, 1997, 1999). Corpus research has also highlighted types of collocation which had not previously been recognised, such as discontinuous sequences (Renouf and Sinclair 1991; Butler 1998), semantic prosody (cf. Louw 1993, Stubbs 1996), and multiword sequences (cf. Altenberg 1993, 1998; Altenberg and Eeg-Olofsson 1990; Butler 1997).

3.2 Corpora and translation

Corpora have, until recently, rarely been exploited in translation studies, while, conversely, translated text has received unfair treatment in corpus linguistics, being considered an atypical form of language (see Baker 1996, p. 175 for discussion of this). In recent years, this situation has begun to change as translation studies has become aware of the potential of corpora, and corpus linguistics has developed its applications to translation studies.[51]

Since the late 1970s translation studies has undergone something of a change of focus which has opened up the way for the exploitation of corpus methodology. Baker (e.g. 1993, 1999), perhaps the leading proponent of corpus linguistics in translation studies, believes that the field is close to reaching a turning point in its development as a discipline, broaching the divide from prescriptive to descriptive, and that this is a direct consequence of corpus methodology. In recent years, translation studies has moved in the direction of authentic data and pragmatic equivalence (cf. Toury's work in Descriptive Translation Studies, discussed in Baker 1993), and towards an appreciation of the target text, and the place of the translation in the target text system. Baker's own research, on the Translational English Corpus at UMIST, developed these lines of thinking, in laying the groundwork for analysis of the distinctive features of translated text through monolingual comparable corpora, thereby freeing the researcher completely from the source text. Baker considers translated texts to be different, because of their different contexts of production and reception, but not deviant or corrupt (Baker 1999, p. 282-3). Her work has begun to redress the balance in studies of the translation process and in the analysis of the distinctive features of translated texts, such as conservatism, and 'levelling out' (*ibid.*, pp. 176-7, see also Chapter 7), but much remains to be done on the product of translation with multilingual corpora.

Baker's findings on the specific characteristics of translated text should not rule out the presence of such texts in a corpus, although they are clearly important to bear in mind. In the case of the administrative language of a supranational organisation there are many reasons why it would be unrepresentative to *exclude* translated text, especially as the EU recognises equal legal status for all language versions of a text. While Goffin claims that "les versions traduites laissent transparaître en filigrane les modes d'expression du modèle, tant est forte la

---

51 This is especially the case for studies which focus on the process of translation: cf. Baker 1993, 1996; Kenny 1997a, 1997b; and Hansen 2000 who treats translations as a text-type in their own right. For examples of investigations into the product of translation, see Partington's (1998) investigation of false friends; Tognini-Bonelli 1996; Gledhill 1999.

prégnance du texte originaire" (1997, p. 70), a multilingual context of production is quite simply a feature of EU administrative texts.

In the EU context, there is no neutral ground. Even the fact that a text is originally produced in a particular language does not guarantee 'nativeness'. Indeed one could argue that a translated version, having at least been produced by a native speaker of the target language (as EU translators translate into their native language) may be more likely to represent authentic French, or English. Translation is the norm rather than an exception. Given the complexity of the situation, then, the best policy is to follow the EU in accepting each language version of a text as a linguistic as well as a legal equivalent. Phillipson explains that "In theory there is no text in one language that the others are translations of, even if most texts originate in either French or English. This principle reflects a complicated production process with no single author and the reality of many contributing to the words finally agreed on" (Phillipson 2003, p. 131).

3.3 French corpus linguistics

Section 3 above suggests that English has been the main focus of corpus work. For a long time this was certainly true. With regard to French, it is useful to distinguish between the corpus linguistics of French, that is, corpus-based analysis of the French language, and French corpus linguistics, or corpus linguistics as it is carried out in France and other Francophone countries. The two do not always coincide, as much research on the French language has been carried out in other countries (e.g. Sweden, cf. Gellerstam 1992; Engwall 1996), just as a lot of work on English has been carried out in non-Anglophone countries, especially the Netherlands and the Scandinavian nations. French corpus linguistics has tended to be of a different nature from Anglophone corpus linguistics, and often has different aims.

Claire Blanche-Benveniste, in a special issue of the *Revue française de linguistique appliquée* on corpus linguistics (1996) has asked:

> Qu'en est-il pour le français? [...] on n'a pas développé, en France, des corpus conçus comme ceux des autres pays d'Europe. Les corpus écrits à base littéraire y tiennent une bien plus grande place. (Blanche-Benveniste 1996, p. 26)

France may have been slow to start, but this is not to say that there is not a great deal of research to be taken into account. Corpus containing French language texts, whether monolingual corpora of French or multilingual corpora with French as one of the components include: the Aarhus Corpus of Contract Law (Danish, English and French); the Canadian Hansard corpus (Canadian parliamentary transactions in English and French); the CRATER corpus (a domain-specific corpus of telecommunications language in French, English and

Spanish); the European Corpus Initiative corpus (which contains a sub-corpus of four million words of French journalistic texts). As regards spoken corpora, Gabriel Bergounioux's *Corpus d'Orléans* (1966-1970) "avait l'ambition de refléter une parole collective, celle qu'entendaient, à la fin des années 60, les Orléanais" (Bergounioux 1996, p. 87). Gougenheim et al. (discussed in McEnery and Wilson 1996, p. 2 and also Wise 1997, p. 16) created a corpus of transcribed spoken French from 275 informants, investigating high frequency lexical and grammatical choices, and used this as the basis of the *Dictionnaire du français fondamental* which aims to capture the 'core' of the language. Similarly the *Groupe Aixois de Recherches en Syntaxe* (GARS) has been compiling since the mid-1970s a two-million word corpus of spoken French at the University of Provence (Blanche-Benveniste 1996, p. 27).

The *Trésor de la langue française* has been compiled since the 1960s on the basis of FRANTEXT, a text archive of 160 million words (Habert et al. 1997). This massive archive contains a range of genres and periods, and is currently the closest French equivalent to the BNC or Cobuild corpus. However, it has a strong bias towards literary texts which these Anglophone corpora do not. Ayres-Bennett claims that "most histories of the French language have been based on predominantly *literary* texts" (1996, p. 2, the emphasis is Ayres-Bennett's). The same would seem to be true of most dictionary descriptions of the French language, and Frey and Latin confirm this: "[la lexicographie] a tout d'abord privilégié les textes littéraires considérés comme illustrant le mieux la norme valorisée de la langue" (Frey and Latin, eds. 1997, p. 21). Frey and Latin's volume gathers together a collection of lexicographical studies of national varieties of French, such as Cameroon French and Nigerian French. Nor is lexicographical work is limited to the 'general' language: as Chapter 2 indicated, Geoffrey Williams has carried out a corpus study of terminology in the field of plant biology, the aim of which is to improve the content of specialised dictionaries for the benefit of learners (G. C. Williams 2001a).

While there have been corpora in France since the 1960s, Habert et al. claim that what is new is annotation, an increase in corpus size, and better accessibility of corpora and tools (cf. Habert et al. 1997, p. 7). In their introduction to *les linguistiques de corpus*, they concentrate almost totally on annotated corpora, of which there are still relatively few, especially compared to English: "Les corpus enrichis sont aujourd'hui majoritairement de langue anglaise ou américaine." (*ibid*., p. 14). Habert described the contemporary situation in French corpus linguistics as follows:

> La conjoncture actuelle tient, semble-t-il, à la rencontre d'une tradition anglosaxonne de linguistique descriptive s'appuyant sur les corpus électroniques et d'un profond changement de cap en traitement automatique du langage naturel. (*ibid*., p.8)

French is somewhat behind English in the field (*ibid.*, p. 14). English has dominated because of the long history of Anglo-Saxon corpus-based descriptive linguistics and the place of British and American English in Natural Language Processing projects.

3.4 Issues in corpus linguistics

As the previous sections have indicated, corpora today come in many shapes and sizes, and vary according to a range of dimensions. Approaches to corpus linguistics also differ considerably. In Anglophone corpus linguistics, there are three main theoretical approaches (cf. Hunston 2000b), which can be referred to by their principal places of origin. The Birmingham approach, which is behind the pioneering Cobuild project, concentrates predominantly on phraseology and patterning in language, following John Sinclair's 'clean-text' policy (Sinclair 1991, pp. 21-22), according to which the corpus is not permanently marked up, as this would impose a theory on the data. The Cobuild corpus does, however, have a limited level of tagging, termed 'light mark-up' (Clear et al. 1996, p. 306). The Lancaster approach (cf. work by G. Leech, e.g. 1993, 1997), on the other hand, advocates tagging and mark-up of various kinds, such as lemmatisation, word-class tagging, or even semantic tagging. Finally, in Douglas Biber's approach to corpus linguistics in the USA (e.g. Biber 1988, Biber, Conrad and Reppen 1998), the focus is on register analysis and comparison. Biber's approach, as we saw earlier, is multidimensional, seeking to describe registers along a range of axes according to the clustering of linguistic variables.

The issue of whether or not to mark-up or tag a corpus is a highly contentious one in corpus linguistics, and indeed humanities computing generally (see Hockey 2000). Each approach has value for different research aims. For the present study of phraseology and collocation, predominantly surface features of language, I adopt Sinclair's clean-text policy. Annotation is especially useful for the study of syntax, semantics, prosodic features or discourse. For a study of phraseology, however, careful manual analysis of the data produced by a good analysis tool, can take us a long way. Stubbs and Gerbig advocate untagged text, saying that "it is easy to underestimate what can be done with concordances of untagged text" (1993, p. 79). They give examples, such as the identification of sentence-initial units, and show that with untagged text "the pattern matching of concordance programs can identify important syntactic patterns" (*ibid.*). While some investigations simply cannot be carried out with untagged text, they insist that "one does not abandon a very powerful observation method because it is not perfect" (*ibid.*). There is a balance to be drawn between the advantages of annotation for certain types of analysis, and the time needed to afford such annotation.

A perennial problem in corpus linguistics which remains to be dealt with in the context of this study is that of corpus representation. Although sometimes regarded as synonymous with the issue of size, the two are independent. The problem is circular: in order to generalise from a corpus to a whole language, register or genre, the corpus needs to be a representative sample: however, it is impossible exactly to define the parameters of a total population of texts (except the complete works of an author, the extant texts of a dead language) without resorting to artificial means, such as defining the population as, for example, 'all the texts printed in 1961 in the United States' (the definition underlying the design of the Brown corpus). In that case, the issue becomes one of whether the artificially-restricted 'population' is representative of the whole language, register or genre. It should be noted in addition that compiling a corpus of whole texts and not fixed-size samples is to take for granted that a language or register is effectively a collection of texts - a collection of instances and not an abstract faculty of the mind. In terms of Halliday's analogy (e.g. Halliday 1991), texts are 'the weather', instances of which build up over time to constitute language, or 'the climate'.

So it is better to begin instead with the question of what a corpus is to represent. The design of the administrative corpus here makes a compromise between a proportional corpus and a corpus for studying variety, the specific design being influenced by text availability. These two types of corpus are distinguished and discussed by Biber, Conrad and Reppen:

> [...] a proportional corpus would be of limited use for studies of variation, because most of the corpus would be relatively homogeneous. That is, most texts in a proportional corpus would be from conversation, [...]. In most corpus studies, we are interested in the range of linguistic variants that occur in a language or in describing one variety of a language relative to another variety. (Biber, Conrad and Reppen 1998, p. 247)

Proportional corpora themselves may represent *reception* or *production* of language (Clear 1992, p. 24). A general corpus designed to reflect language reception will exaggerate the importance of a small proportion of texts (literature, journalism etc.), whereas in a corpus reflecting language production these important texts will be overwhelmed by spoken language, particularly conversation.

In the case of administrative language, a 'production' corpus would be composed predominantly of documents such as press releases, especially those issued by the European Commission, and Presidential speeches, which are many times more frequent than documents such as treaties, which appear only once every five years or so on average. A 'reception' corpus, on the other hand (one reflecting the texts read or heard by an audience like the general public) would have to give much greater weight to treaties and other such primary legislative texts which are used as reference documents by a large number of people, but read in their entirety by very few people.[52] Relatively few texts have a really lasting influence, and it is impossible to gauge the influence of any single text. Decisions regarding corpus compilation will necessarily be based on estimations, although this is not meant to imply that it is futile to attempt a careful design.

A corpus designed for studying genre variety, on the other hand, might contain equal quantities of the genres within the register of administrative language (press releases, speeches, reports, legislation etc.). One advantage of this type of corpus is the ease it affords in analysing the differences between genres. A serious disadvantage, however, is that there is no weighting to reflect the different frequencies of publication and varying degrees of linguistic influence exerted by the different genres or individual texts. On a more practical note, text availability causes problems for such an approach, as some genres are only available in very small quantities and large differences in text length between genres means that long texts would be represented by only a few texts and would therefore cover only relatively few subject areas, while press releases and other relatively short texts would have to be present in huge quantities to provide balance and would as a result cover many more fields of discourse.

The compromise nature of my corpus aims to reduce such problems. At the end of the day, as Leech notes: "We should always bear in mind that the assumption of representativeness must be regarded largely as an act of faith" (1991, p. 27). This compromise design aims to give due weight to important texts in order not to misrepresent the register and at the same time to enable comparison of genres, from the point of view of collocation and phraseology. The corpus can therefore provide insights into the relative frequency of patterns and the quantitative importance of particular genres.

Although corpus linguistics has come a long way since he wrote it, Sinclair's caution still holds true:

> The results are only as good as the corpus, and we are at a very primitive stage of understanding the character of corpora and the relation between decisions on the constitution of the corpus and information about the language derived from the corpus. (Sinclair 1991, p. 9)

This caveat holds for all of the analysis carried out here. It is only in the light of experience and analysis that it is possible to refine corpus design.

---

52 Compare Swales (1990a, p. 14) who has shown that even those scientific papers which are widely read are probably not read in their entirety, at least in the order intended by their presentation on the page.

3.5 Tools for corpus analysis

Regardless of its design and claims to representation, an electronic corpus in itself is scarcely of more use than a paper collection of texts. In order to benefit from the huge advances in technology made in the last fifty years, a corpus must be combined with some form of analysis tool. Generally speaking, progress in available interrogation software fails to keep pace with the demands of linguistic researchers: there are, however, very useful packages and programs available. McEnery and Wilson (2001), Oakes (1998) and Biber, Conrad and Reppen (1998) contain guides to corpus analysis tools, and the Internet is invaluable for continually updated information.

The program chosen for use in this research is Scott's WordSmith Tools package (Version 3, OUP 1999). WordSmith Tools represents a logical step forward from Scott's earlier Microconcord and Wordlist programs, combining a suite of facilities in one meta-tool: Concord, a concordance program which retrieves specified strings of characters from the corpus; WordList, which generates alphabetical and frequency-ordered wordlists, based on either single words, or sequences of between two and eight words; and Keywords, which identifies words with salient frequency in one text or corpus compared with another. An invaluable feature is the ease with which one can toggle between the Concord, WordList and Keyword programs in order to analyse text from these different perspectives at once.

4. The administrative corpus

One might argue that it is better, as a general rule, to make use of existing resources where possible. This allows for more direct comparison of findings. However, the lack of suitable corpora of French made it necessary in this case to build a personal corpus of administrative language. At this relatively early stage in the exploitation of corpora for French register analysis, this is methodologically useful: it is only through practice and repeated experimentation that corpus designs can be compared and evaluated, in terms both of the hypotheses that corpus analysis can make about language, and also their potential shortcomings. A second advantage of starting afresh is that it is possible to dictate exactly which genres are represented and which texts included in the corpus: the corpus can be designed to be maximally suitable to the needs of the research. Less of a distance is enforced between the analyst and the text: this, according to Svartvik (1992b, p. 10), is the greatest danger of a heavy dependency on corpus data. Had there already been corpora of French administrative language, the temptation to exploit these for the sake of the advantages to be gained in mark-up and existing peer-criticism of the corpus in question might have been overwhelming, even if they did not otherwise fit the criteria of this research quite perfectly.

In the event, however, there was no suitable corpus. Various projects could offer useful data but not a whole corpus. For example, the European Language Resources Association (ELRA) has a corpus of 7.1 million words in French (and in another eight languages) of debates and minutes of the European Parliament. This is a useful corpus in itself, but not one that could be said to represent more than a small part of the register of administrative French. Similarly, the Hansard French/English corpus represents a single genre of Canadian French. FRANTEXT comprises a vast amount of text, but only a small fraction is 'administration publique', the overwhelming majority being literary texts. For this reason, therefore, it was decided at the start of this period of research to create a new corpus.

4.1 Text sources

All of the texts in the administrative corpus were obtained from the Internet between March and September 1999. The key web resources used are listed in Appendix 1. Both the French governmental sites and the European Union sites allow a copy of their texts to be stored for personal research.

4.2 Design of administrative corpus

Appendix 1 details the textual contents of the complete French administrative corpus (referred to here as "FRADCO"). The full corpus contains over two million running words, equally divided between European Union and French national government texts. It is made up of 1,086 whole texts of varying lengths, again equally divided between the two halves of the corpus. Although a two-million word corpus is small compared with corpora for lexicographical work, such as the BNC, the Bank of English, or FRANTEXT, it should be remembered that these are general corpora, which seek to represent the language in question as a whole, or at least as a set of varieties, while the administrative corpus is simply that: a corpus of texts sampling a single register of French. In this light, its representative power suddenly becomes much greater. The whole of the 'Miscellaneous' category of the Brown Corpus, which contains government documents, industry reports, college catalogues and similar, for example, comes to roughly 60,000 words. For a register-specific corpus, two million words is substantial: certainly large enough, if carefully designed, to provide information on the typical phraseology of the register.

The corpus is a roughly synchronic sample of the register. The majority of the texts date from late-1997 to mid-1999, although a few older texts, such as treaties and constitutional texts, have been included on the basis of their continuing relevance. In addition to the short time-period from which the texts are drawn, an effort was made during compilation to sample texts evenly throughout the calendar year where possible, in order to avoid the possibility of a surfeit of texts all referring to events at a particular time in the administrators' working year.

As Appendix 1 shows, each half of the corpus is made up of a wide range of textual categories - nineteen in the EU part of the corpus ("FREUCO") and eighteen in the French national part ("FRNACO"). Whether or not some of the categories which appear under the same name in both halves of the corpus (e.g. *communiqués de presse*), or more than once in the same half (e.g. the various categories of administrative speech) represent in fact the 'same' genre is debatable. However, there is considerable overlap in these respects, so that the thirty-seven categories do not equate to thirty-seven different genres. The concern to sample the population of available documents means that there is not a one-to-one pairing of genres between the two halves of the corpus.

The tables also show that the corpus contains texts of varying degrees of formality, and both written texts and texts which were written to be read aloud (speeches). The latter category was included for three main reasons. Firstly, even within the written mode there are variations: some texts are written to be read in their entirety, while others are written to be consulted (e.g. primary and secondary legislation). Secondly, there is no clean division between the written and spoken modes. As we have seen, Douglas Biber has found that there is "no single parameter of linguistic variation that distinguishes among spoken and written genres" (1988, p. 55). Finally, although the written mode is arguably more central to the administrative function - perhaps one of the main differences between administrative and political language - speeches usually originate in writing and are then subsequently delivered orally. Indeed, the text of EU speeches is made available on the websites on a 'check against delivery' basis: that is to say there is no guarantee that they do not differ from the version delivered. This would seem to be an acknowledgement that they are to all intents and purposes written texts.

In addition to covering a wide range of genres, the available texts were also sampled to cover a wide range of subject matter. Although the sampling is essentially random, in this way it is also partially stratified in order to avoid bias which could influence the analysis. Larger texts (treaties, Assemblée Nationale debates, etc.) tend to cover more than one subject area, or at least different sub-fields within a general area, so despite their large size these do not strongly bias the subject matter of the corpus. However, a corpus of any size is necessarily biased to a certain extent: this is simply a result of the context-dependence of human language and the lack of an easily identifiable population of texts. With the exception of authorship studies which analyse the complete œuvre of a writer, it is rarely possible in corpus research to apply the tried-and-tested sampling methods of the social sciences, which require a finite and clearly-defined total population.

With regard to the comparative analysis which the structure of the corpus makes possible, the two halves of the corpus contain similar quantities of material which was written to be spoken (184,229 words EU, and 184,371 words National). This allows direct comparison to be made between the two halves of the corpus, and also between these and purely written texts. The French national half of the corpus also contains about 50,000 words which are a mixture of written text and transcribed debate from the Assemblée Nationale. An equivalent was not available for the European Union half of the corpus, but as the genre is clearly an important one, it was considered appropriate to include it in a corpus which seeks to represent the whole register. Both halves of the corpus also contain large quantities of press release material. Although the quantities are not equal in this case, they may be indirectly compared since each part is substantial, and when the two halves are combined, the press release genre as a whole can be compared with the rest of the corpus taken as a whole, or with a well-defined section of it, such as the speeches. As Biber, Conrad and Reppen say:

> the representativeness of a corpus can be investigated empirically - and it is through these sorts of investigations that we can learn to build better corpora in the future. (Biber, Conrad and Reppen 1998, p. 250)

With retrospect it may become clear that an alternative corpus design would be more appropriate: the present corpus, however, is the result of careful design, and opens the way for many types of comparative analysis.

4.3 The comparator corpus

Corpus-based analyses, especially corpus-based register analyses, are of little value without some element of comparison. Much of the analysis of the administrative register in this study is already internally comparative. The analysis in Chapter 5 also effectively sets up a comparison between the administrative corpus and a corpus-based dictionary of locutions (Rey and Chantreau 1993). At other times it is desirable to be able to carry out comparative analyses with a more general corpus of French texts, or at least a sample of different registers. This study has sought to overcome the problem of the lack of a large general corpus of French by compiling a small corpus, made up of texts from a range of genres which are freely and generally available. This corpus merely provides a selection of 'other' French, made up of non-discipline specific texts in the standard language: it does not claim representation.

While the design and compilation of a large general corpus would constitute an enormous project, well beyond the scope of a study by a single researcher, a small corpus can be assembled quite rapidly, using texts already in electronic format, on CD-ROM or from the Internet, for instance. I call this a 'comparator corpus'. The term 'control corpus', while more generally used, implies a more representative sampling of a language, covering a greater number of genres, ideally including the conversation which makes up such a large proportion of the language we both produce and are exposed to in daily life. A control corpus, in other words, should seek to represent the language as fully as possible. The comparator corpus compiled here, on the other hand, seeks merely to provide a point of reference beyond the register of administrative language.

With roughly two and a quarter million words of text (see Appendix 1), the comparator corpus is of a similar size to the complete French administrative corpus. It contains four genres: journalism (*Le Monde*, covering the subgenres *biographie*, *courrier*, *marché financier*, *nécrologie*, and *libre opinion*); non-fiction (prose texts on a range of topics); fiction;[53] and biblical texts (five books from the Old and New Testaments of a twentieth-century edition of the Bible). The journalism section is by far the largest. While the limited range of genres is a weakness of the comparator corpus, the inclusion of a large proportion of journalistic text does increase its variety. Journalistic language has the advantage of being a very wide genre: what one might, following David Lee (on the Corpora electronic mailing list on 31 August 2000), call a 'supergenre', embracing many genres and subgenres and a potentially unlimited variety of subject matters. Burr (1996, cited in Hockey 2000, p. 21) has argued that journalism is a fusion of literary and spoken and special purpose language, and as such represents the modern language as it is. In other words, the internal heterogeneity of the journalism section goes some way towards compensating for the restricted range of genres in the comparator corpus as a whole.

5. Conclusion

This chapter has set out the tools, both theoretical and methodological, which are necessary for an examination of collocational and phraseological patterning in administrative language. Before arguing for the value of corpus methodology for this research, we first discussed the object of study, administrative language, in theoretical terms. At the most abstract level, administrative texts are united by situational features, that is by register, in a Hallidayan sense: the texts all mediate in some way between administrative institutions and citizens. One subset of this register is the language of the European Union, the principal focus of this research. Another is French national administrative language. These two particular ways of viewing the function of administration, and of dividing up the sphere of influence of their institutions, can be seen as separate discourses. Each of the two discourses employs a number of types of text (genres, with a common communicative purpose) in order to fulfil its function: these differ between the two discourses although there is a large degree of overlap.

---

53 Only texts which are no longer in copyright can be used. An arbitrary cut-off date of 1900 has been adopted.

Chapter 4

Multiword Sequences

Then we get to the real nitty-gritty.
DAVID LODGE, SMALL WORLD: AN ACADEMIC ROMANCE

1. Introduction

Following the order of approach set out in Chapter 2, this chapter focuses on phraseology as the creation of the users of administrative language. The method adopted enables us to identify phraseological patterning directly from the corpus, rather than imposing prior expectations on it. The starting assumption of this 'macro' approach is what has been called the 'strong hypothesis' of collocation: namely, that every syntagm is a collocation (cf. Gledhill 1999, p. 226). While this is a more open definition of collocation than is often admitted, it is a convenient starting point.

Since administrative documents rely to a relatively large extent on formulae, terms and intertextual reference, analysis which concentrates on relatively long repeated sequences of words is likely to highlight these features of language as well as revealing the typical phraseology of the register. The largely synchronic nature of the corpus used here means that the extent of intertextuality may not be as apparent as it would be in diachronic analysis, but we can still expect a high number of repeated sequences compared with other registers.

The WordList facility of WordSmith Tools (Scott 1999) enables the researcher to make wordlists, ordered either alphabetically or by frequency, both for single words in a corpus, and also for repeated sequences of between two and eight words, which WordSmith terms 'clusters'. The analysis in this chapter is based on wordlists of multiword sequences: for the purposes of reference and comparison, however, Appendix 3 contains wordlist statistics for single words, and tables of the most frequent 100 words, for the complete administrative corpus (FRADCO) and the two sub-corpora individually (FREUCO and FRNACO), as well as the comparator corpus. It is worth considering the different single-word lists briefly: a comparison of FREUCO and FRNACO shows that while the most frequent word forms in both sub-corpora are grammatical or function words, FREUCO also contains four content words in its top thirty most frequent word forms - these are 'Commission', 'Conseil', 'articles', 'membres' - but the equivalent list for FRNACO contains only grammatical words. Compared with the more general comparator corpus, however, FRNACO does contain some highly frequent content words. This finding appears to blur the distinction between function (closed-class) and content (open-class) words in the context of the administrative register. There is an overlap in the role of function words and frequently occurring lexical words which serve to structure discourse and identify register. This suggests that the boundary between grammatical and content words may shift depending on register or discourse issues. In any case, these wordlists indicate that we should not limit our focus solely to lexical words, in the sense of nouns, verbs, adjectives and adverbs, as most phraseological and collocational research does, or indeed solely to grammatical words (cf. Gledhill 2000, p. 17-18). This chapter and Chapters 5 and 6 concentrate predominantly on the top end of the wordlists: this requires an approach which is open to both lexical and grammatical words as they are traditionally defined.[54]

This approach makes it possible to highlight different types of patterning in the different lengths of sequence, which enables the identification of core phraseology. It does, however, have certain shortcomings; in particular, only those sequences which recur in *identical* form are highlighted. It is not true to say that variation is completely overlooked: while free variation is certainly invisible to this method, consistent and frequent variations are recorded, although it is difficult to accord due weight to them. Nevertheless, this particular approach has the potential to give many insights into the phraseological patterning of the register, especially when considered in conjunction with the complementary approaches taken in Chapters 5 and 6.

1.1 Procedure

The WordList facility of WordSmith Tools has been used to carry out this analysis. WordList is able to extract exactly repeated sequences of between two and eight words in length: in addition it is possible to identify longer sequences from the 8-word sequences.[55] As regards sentence and clause boundaries, WordList does not recognise clusters which occur over a punctuation boundary. It is highly likely, given the formulaic nature of administrative documents, that

---

54 Notwithstanding the unusually high frequency of some content words in the corpus, and especially the EU sub-corpus, the data in both sub-corpora fit the A-curve (developed from Zipf's Law, cf. Zipf 1949) which Kretzschmar and Tamasi (2001) have found to describe variation not just in the vocabulary of a written text but also in the lexicon of the spoken language and speech sounds. These A-curves demonstrate that the appearance of high-frequency lexical items where only grammatical items might be expected is not an artefact of the data or the corpus design, but a phenomenon of language (specifically of the administrative register) which must be accounted for.

55 See also Biber et al. (1999) for discussion of multiword sequences, or 'lexical bundles', in English.

some recurrent sequences do occur over such boundaries in the corpus, but these are unlikely to constitute phraseological elements, if they occur over clause boundaries. This approach does not correspond to that of Butler (1997), whose study takes no account of sentence boundaries in extracting repeated sequences, although he suggests that sequences which occur only or predominantly over sentence boundaries are unlikely to be very frequent in his texts (1997, p. 64-65).

Given the extremely large number of recurrent sequences in the corpus, and the particular interest here in the typical, core phraseology of the register, the analysis has been restricted to sequences which occur at least a specified minimum number of times, the actual frequency varying according to the size of the sub-corpus used. Although this excludes some sequences which would otherwise appear simply because of their frequency in a single text, as Altenberg notes: “Neither length nor frequency is a criterion of phraseological status, but the frequency threshold gives at least some guarantee that the selected word-combinations have some currency […] and that they are of some interest from that point of view” (Altenberg 1998, p. 102).

A further reason for restricting myself to the most frequent sequences relates to the hardware and software limitations: WordList is very demanding on memory when dealing with sequences of words, especially longer sequences, and low frequencies are occasionally unreliable. This can be alleviated by increasing the minimum frequency of occurrence of the sequences one is interested in, or by running the software over smaller sub-corpora.

In producing a list of sequences for a particular corpus, the most immediately obvious feature is the large proportion of overlap between lengths of sequence, and it is convenient to reduce the lists to eliminate repetition: for example, to disregard the 3-word noun phrase sequence ‘traité sur l’Union’ where the complete unit is clearly the 4-word ‘traité sur l’Union européenne’. It is no simple matter to prune frequency lists in this way, however. It is not possible merely to exclude those sequences which are part of longer sequences, as sometimes the frequency of a 3-word sequence will be significantly higher than, say, a 4-word sequence in which it is included. This highlights the fact that language, neither spoken nor written, is not produced by clipping together sequences of words like building blocks, but rather there is a constant fluctuation between the open choice principle and the idiom principle (cf. Sinclair 1991, and Chapter 2 above).

There are often co-occurrence tendencies or preferences, for example for conjunctions, discourse markers, positive or negative words, rather than particular words to each side of the individual sequences. This is the phenomenon to which Sinclair was referring in his discussion of the phrase ‘set eyes on’:

> Many phrases have an indeterminate extent. As an example, consider *set eyes on*. This seems to attract a pronoun subject, and either *never*

> or a temporal conjunction like *the moment*, *the first time*, and the word *has* as an auxiliary to *set*. How much of this is integral to the phrase, and how much is in the nature of collocational attraction? (Sinclair 1991, p. 111)

The phenomenon of overlap between lengths of sequence has been recognised and formally measured in statistics, using the concept of cost criteria.

1.2 The concept of cost criteria

Working in the area of collocational knowledge acquisition, Kita et al. (1994) have suggested a measure for dealing with such overlapping in multiword sequences of varying lengths. Their measure, which they term 'cost criteria', is related to the measure of Mutual Information (cf. Kita et al. 1994; Jelinek 1990[56] cited in Kita et al. 1994; Oakes 1998) as both are concerned with identifying collocations in a corpus. Cost criteria, however, is based on absolute frequency rather than relative frequency.[57] In this way, cost criteria accords due weight to high frequency collocations, but does not artificially inflate the importance of low frequency ones. From their work on the ATR Dialogue Database Corpus, Kita et al. (1994) demonstrate that while Mutual Information tends to extract compound noun phrases in both English and Japanese, such as 'slide projector' and 'Wall Street' (*ibid.*, p. 61), the cost criteria measure tends to extract frozen phrase patterns, such as 'may I have your name and address' and 'so please hold the line' (*ibid.*, p. 61).

2. FRADCO - the complete administrative corpus

Owing to hardware and software limitations as outlined above, it was impossible to obtain perfectly consistent results for multiword sequences for the complete two million word corpus. This means that it is not possible to state precisely the number of sequences of each length which appear in the complete corpus, or to calculate the proportion of the corpus which is made up of such sequences. It is possible, however, to discuss the highest frequency sequences, since the memory limitations do not affect these.

---

56 The measure of Mutual Information can only identify collocations of two words in a corpus. Jelinek 1990, however, (cited in Kita et al. 1994, Oakes 1998) has proposed an iterative form of Mutual Information which allows longer sequences to be extracted.

57 The formula for the reduced cost of a word sequence α is: $K(\alpha) = (|\alpha| - 1) \times (f(\alpha) - f(\beta))$, where β is a longer sequence which includes α. $|\alpha|$ is the length of α in words. A high value of $K(\alpha)$ suggests that α is a full collocation, or has a greater unity as a collocation than β.

The following are the twenty most frequent 8-word sequences in FRADCO:

Table 4.1: 8-word sequences in FRADCO

	Sequence	**Freq.**
1	ARTICLE # ARTICLE # ARTICLE # ARTICLE #	259
2	DE LA LOI NB #-# DU #	106
3	CONFORMÉMENT À LA PROCÉDURE VISÉE À LARTICLE # [58]	75
4	DE LA LOI NO #-# DU #	69
5	STATUANT CONFORMÉMENT À LA PROCÉDURE VISÉE À LARTICLE	67
6	LOI NO #-# DU # JUILLET #	66
7	ARTICLE # DE LA LOI NB #-#	57
8	LA MINISTRE DE LEMPLOI ET DE LA SOLIDARITÉ	55
9	LARTICLE # DE LA LOI NB #-#	52
10	VU LA LOI NO #-# DU #	50
11	A PRÉSENTÉ SES CONCLUSIONS À LAUDIENCE DE LA	48
12	LA LOI NO #-# DU # JUILLET	45
13	MINISTRE DE LA CULTURE ET DE LA COMMUNICATION	44
14	SUR PROPOSITION DE LA COMMISSION ET APRÈS CONSULTATION	44
15	LA LOI NB #-# DU # FÉVRIER	42
16	LOI NB #-# DU # FÉVRIER #	42
17	A MANQUÉ AUX OBLIGATIONS QUI LUI INCOMBENT EN	41
18	DE LA RÉFORME DE LETAT ET DE LA	41
19	LA RÉFORME DE LETAT ET DE LA DÉCENTRALISATION	41
20	MANQUÉ AUX OBLIGATIONS QUI LUI INCOMBENT EN VERTU	41

The hash symbol (#) indicates any number. While numbers have been shown to have interesting collocational patterns of their own (cf. Hoey 2000), it was felt that in documents of this sort, numbers would not as a general rule have significant patterns of collocation, since they are predominantly used in dates, document numbers, reference numbers of laws etc., as can be seen from the list above. Thus, to treat numbers individually in making a wordlist would obscure many otherwise important sequences. Months of the year sometimes collocate with other words for pragmatic reasons; for example, meetings which happen at

58 WordList has been set to consider apostrophes as part of the word (i.e. l'article = 1 word, and shown as 'larticle' in the list).

particular times of year such as European Councils which are usually held in December and June, at the end of a national Presidency.

These sequences are clearly characteristic of the administrative register rather than the general language. Moreover, the majority of the more frequent long sequences come from legislative texts, or refer to these. Numbers 8 and 13 in the table above demonstrate that this analysis can highlight terms in the various component fields, and the names of organisations, bodies, individuals, and, as in these cases, ministries. As mentioned briefly in Chapter 2, terminological work has so far only rarely been based on corpora (cf. Pearson 1998), although it does rely on authentic texts: while corpora are ideal for retrospective analyses of terms used, they have been seen as unsuitable for the purposes of building terminological databases, which by their nature are required to be very up-to-date. Frequency of occurrence is much less important in terminology too, indeed it is rare terms and neologisms which are the centre of attention: these are not readily highlighted by the type of analysis carried out here.

The comparator corpus contains far fewer long sequences. Only forty-four 8-word sequences are repeated at least ten times, as compared with around 500 in FRADCO. This is due in large part to the heterogeneity of the corpus, and the fact that it is small for a corpus which is not register-specific. The great majority of these long sequences in the comparator corpus are from a single genre: the *Conseil* genre of *Le Monde* texts. These texts constitute reports of the French Council of Ministers, partly based on Press Releases issued by this body. Another is the sequence 'et il engendra des fils et des filles', repeated 17 times in the book of Genesis.

Shifting our attention to the other end of the scale, the twenty most frequent 3-word sequences in FRADCO are listed below, with their respective frequencies and also their frequencies in the comparator corpus (obtained using the Concord facility of WordSmith Tools).

Table 4.2: 3-word sequences in FRADCO

	Sequence	**Freq.**	**%**	**Freq.in comp. corpus**
1	DE LA COMMISSION	1,927	0.09	121
2	ET DE LA	1,854	0.09	734
3	DANS LE CADRE	1,480	0.07	111
4	LA MISE EN	1,347	0.06	154
5	À LARTICLE #	1,316	0.06	11
6	EN MATIÈRE DE	985	0.05	126
7	LES ÉTATS MEMBRES	955	0.05	4
8	DE LA COMMUNAUTÉ	889	0.04	127
9	DE LARTICLE #	881	0.04	13
10	MISE EN OEUVRE	846	0.04	69

11	LA COMMISSION A	828	0.04	1
12	DANS LE DOMAINE	821	0.04	96
13	CE QUI CONCERNE	804	0.04	101
14	DE LUNION EUROPÉENNE	772	0.04	4
15	EN CE QUI	767	0.04	89
16	LE CONSEIL EUROPÉEN	763	0.04	7
17	LE CADRE DE	693	0.03	42
18	ET À LA	643	0.03	196
19	DE LA RÉPUBLIQUE	634	0.03	445
20	DE LA POLITIQUE	593	0.03	165

Unlike the list of 8-word sequences above, the majority of these sequences are not restricted to the administrative register, and indeed every one appears at least once in the comparator corpus, although some clearly refer to administrative and political bodies (e.g. 'la Commission', 'l'Union européenne', 'le Conseil européen'). Instead, many are grammatical or partly grammatical sequences which are frequent also in the general language ('mise en œuvre', 'dans le domaine', 'en ce qui concerne', 'et à la'). Below are the most frequent 3-word sequences in the comparator corpus. Because of the heterogeneity of the corpus, the most frequent sequences in the comparator corpus occur with a much lower frequency, despite the roughly comparable corpus size.

Table 4.3: 3-word sequences in the comparator corpus

	Sequence	**Freq.**	**%**	**Freq. in FRADCO**
1	IL Y A	1,372	0.06	513
2	ET DE LA	734	0.03	1,854
3	CONSEIL DES MINISTRES	598	0.03	214
4	IL NY A	480	0.02	151
5	CE NEST PAS	472	0.02	92
6	DE LA RÉPUBLIQUE	445	0.02	634
7	DE # À	424	0.02	214
8	PRÉSIDENT DE LA	380	0.02	504
9	DE #	365	0.02	357
10	DU # AU	350	0.02	66
11	CEST-À-DIRE [59]	348	0.02	198
12	EST-À-DIRE	348	0.02	198
13	NE SONT PAS	342	0.02	414
14	DE PLUS EN	304	0.01	192
15	PLUS EN PLUS	301	0.01	189
16	TOUT LE MONDE	293	0.01	39

59 In addition, 'c'est à dire' (non-hyphenated) appears in both corpora.

17	DE LA GUERRE	292	0.01	30
18	MINISTRE DE LA	290	0.01	280
19	DE LA FRANCE	289	0.01	238
20	À LA FOIS	288	0.01	302

Although only two sequences ('et de la' and 'de la république') are common to the lists of the top 20 sequences of both corpora, many more from the FRADCO list appear with a lower frequency in the comparator corpus list. This highlights the fact that a register employs the resources of the general language to a greater or lesser extent, but is not a highly isolated 'sublanguage' like the language of air traffic control, or weather reporting.

It is clear from the 8-word sequence lists that in many cases even longer sequences are present in the corpus, with or without variation. In order to investigate this, all of the sequences which appear at least ten times in the whole corpus were taken and grouped them into related 'families'. The following sequences and sentence stems came out as most typical of the register as a whole. The words outside brackets are more central to the sentence stem, while the words in brackets are optional expansions. A slash separates alternatives within a sequence.

[statuant] conformément à la procédure fixée / prévue / visée à l'article # [et après consultation du comité économique et social et du comité des régions]
a présenté ses conclusions à l'audience de la [sixième chambre [du # MONTH #]
sur proposition de la Commission et après consultation [du Parlement européen et du Conseil du #]
[le Royaume de Belgique] a manqué aux obligations qui lui incombent en vertu [de l'article # / ladite directive]
statuant à la majorité qualifiée sur [proposition / recommandation de la Commission]
réglementaire et administratives nécessaires pour se conformer à la directive [#CE du / #CEE du Conseil]
[la Commission] a décidé de saisir la Cour de Justice
[jour suivant celui de] sa publication aux Journal Officiel des Communautés européennes
[dans un délai de trois mois / cinq ans] à compter de la [date d'entrée en vigueur du règlement]
le paragraphe # / l'article # / le premier alinéa est remplacé par le texte suivant
[le présent règlement est obligatoire dans tous] ses éléments et directement applicable dans tout état membre
la Commission des Communautés européennes a introduit un recours visant à faire constater que

la majorité qualifiée est définie comme la même proportion des voix pondérées des membres
[le comité émet son avis sur ce projet] dans un délai que le président peut fixer en fonction de l'urgence [de la question en cause]

sera publiée au Journal Officiel de la République française
[à] la date de publication de la loi NB [# du #]
vous pouvez consulter le tableau dans le JO NB # du ### page # [à]
le président de la République promulgue la loi dont la teneur suit
[la commune] dont la population est supérieure à la moitié de la population totale [de celles-ci / concernée]

à la majorité des deux tiers de ses membres
des émissions de gaz à effet de serre

Although this list was made on the basis of the whole corpus, it is notable that few long sequences appear in both sub-corpora. In fact the top group is drawn exclusively from FREUCO, the middle group from FRNACO, and only the last two sequences occur in both sub-corpora with a frequency greater than ten.

There is much greater overlap between the sub-corpora at the level of 3 and 4-word sequences, which tend to be grammatical in nature. Of the top fifty 3-word sequences in FREUCO by frequency, 13 occur also in the equivalent list for FRNACO. In descending order of frequency in FREUCO, and with comments following where the usage differs greatly between the sub-corpora, these are:

de la Commission
à l'article
dans le cadre
la mise en
et de la
en matière de
mise en œuvre
ce qui concerne
dans le domaine
de l'article #
le cadre de
de la politique
et à la

Although 'de la Commission' appears in both sub-corpora, it is about five times less frequent in FRNACO, and in less than 20 cases refers to the European Commission, but more often to such commissions as 'la Commission générale de terminologie et de néologie', and various 'commissions départementales'. With regard to 'ce qui concerne', the top 50 most frequent sequences in FREUCO also contains ‘en ce qui’, with a frequency of 584 (compared with 607 for ‘ce qui concerne’). It might be expected that the two sequences would both appear with the same frequency. The examples of ‘ce qui concerne’ which are not immediately preceded by ‘en’ (29) in FREUCO instead form part of the expression ‘pour ce qui concerne’: there are 578 instances of ‘en ce qui concerne’ compared with 29 of ‘pour ce qui concerne’, a ratio of roughly 20:1. There are also a few examples of ‘en ce qui’ immediately followed by an object pronoun (‘en ce qui me / le / la concerne’). In FRNACO, however, the picture is different: there are 155 instances of ‘en ce qui concerne’ and 39 of ‘pour ce qui concerne’, a ratio of roughly 4:1.

The same procedure was then carried out with 4-word sequences. Of the top 50 in each sub-corpus, only five are shared:

en ce qui concerne
dans le cadre de
la mise en œuvre
dans le domaine de
la mise en place

These are all relatively grammatical in nature, and are common in other registers too. Indeed, they are unlikely to be identified as typical of the administrative register.

As regards 5-word sequences, there is little overlap between the sub-corpora at the top of the frequency list:

dans le domaine de la
la mise en œuvre de
dans le cadre de la

All of these are extensions of the 4-word sequences above. There are no shared 6 or 7-word sequences.

There are also, not surprisingly, clear semantic and discoursal similarities even where sequences are not identical, such as between ‘est remplacé par le texte suivant’ in FREUCO and ‘sont remplacés par les mots’ in FRNACO, indicating document revisions, and between ‘publication au journal officiel des communautés européennes’ and ‘au journal officiel de la République française’.

While much of the difference in multiword sequences can be attributed to the discourse or context of production of the texts (whether EU or national), other differences appear to stem from finer distinctions. Indeed, many sequences occur exclusively in a single genre, or a couple of closely-related genres. For this reason it was decided to run the WordList procedure over defined parts of the corpus individually.

3. Sequences in speech genres

The groups of speech genres in the two sub-corpora are of similar size. Wordlists were compiled for sequences of between three and eight words with a frequency of occurrence of at least ten, for both European Union and national speeches.

Table 4.4: Sequences in FREUCO speech genres

FREUCO	Types	Tokens
8-word sequences	1	17
7-word sequences	6	109
6-word sequences	17	318
5-word sequences	53	939
4-word sequences	181	3399
3-word sequences	710	14338

Table 4.5: Sequences in FRNACO speech genres

FRNACO	Types	Tokens
8-word sequences	2	23
7-word sequences	4	53
6-word sequences	7	101
5-word sequences	16	259
4-word sequences	68	1227
3-word sequences	443	8486

Few long sequences occur with a frequency greater than ten. The European Union sub-corpus has more sequences at almost every length, in terms of both types and tokens, with the exception of 8-word sequences, where the difference is minimal. This suggests that the speeches of this sub-corpus rely more on formulae and set expressions, including reference to institutions, people, etc.

3.1 The overlap between lengths of sequence

In order to investigate the extent of overlap between lengths of sequence, three types of sequence were marked for each of the sub-corpora:

a) not part of a longer sequence (with a frequency of occurrence ≥10) - that is to say, sequences which could be said to have a degree of unity at the length in question;
b) ONLY part of a longer sequence - that is to say, sequences which have no particular unity at the length in question;

c) part of a longer sequence, but also have some unity at the length in question - in other words, shorter sequences which have a greater frequency of occurrence than the longer sequence of which they are a part.

In this way, sequences which have a potentially greater role in the register as a whole are not hidden in a mass of data.

Table 4.6: Sequence overlap in FREUCO

FREUCO Length of sequence	A. not part of longer sequence (with fr. >10)	B. only part of a longer sequence	C. part of longer seq. but with greater frequency at this length
8	1/1 - 100%	0/1 - 0%	0/1 - 0%
7	4/6 - 66.7%	2/6 - 33.3%	0/6 - 0%
6	6/17 - 35.3%	8/17 - 47.1%	3/17 - 17.6%
5	26/53 - 49.1%	17/53 - 32.1%	10/53 - 18.9%
4	100/181 - 55.2%	43/181 - 23.8%	38/181 - 21.0%
3	455/710 - 64.1%	69/710 - 9.7%	186/710 - 26.2%
Totals	592/968 - 61.2%	139/968 - 14.4%	237/968 - 24.5%

Table 4.7: Sequence overlap in FRNACO

FRNACO Length of sequence	A. not part of longer sequence (with fr. >10)	B. only part of a longer sequence	C. part of longer seq. but with greater frequency at this length
8	2/2 - 100%	0/2 - 0%	0/2 - 0%
7	1/4 - 25%	2/4 - 50%	1/4 - 25%
6	1/7 - 14.3%	3/7 - 42.9%	3/7 - 42.9%
5	6/16 - 37.5%	5/16 - 31.3%	5/16 - 31.3%
4	43/68 - 63.2%	6/68 - 8.8%	19/68 - 27.9%
3	336/443 - 75.8%	31/443 - 7.0%	76/443 - 17.2%
Totals	389/540 - 72.0%	47/540 - 8.7%	104/540 - 19.3%

Those sequences which appear in a list because they are part of a longer sequence with the same frequency of occurrence (Column B) are least interesting from a linguistic perspective. It is revealing, however, to look in more detail at the sequences which are not part of a longer sequence and at those which form part of longer sequences with a lower frequency of occurrence.

The following sequences are not part of a longer sequence:

FREUCO

8-word seq.: Yves-Thibault de Silguy Membre de la Commission
7-word seq.: Jacques Santer Président de la Commission européenne
le pacte de stabilité et de croissance
les chefs d'état et de gouvernement ont
le maintien de la stabilité des prix
6-word seq.: je vous remercie de votre attention
des chefs d'état et de gouvernement ont
au sein de la zone euro
de maintenir la stabilité des prix
Conseil des gouverneurs de la BCE
politique monétaire axée sur la stabilité

FRNACO

8-word seq.: de monsieur Jacques Chirac président de la République
monsieur Jacques Chirac président de la République a
7-word seq.: la déclaration universelle des droits de l'homme
6-word seq.: de la politique de la ville

The longer sequences in both sub-corpora tend to refer to the major figures in the administration and various institutions, or to indicate the main concerns of the European Union and French government. The sequence 'je vous remercie de votre attention' is a politeness formula used at the end of official speeches: it only occurs as the final words of a text. Many of the shorter sequences are also names of individuals, bodies, institutions, laws, etc. Others, examples of which are given below, are either more grammatical in nature, and are used to structure texts and ideas, or else, while clearly still typical of the administrative register, are more general and can be used in a wide range of contexts.

FREUCO

5-word seq. (examples): mesdames et messieurs les députés
dans le domaine de la
taux de change de l'euro
dans le cadre de la
la mise en place de
la mise en œuvre de
c'est la raison pour laquelle
4-word seq. (examples): dans la zone euro
en ce qui concerne
de plus en plus
un certain nombre de
la création de l'euro
pour la première fois
le traité de Maastricht
3-word seq. (examples): Monsieur le président

des états membres
à la fois
introduction de l'euro
dans ce contexte
en faveur de
des fonds structurels

FRNACO

5-word seq.: le président de la République
le passage à l'an #
dans le domaine de la
dans le cadre de la
la mise en œuvre de
mesdames et messieurs les ministres

4-word seq. (examples): de plus en plus
en ce qui concerne
la société de l'information
pour la première fois
je suis heureux de
entre nos deux pays
dans le même temps

3-word seq. (examples): monsieur le président
de la France
en matière de
je souhaite que
de notre pays
il nous faut
je vous remercie
de nos concitoyens

Some of these are almost completely specific to speeches, such as those containing the first person pronouns (singular or plural), as well as the speech formulae.

3.2 The overlap between sub-corpora

In order to investigate the overlap between sub-corpora when considering speech genres, again three types of sequence have been marked:

a) Sequences unique to one sub-corpus (or with frequency <3 in the other sub-corpus) - that is, sequences which are near discourse-specific in the corpus, and potentially specific to one particular context of administrative language;
b) Sequences with frequency ≥10 in one corpus, but smaller (≥3 but <10) in the other, about which it is not possible to say very much in a corpus of this size;

c) Sequences with frequency ≥10 in both sub-corpora - that is, sequences which might appear to be common either to the speech mode in the administrative register, or to the administrative register as a whole, regardless of 'discourse'. Above all, these tend to be grammatical sequences ('en ce qui concerne', 'le domaine de la', 'il y a', and formulae specific to speeches - 'mesdames et messieurs').

Table 4.8: Overlap between sub-corpora – FREUCO

FREUCO Length of sequence	a. Sequences unique to sub-corpus	b. EU fr. ≥10 NA fr. <10 (≥3)	c. Seq. with fr. ≥10 in both sub-corpora (as proportion of EU)
8	1 - 100%	0 - 0%	0 - 0%
7	6 - 100%	0 - 0%	0 - 0%
6	16 - 94.1%	1 - 5.9%	0 - 0%
5	40 - 75.5%	10 - 18.9%	3 - 5.7%
4	117 - 64.6%	41 - 22.7%	23 - 12.7%
3	292 - 41.1%	251 - 35.4%	167 - 23.5%
Totals	472 - 48.8%	303 - 31.3%	193 - 19.9%

Table 4.9: Overlap between sub-corpora – FRNACO

FREUCO Length of sequence	a. Sequences unique to sub-corpus	b. EU fr. ≥10 NA fr. <10 (≥3)	c. Seq. with fr. ≥10 in both sub-corpora (as proportion of EU)
8	2 - 100%	0 - 0%	0 - 0%
7	3 - 75%	1 - 25%	0 - 0%
6	5 - 71.4%	2 - 28.6%	0 - 0%
5	10 - 62.5%	3 - 18.8%	3 - 18.8%
4	24 - 35.3%	21 - 30.9%	23 - 33.8%
3	103 - 23.3%	173 - 39.1%	167 - 37.7%
Totals	147 - 27.2%	200 - 37.0%	193 - 35.8%

There is a general tendency for shorter sequences to be more likely to appear in both sub-corpora. The main reason for this is that shorter sequences, of 3 and 4 words in length, are more likely to be grammatical in character, while longer ones tend to be real-world references (institutions, legal instruments, names of individuals etc.). There are no sequences longer than 5 words which appear in both sub-corpora, with a frequency of at least 10 occurrences in both. There is a total of 193 shorter sequences (3, 4 and 5 words in length) shared by the sub-corpora. These are listed in Appendix 4.

A total of 472 sequences are unique to FREUCO and only 147 sequences to FRNACO, which again implies that the EU discourse relies more on such prefabricated expressions. Often the reason why a particular sequence should be discourse-specific is evident, as in the example 'Jacques Santer Président de la Commission' in the EU sub-corpus. In such cases, there is often an equivalent sequence in the other sub-corpus: in this case 'Jacques Chirac Président de la République'. This holds also for names of bodies and institutions, and policy areas, since the EU and French administration have different spheres of interest and power, and other such references to real-world entities. In other cases, it is equally clear why the sequence should appear in one context only, such as 'mes chers compatriotes' (FRNACO), 'millions de francs' (FRNACO), and 'pour notre pays' (FRNACO), since EU speakers only rarely speak to, or on behalf of, a single member state.

More interesting from a linguistic point of view are those sequences which are more grammatical in character and yet only appear in the speeches of one sub-corpus, or where there is a large disparity in frequency between the two. Such anomalies may merely be related to the size or balance of the corpus, or else simply to chance. On the other hand, these sequences may be the manifestation of more fundamental phraseological differences between the French of the European Union and national administration. Larsen (1997, cf. also Chapter 1) claims that political discourses in the European Union domains he investigates are national, and that international texts, moreover, are made up of fragments of different discourses. Furthermore, Gaffney (1999), as we have seen, has suggested that there may as yet be no fully-formed EU-level political discourse, owing partly to the lack of strong central institutions. The EU is lacking in the mythology and symbols which lie behind national discourses, and it is often the case that EU-level issues only impinge on the general public if they contradict national approaches. What is more, the European Union is of course not designed for leadership in the same way as national political and administrative frameworks. Thus the national and EU contexts have different foundations, draw on different resources for their discourse, and represent a different type of leadership. For these reasons, it would not be surprising were French national and European Union language found to differ both in terms of phraseological units of a grammatical nature and their typical collocational patterns.

In FREUCO, there are a number of cases where there is a disparity in the frequency of certain grammatical or semi-grammatical sequences in the speeches, which is consistent with the rest of the corpus, although sometimes to a lesser degree. These sequences appear therefore to be typical of the discourse (EU or national), but are not specific to speeches. Some of the most salient examples are:

'en matière de politique' - There is no significant difference in usage between the two sub-corpora, except for the fact that FREUCO uses this sequence about three times more frequently. It generally collocates with an adjective relating to a policy area: 'régionale', 'budgétaire', 'agricole', 'douanière', 'fiscale', etc.

'sur la base de' - FREUCO uses this sequence most often in the context of legislation (e.g. 'sur la base de l'article J4', 'sur la base de l'accord signé à Luxembourg', 'sur la base de la loi no. 1398'), and it is this difference which results in the disparity in frequency between the two sub-corpora. This is rare in speech genres, where the difference appears to be due to chance.

'à moyen terme'[60] - This sequence is used only twice in FRNACO speeches, compared with over 40 times in FREUCO. It is used in the European Central Bank speeches in the context of 'le maintien de la stabilité des prix à moyen terme', and also in the Commission speeches, but only rarely here in a financial or budgetary context.

'de premier plan' - This sequence collocates frequently in the EU sub-corpus with the phrase 'jouer un rôle' (e.g. 'jouer un rôle de premier plan dans les négociations').

'l'entrée en vigueur' - Although this sequence is used in both sub-corpora, and in similar ways (generally referring to the entry into force of various treaties, agreements and laws), it is much more frequent in EU discourse (139 occurrences compared with 22).

In other cases, the sequence appears only in the speech genres of the EU discourse. This is true for 'je vous remercie de votre attention', used to mark the end of a speech, and also the sequence 'risque de change', which in all but one case occurs in FREUCO and in all but one of these in Commission speeches. This is because the term is particularly appropriate to the EU context - translated as 'exchange risk' in the Glossary of the European Communities (1990).

In several cases, the anomaly only appears in the speeches, although the sequences in question are not unique to these genres. We might describe these therefore as characteristic of the speech genres and the EU discourse.

'en termes de' - In the corpus as a whole, the frequencies of this sequence are consistent across the sub-corpora. In the speeches, it occurs once only in FRNACO, and 18 times in FREUCO, in a wide range of contexts: 'les moyens suffisants en termes de personnel', 'un poids du passé plus lourd en termes de dettes', 'les objectifs fixés en termes de PNB', etc. There are no significant clusters.

---

60 See also Chapter 5.

'à la baisse' - The disparity in use of this sequence is due to the phrase 'révision à la baisse' ('revision of figures downwards'), which appears predominantly in speeches by the Commissioner responsible for economic, monetary and financial affairs.

'de l'ordre de' - This sequence, which is almost always used in the context of numbers and figures (e.g. 'l'inflation est de l'ordre de 1%'), tends to appear in speeches in the EU sub-corpus and official reports in FRNACO.

'en fonction de' - This sequence often occurs in the longer set phrase 'un délai que le Président peut fixer en fonction de l'urgence de la question en cause' in EU legal texts. When it occurs in speeches, its usage is more flexible: 'adapter la coopération en fonction de l'évolution des besoins', 'une approche qui varie en fonction de son expertise'.

In FRNACO, there are also some, although fewer, grammatical or semi-grammatical sequences which occur with a much higher frequency than in FREUCO. In the following set of sequences, there is a disparity in frequency between the speeches of the two sub-corpora, a disparity which is consistent with the rest of the corpus, sometimes to a lesser degree, but which cannot be explained with reference to its being the subject of a single text:

'le passage à l'an #' - The year in question is in every case 2000, which is seen as a milestone. The EU sub-corpus is particularly concerned with problems which will arise because of the dawn of the year 2000, especially in information technology. In the national sub-corpus, on the other hand, the year 2000 is described as something to be celebrated: 'nous fêterons tous ensemble le passage à l'an 2000', 'le passage à l'an 2000 constitue un évènement important'. Even where the reference is to potential computer problems, the tone is one of optimism and responding to a challenge: 'maîtrisons ensemble le passage à l'an 2000'.

'entre nos deux pays' – Not surprisingly, this sequence does not occur at all in FREUCO. European speakers do not seek to foster links between pairs of individual countries, but rather between the EU as a whole and third parties. The corpus shows, however, that French administrative speeches frequently refer to problems, similarity of views, and cooperation between France and other countries.

'la prise en charge' - Although this sequence does not collocate frequently with other individual words or phrases, it is much more common in FREUCO (53 occurrences compared with 5, and 11 to 1 in the speeches).

'la conviction que' - When this sequence is used in FREUCO, its subject is most frequently 'le Conseil européen', whereas in FRNACO, its subject is more often than not in the first person ('je' or 'nous'). It would seem that the disparity is related to the tendency for EU speakers not to use the first person, but rather to speak on behalf of an institution.

'dans cette voie' – The disparity here may merely be due to chance since the difference between the relative frequencies is not particularly large. There are common collocations in the texts with the verbs 'poursuivre' (e.g. 'il nous faudra poursuivre dans cette voie') and 's'engager' (e.g. 'sera imprudent de s'engager dans cette voie').

In two cases, the sequence is specific to the speech genres of FRNACO. These are 'il nous faudra' and 'je le sais'. There is a tendency for texts in the national sub-corpus to use first person pronouns more than those in the EU sub-corpus. In addition, FREUCO uses them more in a number of formulae, in particular 'je vous remercie de votre attention', while FRNACO uses them in a wider range of contexts, the most frequent being 'je souhaite que...', 'je suis heureux...' 'je sais que...' and 'je tiens à...'. In a single case, while the sequence occurs in other genres, the anomaly only appears in the speeches. This is the sequence 'de veiller à', which is on the whole more frequent in the EU sub-corpus, but has a much greater frequency in the speeches of FRNACO than those of FREUCO. This disparity is not due to a single common usage in the sub-corpus: rather it is used in a wide range of contexts, such as 'veiller à l'épanouissement de l'enfant' and 'veiller à la qualité du recueil'. It tends to be preceded by an impersonal expression, ('il convient de', 'il lui incombe de', 'il est important de', 'il nous appartient de').

4. Sequences in individual genres

As each genre category in the corpus is of a different length, with varying numbers of texts, the numbers of sequences found in them differ considerably, and quantitative analysis is not viable. For this reason, it is difficult to compare pairs of genres: instead, this section looks at each of the genre categories individually, highlighting both quantitative and qualitative features of interest, for example where a genre which is represented by a small quantity of text contains a high number of sequences, and where these differ markedly from the equivalent list of sequences in the whole corpus. Further details about each of the genres are contained in Appendix 1. This discussion reveals the main concerns, and the most frequent formulae and phraseological patterns of each genre. While there are similarities among the genres, and therefore commonalities at the level of register, there are also significant differences. In other words, considerations of genre also have an effect on the language used in different contexts.

This approach also enables us to see how the different genres relate to each other: to what extent are the Press Release genres similar as regards multiword sequences, and to what extent do they differ as much among themselves as they do when compared with separate genres. Multiword sequences at the two extremes are discussed, that is to say, the longest sequences (of 7 and 8 words in length, occurring with a frequency of at least 5), and 3-word sequences (with a frequency of at least 10). The figures given are for types rather than tokens of sequence in the genres in question. It is very difficult to arrive at an accurate assessment of the quantitative role of such sequences (their tokens in each genre), because of the overlap among lengths of sequence. Those genres with high proportions of multiword sequences therefore rely to a large extent on *different* sequences. The discussion which follows, however, takes into account features of some genres related to sequence tokens, for example, where a genre contains both a number of highly frequent sequences, and also numerous sequences with a much lower frequency. This can happen when a genre uses a limited number of exactly repeated sequences, for example at the very start or end of a text. For the shorter (3-word) sequences, and where the genre has a sufficiently large number of these, the WordList Comparison feature of WordSmith Tools has been used to compare this wordlist with that of FRADCO as a whole. This reveals the major disparities between the two wordlists: for example, sequences which are particularly important in the genre but not in the whole corpus.

4.1 FREUCO

PRSP: Speeches - Commission

Long sequences: Although this genre is the second largest in FREUCO, it is only eighth in terms of number of long sequences. This points to a low proportion of such sequences in the genre, which is confirmed by a standardised figure: the genre is ranked thirteenth in terms of frequency of long sequences per 10,000 words, with only 1.01 8-word sequences, and 1.78 7-word sequences. The sequences tend to feature the names of Commissioners and their position, such as Yves-Thibault de Silguy, the Commissioner responsible for economic, financial and monetary affairs, Edith Cresson, responsible for research and innovation, and Jacques Santer, the President of the Commission.

Short sequences: As in the whole corpus, the sequence 'de la Commission', which occurs here 240 times (0.14%, compared to 0.09% in FRADCO), is the most frequent. As regards those sequences which are key in the genre as compared with the whole corpus, 'la zone euro' stands out, followed by sequences referring to Jacques Santer as President of the Commission, and the speech formula 'Mesdames et Messieurs'. Of course there are also many frequent grammatical sequences, although these are not key in the genre. The negative 'key sequences' (those which occur with an unusually low frequency in the genre as compared to the main corpus) include intertextual references to articles and legislation.

PASP: Speeches - Parliament

Long sequences: This genre contains only one 7-word sequence: 'Messieurs les Chefs d'État et de gouvernement', which occurs 7 times. This formula serves to address the audience at the start of a speech.
Short sequences: By far the most frequent 3-word sequence is 'le Parlement européen'. Others are the names of other institutions. As compared to FRADCO, the grammatical sequences 'au cours de' and 'il convient de' are especially important in this speech genre.

ECB: Speeches - European Central Bank

Long sequences: Of the three speech genres in FREUCO, this genre has the highest proportion of long sequences: 7.07 7-word sequences and 2.36 8-word sequences per 10,000 words. As the genre is relatively small, however, this equates to only three 7-word and nine 8-word sequences. Unlike the other two speech genres, these relate neither to the principal actors in the European Union, nor to the formalities of giving a speech. Rather, they serve to highlight the main concerns of the ECB: the strategy of monetary policy and the stability of prices in the medium term.
Short sequences: As one might expect from the ECB speech genre, a number of money- or finance-related sequences are foregrounded, such as 'la zone euro', 'la stabilité des prix', 'taux de change', 'la politique monétaire', 'valeur de référence', 'la croissance monétaire' and 'les banques centrales', among others. There are also a number of sequences related to deadlines or future plans: 'à moyen terme', 'maintenir la stabilité', 'à long terme' and 'à court terme'.

PRIP: Press releases - Commission

Long sequences: The long sequences in this genre point to the Commission as the principal actor: as is to be expected from the function of press releases, the longest sequences are clearly narrative, placing an event (usually the Commission referring a matter to the Court of Justice, or sending a reasoned opinion - 'avis motivé' - to one of the member states) firmly in space and time.
Short sequences: The shorter sequences support the comments above. The name of 'la Commission européenne' is most key, followed by sequences where the Commission is subject of a number of different verbs. Again, references to legislation feature most strongly in the negative key sequences.

PRPRES: Press releases - Council

Long sequences: This genre has only a small number of long sequences, none of which occurs more than 6 times. Those which do occur refer mostly to bodies or organisations, such as the 'Forum Euro-Méditerranéen de l'énergie', the 'Banque Centrale Européenne' and, not surprisingly, the Council of the European Union.
Short sequences: The 3-word sequences of this genre similarly show a preoccupation with cooperation with other groups, such as various 'Conseils d'association', the 'Forum Euro-Méditerranéen' mentioned above, and foreign

affairs generally. Grammatical or structuring phrases are also particularly frequent in this genre.

PRCES: Press releases - Ecosoc

Long sequences: The Economic and Social Committee press release genre contains only two 8-word sequences with a frequency of at least 5. These are 'le # septembre # le Comité Économique et' and 'septembre le Comité Économique et social européen' (where the hash once again indicates any number, in this case, dates and years). Given that their frequencies of occurrence are identical (5), it is clear that these two 8-word sequences actually constitute one longer, 10-word, sequence. The 7-word sequences which occur are also based on this longer sequence. Although there are insufficient examples on which to base a strong claim, this genre appears to share with the Commission press releases the fact that the longer sequences indicate the principal actor - in this case, of course, EcoSoc.

Short sequences: Although there are six 3-word sequences with the minimum frequency, five of these combine to make up the 8-word sequences above, and the only different one at this length is 'la société civile', which occurs 10 times, over four different texts, in four cases followed immediately by 'organisée' (translated as 'organized civil society'). One text deals in some detail with the concept, attempting to refine the vague, catch-all definition, as those outside the institutions of the European Union and their relation to it, through the ESC.

OMBPR: Press releases - Ombudsman

Long sequences: This genre, the smallest in FREUCO, contains no sequences of 7 or 8 words with a frequency of at least 5.

Short sequences: It is also the only genre in FREUCO to contain no examples of 3-word sequences with a frequency of 10 or more.

RG: General report - introductions

Long sequences: Like OMBPR above, this genre contains no long sequences with a frequency of greater than 5 occurrences.

Short sequences: It does contain a small number of 3-word sequences (3) occurring with a frequency of at least 10. These are: 'de l'Union européenne', 'le Conseil européen', and the grammatical sequence 'en matière de'.

OJL: Legislative texts - JO (OJ L Series)

Long sequences: This genre of legislative texts has the third highest proportion of long sequences: 33.45 7-word and 24.66 8-word sequences per 10,000 words. By far the most frequent sequence is a reference to particular issues of the JO: 'Journal Officiel NB L # du ### P'. Of the others, a large number indicate the genre's concern with the entry into force of legislation: '(est obligatoire) dans tous ses éléments et directement applicable dans (tout état membre)', 'à compter de la date d'entrée en vigueur'; and references to other primary and secondary legislation.

Short sequences: The genre is also noteworthy in terms of shorter sequences: with 64.67 3-word sequences per 10,000 words, it has the second highest concentration of such sequences in FREUCO. These reveal similar concerns to those of the longer sequences, that is to say, with other legislation, in comparison with 'le présent règlement'. The most negatively key sequence is 'le Conseil européen'.

COM: COM documents (OJ C Series)

Long sequences: The C Series of the Official Journal, like the L Series, contains a large number of sequences which reveal the extent of intertextuality, and cross-referencing among legislative texts. These include: 'vu le traité instituant la Communauté Européenne', '(sa) publication au Journal Officiel des communautés européennes', 'article # est remplacé par le texte suivant'. There are also multiword phrases indicating the different parties: 'les autorités compétentes de l'état membre d'origine / d'accueil' - the authorities in question act as both subject and object, and also frequently as the agent of a passive verb. Also among the most frequent sequences, however, are technical terms: 'transbordeurs rouliers et engins à passagers à grande vitesse', 'alimentation du moteur au gaz naturel comprimé'.

Short sequences: The short sequences, both in terms of absolute frequency and their relative frequency as compared with FRADCO, are of various types: cross references to other legislation, common sequences with a wide range of different uses like 'de la Commission', grammatical sequences and technical terms. Among the negative key sequences are both 'le Conseil européen' and 'la Commission européenne', and also 'les états membres'.

TREAT: Treaties

Long sequences: The Treaty genre, the fourth largest in the corpus, contains, by a substantial margin, the highest proportion of long sequences per 10,000 words in FREUCO, with a massive 73.2 7-word and 59.27 8-word sequences (equating to 788 and 638 sequences respectively). A large proportion of these serve to structure the text, or make reference to other articles within the same text, or to other legislative texts: 'conformément à la procédure visée à l'article #', '(le) paragraphe # est remplacé par le texte suivant'. The sequence 'article # article # article # article #', which occurs by far the most frequently of the 8-word sequences (259 occurrences) comes almost entirely from a passage in the consolidated Treaty of Amsterdam where articles from previous treaties are re-numbered. It is therefore not particularly interesting from a phraseological point of view, but does demonstrate that legal requirements have a great effect on the language in this type of text. There are also a number of names of institutions and bodies, and names of agreements, policies, etc: for example 'la politique étrangère et de sécurité commune', 'Communauté européenne du charbon et de l'acier', and the 'Acquis de Schengen' appears as part of a number of sequences.

Short sequences: As regards short (3-word) sequences, also, this genre has the highest proportion of any in the corpus, with 82.68 sequences (of frequency 10 or more) per 10,000 words. Among those which are not merely a part of a longer sequence discussed above, many are concerned with the consolidation or updating of treaties, or 'le présent traité', and the entry into force of such. The most negative key sequence is 'la Commission a', which occurs only four times in this large genre, highlighting the fact that the texts in question do not share a narrative style with the Press release genres.

CE: European Council sessions

Long sequences: The most frequent sequence, occurring 25 times, is: 'les gouvernements des Etats membres et la Commission (des Communautés européennes étaient représentés comme suit)'. This almost always occurs at the start of a text, and is followed by a list of representatives from each of the member states and the Commission.

Short sequences: The patterns among the shorter sequences are very different, and indicate that both the Présidence and the European Council as a whole are frequently actors in the clause. Member states are named more frequently than in the corpus as a whole, but as individuals and not collectively: indeed 'les états membres' is the most negatively key 3-word sequence.

PC98: European Council Conclusions of the Presidency

Long sequences: As is to be expected, the European Council itself appears as the main actor in this genre, with a number of 8 and 7-word sequences including its name tied with a limited number of actions: 'le Conseil européen se félicite de ce que / de la décision / des progrès', 'le Conseil européen invite le Conseil (et la Commission) à'. Others once again refer to specific policies: 'la politique européenne commune en matière de sécurité et de défense'.

Short sequences: 'Le Conseil européen' is still most evident (most frequent and most key) at the level of 3-word sequences, and appears as both subject and object.

LB: White papers

Long sequences: In this genre, the longer sequences are notably made up of references to specific directives: (with a number of slightly different wordings) 'la directive concernant [sur] l'aménagement du temps de travail', 'la directive sur le temps de travail', and also the issue of health and safety of workers.

Short sequences: The most significant short sequences refer to particular spheres of action - transport, especially 'les compagnies de chemin de fer' and 'le secteur ferroviaire', patents, health and the safety of workers.

PRCJE: European Court of Justice Bulletin

Long sequences: This genre has the second highest proportion of long sequences: sixty 7-word sequences and 48.51 8-word sequences per 10,000 words. It also contains a couple of highly frequent individual sequences, including 'a présenté ses conclusions à l'audience de la' (referring to particular 'avocats généraux' who have delivered opinions to various different Chambers of the House), and a number of sequences which together form the longer sequence 'le Royaume de

Belgique a manqué aux obligations qui lui incombent en vertu (de l'article # / ladite directive)'.
Short sequences: With 64.37 3-word sequences per 10,000 words, the PRCJE genre has the third highest concentration. Many of the most key sequences refer to legislation, especially directives, since it is when there is a breach of these that a case will be pursued at the Court of Justice. The only negative key sequence returned is 'le Conseil européen', which does not occur at all in the genre. The Commission, on the other hand, is frequently mentioned.

PT: Programme of Work
Long sequences: The most frequent 8-word sequence merely acts as a title: 'programme de travail pour la Commission pour la # [date]'. Others reveal the genre's concern with putting plans into practice: 'la mise en œuvre du plan d'action'; and with adapting legislation: 'modification du règlement de base portant organisation (commune des marchés)' - the five instances of this latter sequence all appear in the same document.
Short sequences: By far the most key sequence is 'la Commission a'. Taken by itself this tense usage may appear surprising, since the object of the texts in the genre is to set out plans for future action, rather than report on action taken in the past. However, on cross-checking with Concord, it becomes clear that the sequence almost always collocates with such words as 'proposé', 'présenté', 'contribué', 'poursuivi', etc. These, material or relational processes, are very different patterns of collocation from such press release genres as PRIP, where the sequence collocates most notably with 'estimé', décidé', 'adopté', 'approuvé', 'examiné' and 'considéré', generally mental processes. A more detailed analysis of the actual instances in this genre, reveals that on many occasions, the Commission has taken preliminary action or make preliminary decisions in order that future action may go ahead.

PRMEMO: Memo - Commission
Long sequences: Despite being relatively large in terms of number of word tokens, this genre contains no examples of long (7 or 8-word) sequences.
Short sequences: The most frequent 3-word sequences tend to be grammatical in nature: 'dans le cadre', 'la mise en œuvre', 'en matière de', or else to refer to institutions of the Union or member states and third countries (those not contracting parties to the agreement or treaty in question). The practice of 'le blanchiment des capitaux' (money laundering) is also key in this genre of the corpus, but this is entirely due to the inclusion of one text on the subject.

PRPESC: PESC - Council
Long sequences: By far the most frequent sequence in this genre relates to the 'déclaration de la présidence au nom de l'Union européenne sur'. In every case, this sequence constitutes the opening words of the text, and is followed by a wide range of topics (such as a particular state, nuclear testing, an agreement, elections and executions). Less frequent sequences denote particular groups of states, such

as 'les pays d'Europe centrale et orientale', 'les membres de l'espace économique européen', 'les pays de LAELE [...]' (EFTA).
Short sequences: Disregarding those frequent sequences which merely combine to make up the longer sequences above, the three word sequences betray a concern with 'les droits de l'homme' and 'la peine de mort'. The European Union is also constructed as congratulating itself - '[l'Union européenne] se félicite de': this collocates with a wide range of nouns, such as 'décision', 'position prise', 'des efforts', 'de cette initiative', and many others.

PA97: Action plans
Long sequences: Once again, this genre contains no instances of 7 or 8-word sequences.
Short sequences: The genre has 16 3-word sequences. These reveal the main concerns of the genre to be 'la société de l'information', and educational multimedia. Alongside grammatical or semi-grammatical sequences also frequent in the whole corpus, such as 'la mise en œuvre' is the similar construction 'la mise en réseau', or 'networking'.

4.2 FRNACO

SPPR: Speeches - President
Long sequences: Of the three speech genres in FRNACO, SPPR contains the highest proportion of longer sequences (1.73 7-word and 1.15 8-word sequences per 10,000 words). However, there is only a slight difference, and long repeated sequences appear in these three genres to a much lesser extent than most of the other genres. Every one of the 8-word sequences and all but one of the 7-word sequences refers in some way to Président Chirac; this is often part of the title of the speech - 'discours / allocution de Monsieur Jacques Chirac Président de la (République, à l'occasion de)'. The remaining 7-word sequence is 'à chacune et à chacun d'entre vous', which tends to come towards the end of a speech as the President is summing up and addressing his audience again, but in many different contexts: 'je salue…', 'alors, bonne chance à…', 'mon amitié à…'.
Short sequences: Many of the most frequent 3-word sequences of the genre combine to make up the longer sequences above. There is also, in particular, a high proportion of first person pronouns and possessive adjectives (je, nous, mes), and a large number of grammatical sequences.

SPPM: Speeches - Premier Ministre
Long sequences: There is only one 8-word sequence in this genre: this is the name of 'la déclaration universelle des droits de l'homme'. Two of the three 7-word sequences are accounted for by this, and the third refers to the sphere of influence of a Ministry / Minister 'de la recherche et de la technologie'.
Short sequences: The range of short sequences in this genre is very similar to the SPPR genre above, combining a range of grammatical sequences, fragments of speech formulae, and references to 'le pays' and 'les concitoyens'.

SPM: Speeches - Ministers

Long sequences: This genre contains no examples of 7 or 8-word sequences, despite its relatively large size.

Short sequences: Once again, the most frequent 3-word sequences in this genre are similar to the other two speech genres above, in that there are many grammatical or partly grammatical sequences, and a relatively high proportion of first person pronouns. Few of the sequences which occur with a frequency of at least 10 are specific to one text - rather, most are common to the speeches generally, or even to the administrative register as a whole.

CPCM: Press releases - Council of Ministers

Long sequences: The Council of Ministers Press release genre has the second highest proportion of long sequences in FRNACO, with 33.27 7-word and 25.74 8-word sequences per 10,000 words. There are a number of sequences with a frequency of 40 (identical to the number of texts in this genre of the corpus): unsurprisingly these tend to combine to form longer formulae for introducing the text, such as 'le service de presse du Premier Ministre a diffusé le communiqué suivant' and 'le Président de la République a réuni le Conseil des Ministres au Palais de l'Elysée (le mercredi)'. Other relatively frequent sequences point to the fact that the Council of Ministers carries out various actions: 'Conseil des Ministres a adopté les mesures individuelles suivantes'. Also, the names of Ministers, Ministries, and policy areas are frequent among the types of sequence.

Short sequences: As regards 3-word sequences, this genre contains the third highest proportion of types in FRNACO, with 55.87 types per 10,000 words. Those which are most frequent (in absolute terms) and most significant (key sequences as compared to FRADCO as a whole) tend also to be fragments of formulae for text organisation. In addition, much reference is made to place and time, to indicate where and when action happened, or decisions were made.

CPPM: Press releases - Premier Ministre

Long sequences: This genre contains only very few longer sequences (in terms of both types and tokens), the majority of which refer to 'la ministre de la culture et de la communication'. Others suggest a highly narrative style, typical of a press release: 'le # septembre # le premier ministre a' (cf. the PRIP and PRCES genres, in FREUCO, above).

Short sequences: There are only fourteen 3-word sequences of the required frequency. Some continue the narrative style of the longer sequences, others are unexceptional grammatical sequences, and a few reveal some of the concerns of the press releases, such as 'l'aménagement du territoire', 'les droits de l'homme' and 'technologies de l'information'.

CPM: Press releases - Ministries

Long sequences: The most frequent long sequences generally contain the names of ministries, while the less frequent (5 or 6 occurrences) indicate a very wide

range of subject matter for the press releases: 'l'accompagnement des personnes handicapées dans leur vie quotidienne', 'la Commission supérieure du service public des postes', 'mission passage informatique à l'an #'.
Short sequences: The 3-word sequences reveal similar concerns, with a wide range of issues, depending on the Ministry in question. Few of the sequences are shared by a number of different texts, except for the grammatical sequences, of which 'et de la' is key in the genre, surprisingly perhaps for a purely grammatical sequence which was also the second most frequent 3-word sequence in the comparator corpus.

CPS: Press releases - Sénat
Long sequences: As in the other press release genres of both sub-corpora, the long sequences of genre tend to refer to ministers, namely the '(ministre) délégué à la coopération et à la (francophonie)' and 'le ministre délégué chargé des affaires européennes', and also to policy areas: 'de la défense et des forces armées'. None is particularly frequent.
Short sequences: At this length, a high proportion of sequences contain the names of certain individuals in the Sénat, and also types of document ('projets de loi', 'communiqué de presse'). The most important concerns are revealed to be 'les affaires étrangères', finance, 'fruits et légumes' (although this owes its salience to a single text on the subject).

RAPO: Official reports
Long sequences: This genre has no particularly frequent sequences - the most frequent is 'la Commission générale de terminologie et de néologie with 10 occurrences, all in a single text. Other sequences on the whole contain the names of ministries, charters, and specialist areas of interest: 'Ministre de la Culture et de la Communication', 'la charte européenne des langues régionales ou minoritaires', 'mission d'étude sur la spoliation des juifs de France', 'et de la lutte contre l'emploi des clandestins'.
Short sequences: The most signficant sequences refer to 'propositions' or proposals. There is also a concern with culture and language, primarily from one or two individual reports. Indeed most of the frequent sequences are text-specific. Given the nature of the genre, it is not surprising that sequences referring to legislation and articles are highly negatively key.

RAPM: Reports
Long sequences: This genre contains a large amount of reference to other texts, and this is evidenced in the longer sequences: 'la loi NB #-# du # janvier', 'décret NB #-# du # octobre #'. Sequences also reveal some of the principal concerns of this type of document: 'la réforme de l'état et de la décentralisation', 'aménagement et de réduction du temps de travail', 'la formation tout au long de la vie'.
Short sequences: While longer sequences tend to refer to other texts and legislation, these are not among the most frequent shorter sequences, or indeed

the most key. Rather, the most key sequences by far are: 'la fonction publique' and 'la formation continue', which reveal some of the concerns of reports rather than their organisation, and intertextuality.

JO: Journal Officiel

Long sequences: As in FREUCO, above, the Journal Officiel genre contains a relatively high proportion of long sequences: 31.45 7-word and 24.1 8-word sequences per 10,000 words. Like the JO genre of FREUCO, here the most frequent sequences tend to be intertextual references to other articles and other pieces of legislation, such as 'vu le décret no. #-# du #', indications of the process of making legislation: 'sera publié au journal officiel de la République française', and the names of Ministries.

Short sequences: When it comes to numbers of 3-word sequence types, the JO genre takes second position in the corpus, with 66.76 types per 10,000 words. Again, both the most frequent, in absolute terms, and most key, consist of intertextual references, and also formulae used in legal texts, such as 'fait à Paris', which comes at the end of a piece of legislation, and 'adoption le # [date]'. The genre also contains a relatively large number of sequences which are unique to it.

DP: Press Dossiers

Long sequences: The longer sequences in the Dossier de Presse genre rarely occur in more than one text, because of the fact that they tend to convey subject matter, and the Dossiers are subject-specific. In this case, more than in any other, sequences are specific to texts, rather than genres, or the register as a whole.

Short sequences: The frequency list of 3-word sequences is dominated by sequences towards the grammatical end of the scale, with the unusual phrase 'mise en ligne' as one of the most frequent and the most key sequence. The other key sequences again tend to convey subject matter and be specific to one text.

TFCONV: Seminal texts - Conventions

Long sequences: There are only two 8-word sequences repeated 5 times or more (in this case 6 and 7 times) in this genre. These are: 'les Etats parties prennent toutes les mesures appropriées' and 'du secrétaire général de l'organisation des Nations Unies'.

Short sequences: The large majority of the 3-word sequences in this genre combine to form the longer sequences above. Those which do not are varied and appear not to have much in common: '[de] la présente convention', references to other articles, and 'de ses parents' (from the 'Convention relative aux droits de l'enfant').

TFCONS: Seminal texts - Constitution

Long sequences: The only repeated sequences are concerned with the modification or consolidation of the constitution, e.g. 'la loi du # novembre # modifie ainsi'.

Short sequences: At shorter lengths, sequences naming institutions, bodies and people are most frequent: 'Président de la République', 'l'Assemblé nationale', 'Conseil des Ministres', 'Cour de Justice', etc. Others are legal expressions: 'magistrats du siège', 'de plein droit',[61] 'projets de loi', 'une loi organique', etc.

TFDH: Seminal texts - Human Rights

Long sequences: This genre contains few long sequences: those that do appear name 'le secrétaire général du Conseil de l'Europe', and evoke the abstract ideal that 'toute personne a droit à la liberté'.

Short sequences: Of those 3-word sequences which do not combine to form longer ones, the most significant is 'la présente convention'. The others tend to refer to administrative concerns, such as contracting parties, committees, legislation and articles.

ANCRs: Account of National Assembly debates - transcription

Long sequences: As might be expected from the only genre which contains transcriptions of authentic debates, the large majority of long repeated sequences are from material inserted in brackets by the transcriber, such as 'applaudissemen[62] sur les bancs du groupe socialiste', 'sur les bancs du groupe démocratie libérale'. There are however a couple of others, which highlight the main concerns of the debates, such as environmental issues: 'émissions de gaz à effet de serre'.

Short sequences: These tendencies are clear from the shorter sequences too, the great majority of which combine to form the longer sequences. Below the most frequent sequences there are many grammatical sequences which are not specific to the administrative register. It appears that while the speech genres are, of course, prepared speech, in these respects they have a lot in common with spontaneous speech.

ANCRw: Account of National Assembly - reports

Long sequences: There are only a few sequences with a particularly high frequency: these tend to be references to other documents, such as 'compte rendu NB # application de l'article #', 'application de l'article # du règlement mardi / mercredi #'. Others express the various Commissions as agents: 'la Commission a repoussé l'amendement NB # de', 'la Commission a adopté un amendement du rapporteur'.

Short sequences: Like the press release genres, and the long sequences above, the 3-word sequences in this genre often express bodies as agents. There are also many references to different types of legislation and other documents: 'projets de loi', 'amendements', 'compte-rendus', 'articles', 'codes', etc.

---

61 This sequence is mentioned in Chapter 5 as a locution.

62 WordSmith truncates words of more than 14 characters, hence 'applaudissemen[ts]'.

ANPL: National Assembly draft legislation
Long sequences: This is the genre with the highest proportion of long sequences in FRNACO: 59.01 7-word and 45.31 8-word sequences per 10,000 words. By far the most frequent sequence is: 'de la loi NB #-# du #' with 89 occurrences, and all of the most frequent sequences refer to particular articles or laws. At a lower frequency, there are also references to the recurrent concerns: 'Conseil de prévention et de lutte contre le dopage'; and also a number of references to deadlines and statistics: 'délai de trois mois à compter de la', 'supérieure à la moitié de la population totale'.
Short sequences: With regard to 3-word sequences also, this genre of draft legislation has by far the highest proportion in FRNACO. It has 80.85 types of 3-word sequences per 10,000 words. 'De coopération intercommunale' has a massive keyness value of over 1000, which indicates that the sequence is very frequent in the genre, and also very infrequent in others. As is to be expected, the genre contains many intertextual references. The sequence 'dans le domaine' is one of few negative key sequences which is not obviously limited to the FREUCO sub-corpus.

CGLM: Letters from PM to the Commissaire au plan (Chief of the French Planning Economic Agency)
Long sequences: This genre contains no instances of either 7 or 8-word sequences. This is likely, however, to be due to its small size.
Short sequences: Again probably owing to its small size, the CGLM genre contains only a very small number of 3-word sequences (three, or 7.65 per 10,000 words), and indeed all of these combine to produce the longer sequence 'le Commissaire général du Plan'.

4.3 Discussion

These mini analyses show that, while different genres contain different types of repeated multiword sequence, the genres fall roughly into distinguishable groups. As a group, the speech genres in both of the sub-corpora turn out to contain relatively few sequences compared with other types of genre. The most frequent longer sequences tend to feature names, of people, institutions and, particularly in the case of the ECB speeches, policies and central concerns. Most key in the genre, as is to be expected, are formulae which are specific to speeches, such as address formulae. The shorter sequences, on the other hand, are predominantly grammatical in nature. Sequences in press release genres are varied, although quite small in number. Notably, they betray the genre's concern with locating events in time and space, and with the actor in the clause, particularly in the case of European Commission press releases. The greatest proportions of multiword sequences are found in genres of a legal nature, whether primary legislation, such as European Treaties (the genre with the highest proportion of both short and long sequences), secondary legislation, such as the Journal Officiel genres in each sub-corpus, and also draft legislation. By far the largest part of these sequences, however, is made up of extensive reference to existing legislation, and cross-reference to articles within the same document. A number of genres also contain repeated formulae which organise the texts and indeed enable the texts to be recognised as of that genre: these include the European Council Sessions, Treaties, programme of work and debate transcriptions.

A similar study has been carried out by Altenberg (1998), in which he found that multiword sequences serve various pragmatic, lexical and grammatical functions. The main tendencies of the sequences in this data support Altenberg's finding. Speech formulae can be seen as the result of a force of pragmatics, names of Ministries, technical terms and policy areas as the result of lexicalisation, and the many grammatical sequences, including subject-verb sequences ('la Commission a proposé') are due to the grammatical function.

5. Correlations between sequence length and type

Sections 3 and 4 have shown that genres and modes of administrative language can be differentiated on the basis of the multiword sequences they contain: in terms of proportions of sequences, types of sequence and individual sequences. Section 4, in investigating sequences at the two extremes of length, also indicated that there is a correlation between sequence length and sequence type.

Not surprisingly, there is increasing variety as the sequences reduce in length, and this is not merely because longer sequences, by definition, contain shorter sequences. Longer sequences are concerned almost purely with the organisation of the text and with reference to particular bodies etc. This is consistent with Butler's conclusions for spoken Spanish: he finds that "in the spoken texts (including the magazine interviews), many of the very frequent sequences are of an *interpersonal* nature, serving either to express agreement or disagreement [...], or to indicate speaker comment, including degrees of modal or illocutionary commitment..." (Butler 1997, p. 69, the emphasis is Butler's). Others are textual in nature, or serve to highlight particular parts of the message. Only a few are ideational / representational, and these mostly temporal, and occur mostly in the written corpus.

At the level of 3-word sequences, some are clearly common to the language as a whole rather than being specific to the administrative register. This shows how the register fits in with the general language, which of its resources it exploits and in what ways it does so. Some phraseological units at this level are composed entirely of grammatical words. Some, however, are units only at this length, rather than being merely part of a longer fixed sequence. These tend to be grammatical sequences, such as 'en matière de'. Many, on the other hand, are very much more frequent in the 3-word sequence list than as part of a longer sequence, thus showing that they are more typically 3 or 4-word sequences, which can be employed in language in a wide variety of contexts. While they regularly form part of longer sequences, they are more adaptable and have a range of typical collocates. For example, 'dans le cadre de' collocates frequently with a range of related nouns: 'programme', 'politique', 'protocole', 'processus', 'procédure'. 'Mise en œuvre', likewise, collocates frequently with 'programme', 'politique', 'plan'. Chapter 6 will develop the discussion of collocation of keywords in the register with related sets of words, as well as with individual words and features of syntax.

This chapter has also touched briefly on the fact that sequences differ in their distribution within individual texts, as well as in their distribution among genres and modes of language. While grammatical collocations tend to be evenly spread through texts, a number of sequences concerned with discourse organisation have favourite positions in texts, most notably at the very beginning or at the end. A more detailed analysis of the positional tendencies of sequences is beyond the scope of this study, but could be usefully carried out within discourse analysis.

6. Conclusions

As was stated at the start of this chapter, it is impossible to put a figure on the number of multiword sequences in the corpus. This is partly due to hardware and software limitations, but more fundamentally because of the indeterminate nature of what constitutes a sequence. It would be possible to quantify all of the sequences of each length in a corpus, but owing to the substantial amount of overlap between lengths of sequence, this figure would be a massive overestimation of the quantitative importance of these sequences. On the other hand, it is arguable that near-identical sequences, or variations of sequences, should be included in the figures, but computer software is only able to retrieve identical sequences, at least from a corpus which is not semantically and syntactically tagged. Despite these unresolvable questions, we can confidently make the generalisation that there is a higher number of repeated sequences in the European Union sub-corpus used here than in its French national counterpart. While subtle imbalances within the corpora can never be entirely ruled out, this suggests that European Union language, partly owing to the complex processes of document translation, is more reliant on formulae and repeated sequences, whether lexical, pragmatic, or grammatical.

Kjellmer has attempted to quantify the role of multiword sequences (which he calls collocations) in the one-million word Brown Corpus, claiming that 336,103 tokens and 84,708 types of such collocations occur. Although this figure would need to be adjusted to account for the overlap between *a moment* and the less frequent *in a moment* (Kjellmer 1987, p. 134), it is still a large proportion. Altenberg, similarly, gives a rough estimation that over 80 percent of the words in his corpus are in some way part of such a sequence (1998, p. 102). This implies a massively important role for multiword sequences, but he points out that "many of these combinations are of little phraseological interest, since they consist of mere repetitions or fragments of larger structures (e.g. *the the* [sic], *and the, in a, out of the*)" (*ibid*., p. 102).

It has been shown in this chapter that different lengths of sequence bring to the fore different types of phraseological patterning, and terminological items particular to the domain of public administration, in the register, not just formulae and conventional expressions created by the discourse, but also grammatical collocations and set phrases. Sequences in the register may be typical of a genre, or be discourse-bound; that is to say that there are notable differences between the European Union and the national French sub-corpora. The shorter sequences (of three and four words in length), have a lot more in common across the different genres and between the two sub-corpora, and might therefore be seen to be characteristic of the register rather than a discourse or genre. Some are also frequent in the general language, although they may differ semantically or pragmatically in general and administrative texts. Longer sequences tend to be specific to the subject matter of texts, and are often motivated by pragmatic factors.

Altenberg has noted that:

> What is perhaps the most striking impression that emerges from the material is the pervasive and varied character of conventionalized language in spoken discourse. The use of routinized and more or less prefabricated expressions is evident at all levels of linguistic organization and affects all kinds of structures, from entire utterances operating at discourse level to smaller units acting as single words and phrases. (Altenberg 1998, p. 120)

It comes as no surprise that administrative language shows similar patternings to Altenberg's spoken discourse. Whether or not the European Union can yet be said to have a discourse of its own, as opposed to just being an amalgam of component national discourses as Larsen has suggested, the differences in multiword sequences, which are not limited to the longer sequences, but also extend to shorter grammatical sequences, indicate that its language can certainly be differentiated on a phraseological level from that of the French national discourse.

Chapter 5

General Language Locutions

'With that tape,' he said, 'we can request the computer to supply us with any information we like about your ideolect.' 'Come again?' I said. 'Your own special, distinctive, unique way of using the English language.

DAVID LODGE, SMALL WORLD: AN ACADEMIC ROMANCE

1. Introduction

The question is now posed as to whether phraseological differences between the two sub-corpora are limited to such multiword sequences, or whether distinctions can be made within the administrative register with regard to phraseological features borrowed from the 'general' language, namely 'locutions' (cf. Chapter 2). Does the picture established in Chapter 4 change when another approach is taken to the corpus, or are the findings consistent?

The approach taken in this chapter compares the general language and the register of administration, owing both to the source of the phraseological patterning investigated and also to comparisons made between the comparator corpus and the administrative corpus (FRADCO). This comparative data is used in particular to investigate the presence, role and function of common locutions in the two corpora, and the distribution of these locutions between the two halves of the administrative corpus (FREUCO and FRNACO), as well as between genres within this corpus. In this way, it can be ascertained whether certain locutions are more genre- or register-bound. It is interesting to see also whether the locutions which are employed have anything in common, in terms of semantics, syntax, pragmatics or discoursal usage.

This chapter therefore takes a 'micro' approach to collocations in the corpus: the starting point is generally-accepted idiomatic phrases of French. As Rey and Chantreau say, "aucun discours ou presque ne peut faire l'économie des locutions, lieux communs éculés ou produits plaisants de l'imagination populaire" (1993, p. xiii). While few varieties of language can do without such phrases, each genre or register draws on the phraseological resources of the French language to a different extent, and possibly for different purposes.

Examples are given, followed, in square brackets, by the sub-corpus from which they are taken and the textual genre (for example, [frnaco\cppmfr] to refer to the 'Communiqué de Presse, Premier Ministre' genre of the national French sub-corpus - see Appendix 1 for details of the abbreviations used). Where it is useful to indicate the number of occurrences of a particular locution in the corpus, this appears before the square brackets (e.g.: 7 [frnaco\cppmfr]). Where it is not otherwise indicated, examples come from the complete administrative corpus.

1.1 The *Dictionnaire des expressions et locutions*

Rey and Chantreau's *Dictionnaire des expressions et locutions* (1993) has been introduced in Chapter 2. Here we should consider briefly the sources of its entries. The dictionary is based partly on existing dictionaries and collections of 'locutions' and partly on a corpus, in a loose sense of the term, of authentic texts. It should come as little surprise, given the history of corpus linguistics in France, that the majority of texts in the corpus are literary in nature: the literary part of the text collection constitutes some 450 texts. However, Rey and Chantreau note that "c'est même une tendance remarquable de la locution française, de nos jours, que d'intégrer des éléments de discours répété, provenant de la politique, de la publicité, souvent véhiculés par les médias de masse" (*ibid.*, p. xv). They give as examples from the field of politics such common phrases as 'le pré carré' and 'l'état de grâce'. In light of this, this second edition of the dictionary extended the range of texts in its reference corpus, with the result of "réintroduisant ainsi dans la phraséologie ce pouvoir social qui dépasse la référence à un créateur individuel et repérable" (*ibid.*, p. xv). Little detail is given concerning this constituent of the source material, but the editors do note that they have made use of articles from a number of newspapers and magazines, including *Charivari*, *Libération*, and *Le Monde* (*ibid.*, p. 816). Given the extent of the time period covered in the reference corpus, it is understandable that the dictionary covers current usage and also older locutions, some of which have now even fallen out of use completely. These are marked *vx* or *vieilli* in the entry. It turns out that few of these appear in the administrative corpus.

Although the dictionary gives no indication of the frequency of the locutions in the reference corpus,[63] in searching for the locution in the administrative corpus this analysis is effectively comparing the register of administrative French with the general language to the extent that it is represented by this reference corpus. In addition, in order to gain some idea of frequency, and more importantly, the function of such locutions in different types of language, these have been compared with the comparator corpus. Although this corpus is relatively small and, like Rey and Chantreau's source base, biased towards literary and

63 Rey and Chantreau do note, however, that their locutions derive a part of their importance from their frequency in the language (1993, p. x). While frequency is not a major consideration for inclusion in the dictionary, it is still recognised that locutions have a quantitatively important role in language.

journalistic textual genres, it is sufficiently varied to provide an additional point of comparison.

Rey and Chantreau's *Dictionnaire* therefore has the advantage of being extensive, including as it does over 11,500 locutions. A definitive collection of such phrases can never be compiled, since new combinations can always be added to the collection, while other phrases drop out of active usage. Furthermore, any decisions as to the frequency required by a potential phrase for inclusion in such a volume must be arbitrary. Nonetheless, its size, generality and authority mean that this dictionary constitutes one of the best starting points for a discussion of collocation in the register in question.

1.2 Procedure

Using the Concord facility of WordSmith Tools, the administrative corpus was searched for all of the locutions as listed in the index to the *Dictionnaire*. The editors highlight the fact that the locutions they discuss are not inflexible in form: they may incorporate interspersed material and can allow substitution of some items, although the item substituted, whether an alternative verb or adjective etc., is far from arbitrary. Some entries suggest alternative forms of the expression, or possible collocates; in other cases these can be found from looking at concordances but are not considered in the relevant dictionary entry.

Inevitably, therefore, the locutions as they appear in the main entry in the dictionary, and in the index, are not necessarily in the form in which they are used in actual text, so some care was required in order to maximise the chances of retrieving all instances of each locution. Rey and Chantreau suggest that, because they are not all formally stable, the expressions "ne sont que très partiellement à la portée de l'ordinateur" (1993, p. xiv). Rosamund Moon, too, recognises this problem in her research, saying:

> Finding exploitations and variations of FEIs is the hardest part of corpus-based investigations, and ultimately a matter of serendipity. Searches are most successful when the query consists of two lexical words, fairly close together. (Moon 1998a, p. 51)

It was necessary therefore to search for expressions on the basis of word forms which were most essential to the phrase, with careful use of wildcard characters to truncate the word where appropriate. When searching for a locution on the basis of a verbal form, it was of course necessary to take account of differently inflected forms. When the word has an accent, two forms were entered, one accented and one unaccented, to counteract the inconsistency in the texts, particularly with regard to accents on uppercase characters. On the whole it was preferable to search on the basis of the minimum form which was considered to be essential to the phrase, and then manually to discard concordance lines which were not in fact instances of the phrase sought, rather than to assume a larger number of elements to be essential to the phrase and risk overlooking some variants. Despite the care taken, some instances of expressions will almost certainly have remained hidden from view, for example because the constituent parts of the locution are separated by more than five words in a particular instance, or because they involve some creative manipulation of the dictionary form of the phrase with the result that only the grammatical structure, below the surface, remains constant (cf. Moon 1998a, p. 92).

In this way, the locutions which appear in the administrative corpus were identified. At this initial stage no distinction was made between those which appeared to be frequent in the corpus, and those which appeared just once. However, by cross-referencing to the main dictionary entries, it was possible to identify instances where the surface form was identical to a locution but where the sequence of words did not have any such phraseological identity.

2. The presence of locutions in the administrative corpus

There are 11,647 locutions and idiomatic expressions in Rey and Chantreau's dictionary. Evidently, this is by no means the extent of this type of phraseological resource in the French language. In searching for the locutions itemised in that work, a number of other expressions with a similar status in the language came to light; these can only be the tip of the iceberg:

(un véritable) cheval de Troie [e.g. freuco\prspfr] (a real Trojan horse)

un effet boule de neige [freuco\prspfr] (snowball effect)

une chasse aux sorcières (aveugle) [freuco\prspfr] (a (blind) witch hunt)

épée de Damoclès [freuco\prspfr] (sword of Damocles)

bonne chance et bon vent [frnaco\spprfr] (goodbye and God speed!)

en être la cheville ouvrière [frnaco\spmfr] (to be the mainspring)

défendre 'bec et ongles' [frnaco\ancrwfr] (defend tooth and nail)

tous les œufs dans le même panier [frnaco\ancrsfr] (all one's eggs in the same basket)

jeter son âme au diable et son tablier aux orties [frnaco/rapofr] (renounce one's calling)

In addition, there were a number of cases of locutions similar, but not identical, to those in the *Dictionnaire*. Generally speaking, if the variation was minor and did not affect the meaning of the expression, such as the replacement of one word with a synonym, the deletion of a word which did not directly affect the core meaning of the locution, or a difference in definite or indefinite articles, for example, then this was counted as an instance of the locution, but if the variation had a greater effect on the semantics or likely pragmatics of the locution, then it was not. There is no way of automatically extracting all of these systematically from the corpus, not least because it is always possible to query their status as locutions. This analysis, therefore, is limited to a discussion of those which appear in the *Dictionnaire*, while recognising that it is potentially only a small sample of the most frequent phrases of French.

Of these 11,647 locutions, only 633 were found in the administrative corpus considered as a whole. This represents 5.43% of the complete list of locutions in the dictionary. Appendix 2 lists these locutions, with their total frequencies across FRADCO.

Table 5.1: Locutions in FRADCO – types

Frequency	Total No. of locution types	% of locutions in Dictionnaire	% of locutions present in FRADCO (633)
0	11,014	94.57	-
1	251	2.16	39.65
2	96	0.82	15.17
3	44	0.38	6.95
4	30	0.26	4.73
5	24	0.21	3.79
6-10	50	0.43	7.90
11-20	42	0.36	6.64
21-50	52	0.45	8.21
51-100	19	0.16	3.00
>100	25	0.21	3.95
	11,647	100.00	100.00

The table above details the presence of locution types in FRADCO, the complete administrative corpus. If one considers locution tokens, the figure is of course much higher, and points to a more important role for this type of collocation in the corpus. As regards tokens, there is a total of 11,673 instances. Approximately two-fifths of the locutions which appear in the corpus do so with a frequency of one, and over 70% appear five times or fewer. Clearly, it is not possible to say much about these, except to draw generalisations regarding their lexical or grammatical tendencies as a group (see Section 4). As is to be expected, the number of locutions with a particular frequency in the corpus falls as the frequency rises. However, there are still a number of locutions which occur with a frequency of over 100 instances (see Section 5 below). Of these, 16 occur with a frequency of between 101 and 200, three between 201 and 300, two between 301 and 400, two between 401 and 500, and two locutions with a frequency of over 500 instances (one with 895 occurrences and one with 1481).

3. Zero-frequency locutions

As Table 5.1 shows, a vast majority (94.57%) of the locutions in the *Dictionnaire des expressions et locutions* do not appear in FRADCO. This is not surprising, given the register-specificity of the corpus used here, and the predominantly literary source of the locutions in the dictionary. While the focus here is on those locutions which *do* feature in the administrative corpus, before discussing these in more detail, a brief consideration of both those locutions which do not appear at all, and sequences which match locutions in their surface form only, is in order.

Over eleven thousand of the locutions in the *Dictionnaire* do not appear in the administrative corpus. Many of these are more at home in the spoken language, or in very informal settings (e.g. 'foutre le bordel', 'en voilà une affaire'). It is not surprising either that the various locutions which are proverbial in nature do not as a rule appear in the corpus. On the other hand, there are many locutions which one can imagine may well appear in a large corpus of administrative language, locutions which one might imagine hearing in a political speech, for example: such as 'c'est le moment ou jamais', and 'cœur de pierre'. It is quite probable that they would occur only a couple of times even in a much larger corpus: it might be expected that the relative frequencies would not vary greatly.

A number of locutions appeared at first glance to occur in FRADCO. Looking beyond the mere surface form to the wider context, however, these turned out not to be occurrences of the locution as it appeared in the *Dictionnaire*, but rather the result of the rules of syntax, or literal counterparts of locutions. This serves to demonstrate the imprudence of relying solely on automatic searches.

A d'autres	Dictionnaire: response to a promise which seems impossible or to lies. ('that's a likely story!') Corpus: part of preposition phrase - 'en faisant appel à d'autres fonctionnaires' [frnaco\rapmfr]; 'par rapport à d'autres services' [freuco\ojlfr]
A la page	Dictionnaire: up to date / in touch Corpus: literal - 'l'internaute ne s'arrête pas à la page d'accueil' [frnaco\dpfr]
De cheval	Dictionnaire: qualifies certain nouns, expressing idea of strength, e.g. 'fièvre de cheval' Corpus: literal - 'la consommation de viande de cheval ou de sanglier' [frnaco\cpmfr]
En avoir	Dictionnaire: euphemistic ('avoir des couilles') Corpus: 'après en avoir informé les autorités' [freuco\comfr]

En béton	Dictionnaire: very solid Corpus: concrete sense only; 'des produits en béton pré-moulé' [freuco\pripfr]
Frapper à toutes les portes	Dictionnaire: seek help wherever one can Corpus: metaphorical, but with the sense of requesting admission / accession - 'onze États frappent à la porte de l'Union' [freuco\prspfr]
Peu de choses	Dictionnaire: describes something unimportant, particularly to devalue something offered Corpus: literal - 'mais peu de choses ont été faites pour l'aménagement de Paris' [frnaco\spmfr]
Un de ces quatre	Dictionnaire: elliptical 'un de ces quatre matins' ('one of these days') Corpus: literal - 'un de ces quatre programmes' [freuco\prspfr]
Vaste programme!	Dictionnaire: Supposed quotation from de Gaulle Corpus: no allusion to quotation - 'un vaste programme de réformes' [freuco\ptfr]

4. Low-frequency locutions

About 70% of the locutions from the *Dictionnaire* which do occur in the administrative corpus occur with a frequency of five or fewer. Given such a low frequency of occurrence for each of these locutions, it is impossible to make valid generalisations about their use individually. At the same time, however, the types of locution which are represented may be investigated.

4.1 Idioms

Gledhill has demonstrated that "science writing is highly devoid of idioms of the traditional kind, but is rich in metaphor and collocational restrictions" (1999, p. 234). Despite their lack of traditional idioms, science texts "employ a system of expression which is as 'idiomatic' (i.e. distinctively fluent) as any other discourse" (2000, p. 2), and instead of conveying subject matter, such idiomatic expressions signal posture in discourse (1995, p. 11). This is broadly consistent with Fernando's finding that idioms differ in their function across different discourse types. As we have seen, she suggests a three-way categorisation of idioms, as ideational, interpersonal and relational (or textual), following Halliday's three metafunctions. Fernando found that:

> The kinds of discourse in which ideational idioms are likeliest to occur are informal speech, journalism, TV and radio broadcasts, the last three powerful vehicles of the newsworthy. They are used more sparingly in academic discourse, spoken and written. To find them,

for example, in legal documents or administrative regulations would be decidedly unusual. (Fernando 1996, p. 101)

While the corpus here is described as an 'administrative' corpus, it is not composed purely of administrative regulations. Rather, a proportion of the texts comprises administrators' speeches, reports, and press releases. Given the communicative aims of these genres, often to persuade an audience, it would not be surprising to find idioms, whether ideational, interpersonal or relational. A number of the low frequency locutions are indeed idiomatic, semantically non-compositional:

Jouer au chat et à la souris (1 occurrence [frnaco\rapofr]) (play cat and mouse)

Vivre de l'air du temps (1 [frnaco\sppmfr]) (to live on air)

Se mettre dans la peau de qqn (1 [freuco\prspfr]) (put oneself in someone's shoes)

Oiseau de mauvais augure (1 [freuco\paspfr]) (literally, bird of ill omen)

Y perdre son latin (1 [frnaco\rapofr]) (not be able to make head nor tail of...)

La politique de l'autruche (1 [frnaco\ancrsfr]) (to bury one's head in the sand)

Poser les jalons (1 [freuco\pc98fr]) (to prepare the ground)

Prendre le taureau par les cornes (1 [freuco\paspfr]) (take the bull by the horns)

Recevoir qqn cinq sur cinq (1 [freuco\prspfr]) (hear someone loud and clear)

Remettre les compteurs à zéro (2 [frnaco\spmfr + rapofr]) (start from scratch)

Rideau de fer (2 [freuco\prspfr]) (iron curtain[64])

It is notable that a large number of these idioms appear in the speech genres of the corpus. All are infrequent, occurring only once or twice in the whole corpus, but it might be expected that these figures would rise with the size of the corpus, and in addition, a number of other idiomatic locutions would also appear in a larger corpus. While it would appear, then, that idioms are infrequent, if not indeed 'decidedly unusual' as Fernando has claimed (1996, p. 101) in such genres as legislation or regulations, they are certainly not exceptional in the discourse of European Union or national French administration as a whole. They may serve to

64 This idiom of course originated in a political context, referring to the notional line which separated Communist from non-Communist countries. It was first used in 1946 in a speech by Churchill, and calqued from English into French.

make an administrative speech more memorable or persuasive for the listener, or indeed reader.

4.2 Proverbial expressions

A number of proverbial expressions are included in the *Dictionnaire*. None of these was found in the administrative corpus. As was noted above, however, the corpus is not completely devoid of such expressions. It is to be expected, therefore, that a larger corpus constructed along the same lines would in fact contain some of the proverbial expressions which Rey and Chantreau gloss. It is also possible, of course, that the administrative corpus does contain examples of these expressions, but that they have been adapted so much to suit the context in which they are being used that they become invisible to a concordancer, at least with a corpus which is not tagged for grammatical categories. This could happen, for example, if only the distinctive grammatical structure remains, and all of the lexical items are modified to suit the immediate context. It has been found, by Moon (1998a, pp. 57 and 131) that proverbial expressions are rarely used in their full or canonical form, but rather are usually adapted.

4.3 Intertextuality

It was seen in Chapter 4 that the administrative register relies to a large degree on intertextuality, or reference to, and quotation from, other texts within the same register. A couple of locutions also demonstrate that the register draws, to a certain extent, on intertextual reference outwith the register, or on broader cultural references. One of these is the successful advertising slogan for Esso petrol: 'avoir/mettre un tigre dans le/son moteur' (to put a tiger in one's tank) (2 occurrences [frnaco\spmfr]). This allusion is exploited twice in the administrative corpus, both times in the same text. The text in question is a speech given at the Sorbonne by Claude Allègre, at the time the minister for national education, research and technology. In it, reference is made explicitly: the minister first recalls the advertising slogan, putting it in inverted commas (and presumably in the speech as it was delivered making it clear that he was quoting), and then uses the slogan as a metaphor, equating the 'tiger', which signifies power and speed, with 'research', and suggesting that research (the 'tiger') can be the force to enable the University to develop over the next century. The allusion, while arguably somewhat laboured, has the effect of making the minister's point more vivid.

The second allusion is the much-quoted line from Voltaire's *Candide*: 'Tout est pour le mieux dans le meilleur des mondes possibles' (2 occurrences [frnaco\spprfr + ancrsfr]). Once again, the quotation is modified. One text, a speech by Jacques Chirac to the young people of Mexico and Latin America, merely states that while the present situation is not 'le meilleur des mondes', it is at least 'un meilleur monde'. Given the impossible optimism of the notion of the best of all possible worlds, 'un meilleur monde' is by comparison realistic and therefore possible, and for that, a more convincing political statement. In the second text (the transcription of a meeting of the Assemblée Nationale), the speaker claims that since the situation in the energy industry does not seem to be heading towards 'le meilleur des mondes possibles', it is necessary to take steps to improve it in the future. Again, the reference adds little, except perhaps for a little cultural colour, to the speech.

4.4 Metaphorical expressions

A large number of the lower frequency locutions which appeared in the administrative corpus are metaphorical in nature. These include:

A la chaîne (1 [freuco\pripfr]) (production-line / churned out)

A la clé (1 [freuco\pa97fr]) (as a bonus / into the bargain)

A cor et à cris (1 [frnaco\rapofr]) (insistently)

A la dérive (1 [frnaco\sppmfr]) (adrift)

A portée de la main (1 [frnaco\ancrsfr]) (within reach / easily accessible)

A reculons (2 [frnaco\spprfr + rapofr]) (backwards)

A bout de souffle (1 [freuco\prspfr]) (out of breath)

A double tranchant (1 [freuco\pripfr]) (double-edged)

A deux vitesses (6 [frnaco\spprfr + rapofr + ancrsfr]) (two-speed)

Aller sur le terrain (1 [frnaco\spprfr]) (in-situ)

Au pied de la lettre (1 [frnaco\rapofr]) (literally / in the strict sense)

Aux abonnés absents (1 [freuco\prspfr]) (absent - metaphor from field of telecommunications)

Avoir voix au chapitre (1 [frnaco\spprfr]) (to have a say in the matter)

Avoir toute latitude pour (1 [frnaco\rapmfr]) (to be at liberty to)

Baisser les bras (1 [frnaco\spprfr]) (to give up)

Contre vents et marées (2 [frnaco\spprfr]) (against all the odds)

Déposer son bilan (1 [freuco\pripfr]) (to go into liquidation)

En dents de scie (1 [frnaco\rapofr]) (serrated / irregular)

Enfoncer une porte ouverte (1 [frnaco\ancrsfr]) (to labour an obvious point)

Entrer en ligne de compte (5 [freuco\lbfr + cefr + ojlfr, frnaco\spmfr]) (to be taken into account)

Être le dos au mur (1 [freuco\prspfr]) (to have one's back to the wall)

Être sur la mauvaise pente (1 [freuco\pripfr]) (to be heading for trouble)

Être de son temps (1 [frnaco\spprfr]) (to be of one's time)

Faire ses premières armes (1 [frnaco\rapofr]) (to make one's début)

Faire du bruit (1 [freuco\prspfr]) (to be important / create a stir)

Faire un tour d'horizon (2 [freuco\prspfr + frnaco\cpmfr]) (to survey)

Faire machine arrière (1 [freuco\prspfr]) (to backtrack)

Faire la navette (1 [freuco\pripfr]) (to shuttle to and fro)

Baptême du feu (1 [freuco\prspfr]) (baptism of fire)

Il y a belle lurette (1 [frnaco\rapofr]) (ages ago)

Jeter aux oubliettes (1 [frnaco\spmfr]) (to discard / shelve)

Le jeu n'en vaut pas la chandelle (1 [frnaco\ancrsfr]) (the game's not worth the candle)

Jour J (1 [freuco\prspfr]) (D-day)

(Re)mettre sur les rails (3 [freuco\pripfr + cefr, frnaco\spmfr]) (to put (back) on the rails)

Occuper le devant de la scène (3 [freuco\prspfr, frnaco\spmfr + ancrwfr]) (to take centre stage)

Pour le meilleur et pour le pire (1 [frnaco\spmfr]) (for better or for worse)

Prendre les devants (1 [freuco\prspfr]) (to make the first move)

Prêter le flanc à (1 [freuco\prspfr]) (to give an adversary an opening / to lay oneself open)

Il doit se retourner dans sa tombe (1 [frnaco\rapofr]) (he must be turning in his grave)

Second souffle (1 [frnaco\sppmfr]) (second wind / new lease of life)

Sonner le glas (de qqch) (1 [frnaco\spprfr]) (to toll the knell)

Tirer au clair (1 [freuco/prspfr]) (to clarify)

Tourner la page (3 [freuco\prspfr, frnaco\spprfr]) (to turn over a new leaf)

Travailler d'arrache-pied (1 [freuco/prspfr]) (work relentlessly)

Little can be said about these individually, since most occur only once in the corpus. However, as a group, metaphorical expressions make up a more substantial category of locutions, and it is useful to bear in mind the range of images drawn upon in administrative language, which has traditionally had a reputation for dryness of expression. A large number of the locutions above occur in speech genres.

4.5 Interpersonal locutions

A couple of the locutions present in the corpus are clearly interpersonal in nature. As might be expected, such formulae also tend to occur in the speech genres:

> Avoir l'honneur de (2 [frnaco\rapofr + freuco\prspfr]) (to have the honour of, for example, contributing to a project, presiding over a meeting)
>
> Bon vent! (3 [frnaco\spprfr]) (goodbye / farewell)

4.6 Legal and political locutions

More crucially, a number of the locutions in the *Dictionnaire* are explicitly marked as having originated in a legal or political context, or as having recently been rejuvenated in a political context. In the general language, these are often used in a metaphorical sense, whereas in the corpus on the whole they retain their original meaning. These include:

> A huis clos (4 [frnaco\tfdhfr + anplfr, freuco\prcesfr + treatfr]) (in camera / behind closed doors)
>
> Au ban de (1 [frnaco\rapofr]) (banished / blackballed)
>
> Avoir gain de cause (2 [freuco\pripfr]) (to win the case, in law)
>
> Avoir force de loi (3 [frnaco\sppmfr + tfconsfr + ancrwfr]) (have force of law)
>
> Bons offices (1 [frnaco\ancrwfr]) (good offices (pol.) (good offices)
>
> Pré carré (1 [frnaco\cpmfr]) (domain / preserve)
>
> Cas de force majeure (6 [frnaco\tfconsfr + jofr + ancrsfr, freuco\ojlfr]) (absolutely unavoidable)
>
> En mon âme et conscience (2 [freuco\prspfr]) (in all conscience)
>
> Dans tous les azimuts (1 [frnaco\rapmfr (all over the place)
>
> Descendre dans la rue (1 [freuco\prpresfr]) (to take to the streets)
>
> Donner acte à qqn (1 [frnaco\rapofr]) (to acknowledge the truth to someone)

Noyau dur (4 [frnaco\spmfr + rapofr + ancrsfr, freuco\prspfr]) (hard core)

En instance (5 [frnaco\jofr + ancrwfr, freuco\prmemo + prpescfr]) (pending)

En lieu et place de qqn (4 [frnaco\rapmfr, freuco\prspfr + ojlfr]) (in lieu of)

Et pour cause (2 [frnaco\ancrsfr]) (with good reason)

Etre juge et partie (3 [frnaco\sppmfr + ancrwfr]) (to judge and be judged)

Faire bloc (1 [frnaco\spmfr]) (to unite)

Faire droit à (3 [freuco\prcjefr + prspfr]) (to grant)

Flagrant délit (4 [frnaco\tfconsfr]) (in flagrante delicto / red-handed)

Mettre en demeure (3 [frnaco\anplfr, freuco\pripfr + treatfr]) (to order, someone to do something)

Le cachet de la poste faisant foi (4 [frnaco\jofr + cpcmfr]) (the postmark to be taken as proof)

Le troisième âge (1 [frnaco\rapofr]) (senior citizens)

Some of these locutions are quite frequent in the administrative corpus (here, the sub-corpus and genre category is only indicated if there is a marked tendency towards one sub-corpus or a particular genre):

A juste titre (20) (rightly)

En connaissance de cause (13) (with full knowledge of the facts)

De (plein) droit (153 [esp. freuco\prspfr, frnaco\anplfr]) (by rights)

D'ores et déjà (118 [esp. freuco\prspfr, frnaco\dpfr + cpmfr + rapmfr]) (already, henceforth)

En tout état de cause (74) (in any case)

En cause (247) (concerned, involved)

En temps utile (28 [esp. freuco]) (in due time)

En vertu de (332 [esp. freuco, esp. prcjefr + pripfr + treatfr]) (in accordance with)

Être / entrer en vigueur (440 [esp. freuco, esp. treatfr]) (to be in force / enter into force)

Sans délai (45) (forthwith, immediately)

5. High-frequency locutions

Table 5.2: Locutions with a frequency over 100 in FRADCO

Locution	Total occurrences in FRADCO	Total as % of locution tokens
Dans le cadre (de)	1481	12.69
Tenir compte de	895	7.67
Entrer / Etre en vigueur	440	3.77
Avoir lieu (de)	408	3.50
Jouer un rôle	338	2.90
En vertu de	332	2.84
A compter de	299	2.56
A l'égard de	251	2.15
En cause	247	2.12
Prendre à sa (en) charge	194	1.66
Sous réserve de	193	1.65
De plus en plus	189	1.62
Dans la mesure de (où)	181	1.55
A long terme	165	1.41
De (plein) droit	153	1.31
Faire face	146	1.25
Etre en mesure de	139	1.19
En revanche	137	1.17
Au plus tard	132	1.13
Donner lieu à	130	1.11
Bien sûr	127	1.09
Tout au (du) long de	121	1.04
D'ores et déjà	118	1.01
Prendre acte de qqch	118	1.01
A moyen terme	107	0.92

By far the most frequent locution in the corpus is 'Dans le cadre (de)', which occurs 1481 times. 'Cadre' as an individual word is the 66th most frequent in the corpus, with 2416 occurrences (disregarding instances of the plural form 'cadres' which is generally used with the sense of 'manager'). The locution 'dans le cadre (de)' accounts for over 60% of the instances of the individual word. In the comparator corpus, 'cadre' is only the 739th most frequent word, appearing 271 times out of 2,223,862 words: this represents 1.2 instances per 10,000 words, whereas in FRADCO 'cadre' occurs just shy of 7 times per 10,000 words. More significantly, 'dans le cadre de' occurs only 111 times in the comparator corpus: therefore the locution accounts for only 41% of the occurrences of 'cadre' as an individual word. It is also notable that all but three of the occurrences in the comparator corpus appear in journalistic texts. This suggests that the use of the locution is highly genre-determined.

5.1 Distribution between sub-corpora

There are significant differences in the occurrence of locutions between the two sub-corpora, FREUCO and FRNACO. As regards types of locution, FREUCO contains 382 of the 633 locutions: this is 60.35% of those locutions which appear in the complete administrative corpus, and 3.27% of the total number in the *Dictionnaire*. FRNACO, by contrast, contains instances of 509 types of locution, or 80.41% of those in FRADCO and 4.36% of the total number. It should be remembered that the two parts of the corpus are almost identical in size. These figures show that the sub-corpus of European Union language makes use of fewer types of locution than the French national side of the corpus. As regards the overlap between the two sub-corpora, only 258 locutions (40.76%) appear in both halves of the complete administrative corpus.

When one looks at the figures for tokens of locutions, however, the picture changes. FREUCO has 6609 instances of locutions, of the 11,673 tokens present in the complete corpus; that is 56.62%. FRNACO, on the other hand, has only 5064 instances of the locutions from Rey and Chantreau's dictionary, or 43.38% of the total. FREUCO therefore can be seen to make heavier use of locutions, considered as tokens. The mean number of occurrences per locution in FREUCO is 17.3, whereas in FRNACO, each locution is used an average of only 9.95 times.

If these figures can be generalised beyond the corpus used here to the administrative register as a whole, it would seem that European Union language makes frequent use of a smaller number of locutions, while the French national equivalent exploits a wider range of locutions, but draws on this particular phraseological resource less frequently. The possibility remains, of course, that FREUCO makes frequent use of locutions which are not present in Rey and Chantreau's dictionary. This would not be surprising, not least because many of the texts in this sub-corpus were not originally drafted in French, but only translated into French, albeit by native-speaker professionals.

The distribution of each locution between the two sub-corpora was then compared. A frequency of five or fewer in the whole corpus was judged an insufficient basis on which to make any claim for unequal distribution. In addition, the higher the frequency of locution, the smaller the possibility that any disparity can merely be attributed to chance. First, locutions of which at least 75% of the instances appear in the European Union sub-corpus are collated:

Table 5.3: Locutions typical of FREUCO

Locution	Occurrences in FREUCO	Total	% in FREUCO
Entrer / Etre en vigueur	361	440	82.05
En vertu de	287	332	86.45
A long terme	134	165	81.21
Etre en mesure de	105	139	75.54
Prendre acte de qqch	107	118	90.68
Entre autres	62	70	88.57
Prendre (bonne) note	65	68	95.59
Avoir l'intention de	59	66	89.39
Avoir trait à	36	43	83.72
De premier plan	28	34	82.35
Ce faisant	28	33	84.85
De sorte que	28	29	96.55
Donner suite à (qqch)	24	28	85.71
En temps utile	26	28	92.86
Sans réserve	18	24	75.00
Suivre de près	18	22	81.82
Tirer profit de qqch	16	21	76.19
En détail	18	20	90.00
Entre temps	16	16	100.00
Donner le signal de (qqch)	11	13	84.62
Mettre à (l')exécution	11	13	84.62
Porter préjudice à qqch	12	13	92.31
Prendre la parole	10	13	76.92
Aller de l'avant	10	12	83.33
Pour peu que	9	12	75.00
Par comparaison (avec)	9	11	81.82
Sur un pied de	11	11	100.00
A bref délai	8	9	88.89
Qui plus est	7	9	77.78
En bonne voie	7	8	87.50
Passer en revue	8	8	100.00
De toute urgence	7	7	100.00
Comme il se doit	6	6	100.00
Dans la ligne	6	6	100.00
Donner à penser	5	6	83.33
Surveiller de près	6	6	100.00

These locutions appear to be more central to the phraseology of European Union discourse than its national French equivalent. The following, by contrast, are the locutions of which at least 75% of instances appear in the national French sub-corpus:

Table 5.4: Locutions typical of FRNACO

Locution	Occurrences in FRNACO	Total	% in FRNACO
Prendre à sa (en) charge	168	194	86.60
Bien sûr	98	127	77.17
Faire appel à	55	70	78.57
A distance	55	69	79.71
Avoir droit à	48	57	84.21
Il est vrai que	36	41	87.80
A son tour	25	32	78.13
Aux côtés de qqn	24	30	80.00
En quelque sorte	22	28	78.57
Avoir raison	19	23	82.61
Mettre à plat (qqn)	19	21	90.48
Rendre service (à qqn)	17	19	89.47
En retour	13	17	76.47
A l'écart (de)	13	16	81.25
Etre en jeu	11	14	78.57
Donner l'exemple	12	12	100.00
En honneur de (qqn ou qqch)	12	12	100.00
Tout de suite	9	11	81.82
Quand même	9	10	90.00
En tout point / en tous points	7	9	77.78
Etre garant de qqch	9	9	100.00
Pas du tout	8	9	88.89
A l'usage de qqn	8	8	100.00
Mettre en doute	6	8	75.00
Prendre garde	8	8	100.00
Sous prétexte (de)	6	8	75.00
De premier (second etc.) ordre	6	7	85.71
Faire (toute) la lumière sur qqch	7	7	100.00
A deux vitesses	6	6	100.00
A la rencontre (de)	5	6	83.33
Au long de	5	6	83.33
Cas de force majeure	5	6	83.33
Il y va de	6	6	100.00
Mettre en jeu	6	6	100.00

These locutions appear to exemplify discourse-based differences within the register of administrative language. Other locutions, however, appear to be characteristic of the register as a whole. The following are those locutions which are fairly evenly distributed between the two sub-corpora (a 45%/55% disparity, or closer). Once again, only those locutions with a frequency of greater than five are considered, and those with a greater frequency have more claim to accuracy.

Table 5.5: Locutions with equal frequency in FREUCO and FRNACO

Locution	Total	FREUCO	FREUCO %	FRNACO	FRNACO %
A compter de	299	150	50.17	149	49.83
A l'égard de	251	137	54.58	114	45.42
En cause	247	132	53.44	115	46.56
Sous réserve de	193	102	52.85	91	47.15
De (plein) droit	153	75	49.02	78	50.98
Tout au (du) long de	121	58	47.93	63	52.07
Faire preuve de	80	44	55.00	36	45.00
En tout état de cause	74	36	48.65	38	51.35
En fait	67	33	49.25	34	50.75
Faire valoir	51	24	47.06	27	52.94
Etre à même de	35	16	45.71	19	54.29
Mettre à profit	33	18	54.55	15	45.45
Pour le compte de	28	14	50.00	14	50.00
Faire défaut	24	11	45.83	13	54.17
A peu près	20	9	45.00	11	55.00
Aller dans le sens de qqn	16	8	50.00	8	50.00
A condition de	14	7	50.00	7	50.00
Autrement dit	14	7	50.00	7	50.00
En connaissance de cause	13	7	53.85	6	46.15
Mettre en chantier	12	6	50.00	6	50.00
A tout prix	11	5	45.45	6	54.55
Sous le signe de	11	6	54.55	5	45.45
Dans une certaine mesure	10	5	50.00	5	50.00
A vrai dire	8	4	50.00	4	50.00
Donner corps à qqch	8	4	50.00	4	50.00
Faire ses preuves	8	4	50.00	4	50.00
Coup d'envoi	6	3	50.00	3	50.00
De longue haleine	6	3	50.00	3	50.00

5.2 Distribution among genres

Just as there is a disparity in the occurrence of locutions between the two sub-corpora, there is also a disparity among genres. At first glance, a number of locutions, of both high and low frequency, show a strong bias towards a single genre. Many other locutions show strong biases towards one or more genres, but are not absolutely restricted to these genres. Generally speaking, locutions have a tendency to occur either in genres of a legislative nature, or in speeches. For example, not surprisingly, 'entrer / être en vigueur' appears most frequently in legal texts, such as Community legislation (ojlfr), European treaties (treatfr), and the French Journal Officiel (jofr). 'A compter de' likewise tends to be used in the two Official Journal genres (ojlfr and jofr). 'Prendre (bonne) note', on the other hand, appears most frequently in the European Council Meetings (cefr), a genre which does not have an equivalent in the French national side of the corpus, and in keeping with this hardly appears at all in this sub-corpus.

On the other hand, some locutions appear in a wide range of genres, and do not appear to be genre-specific. These include some of the most frequent locutions, such as 'dans le cadre de' and 'tenir compte de'. Some of the slightly lower frequency locutions also appear in a large number of genres, including legal texts, speeches, and press releases. These include: 'à long terme'. 'être en mesure de', 'faire preuve de', 'avoir l'intention de' (in a range of genres but particularly in FRNACO), 'mener à bien', 'de premier plan' (in a number of genres but particularly in FRNACO), 'aller de pair avec'.

5.3 Distribution between modes

Since there is no perfect one-to-one mapping of genres between sub-corpora, raw figures cannot be compared directly. Rather, each sub-corpus was divided into two parts: speeches (which are written first and delivered orally) and written texts, while bearing in mind that there is a lot of variation within these two categories. The national French sub-corpus also has a genre composed of transcribed speech with written annotations, a *compte rendu* of Assemblée Nationale debates. This genre is discarded for the purposes of this comparison, since it introduces a different mode of production, that of spontaneous speech.

Table 5.6: Spoken and written genres in FREUCO and FRNACO

Category	Words	% of sub-corpus
FREUCO speeches	196,281	18.42
FREUCO written genres	869,108	81.58
FRNACO speeches (excluding 'ancrs')	198,102	18.76
FRNACO written genres	807,707	76.48

The focus was first on those locutions which appear to be more typical of the speech genres. Since these genres of each sub-corpus account for just under 20% of the total of that sub-corpus, locutions (with a frequency of 20 occurrences or more in the whole corpus) of which greater than or equal to 40% of the occurrences are in speech genres, compared to the whole of the sub-corpus, are highlighted. This allows for the possibility that chance alone accounts for their higher frequency in that genre. Locutions are ordered by their percentage of occurrence in speeches, to bring to the fore those which appear to be most tied to that mode. First, those locutions which are most frequent in the speeches of FREUCO:

Table 5.7: Locutions typical of FREUCO speeches

Locution	Occurrences in speeches	% of occurrences in speeches
A mon sens	14	100.00
Mettre à plat	2	100.00
Bien sûr	27	93.10
A peu près	8	88.89
Vouloir dire	10	76.92
Aller loin	9	75.00
Avoir raison	3	75.00
Il est (n'est pas) question de	5	71.43
En quelque sorte	4	66.67
A côté de	7	63.64
A juste titre	5	62.50
Etre loin de	8	61.54
D'ores et déjà	20	54.05
Etre en train de	16	53.33
A moyen terme	41	51.90
Au fur et à mesure	4	50.00
Aux côtés de qqn	3	50.00
En détail	9	50.00
Tout comme	4	50.00
Rendre hommage à (qn/qch)	8	47.06
A court terme	17	45.95
De plus en plus	30	45.45
Faire défaut	5	45.45
Mettre à profit	8	44.44
Faire preuve de	19	43.18
A son tour	3	42.86
Premier pas	6	42.86
Voir (le) jour	3	42.86
Faire face	38	40.00
Il est vrai que	2	40.00

Second, those locutions which have a high proportion of occurrences in the speeches of FRNACO (an asterisk highlights locutions which also appear in the equivalent list for FREUCO):

Table 5.8: Locutions typical of FRNACO speeches

Locution	Occurrences in speeches	% of occurrences in speeches[65]
Sans réserve	5	83.33
* Avoir raison	13	81.25
Ce faisant	4	80.00
* Aller loin	19	76.00
* A mon sens	6	75.00
Prendre part à	14	73.68
* Rendre hommage à (qqch/qqn)	34	72.34
Avoir l'intention de	5	71.43
* Bien sûr	63	70.79
* Vouloir dire	12	70.59
Tirer parti de	8	61.54
* Voir (le) jour	9	60.00
* A juste titre	7	58.33
Aller de pair avec	5	55.56
* Etre en train de	6	54.55
* Aux côtés de qqn	12	54.55
* Faire défaut	6	54.55
Faire part de qqch à qqn	15	53.57
* A côté de	9	52.94
* A son tour	13	52.00
* Premier pas	3	50.00
* Faire preuve de	13	48.15
Mener à bien	11	44.00
A l'heure	12	41.38
* En quelque sorte	9	40.91

It is notable that although there is a substantial overlap between the two lists - 16 locutions appear in both lists - there is not a total correspondence. Of course, some locutions in each list appear in the other with a percentage slightly below the 40% taken as the cut-off point. Others occur with only a small overall frequency, either in one sub-corpus or both, so percentage figures do not give a clear picture. This accounts for the apparent importance of both 'sans réserve' and 'mettre à plat', in the speeches genres of FRNACO and FREUCO respectively, each of which is apparently below the expected proportion in the

65 Compared with the speeches and written genres of FRNACO as a whole, but not including 'ancrs'.

other sub-corpus. Some, however, show a discrepancy between sub-corpora: 'prendre part à', for example, which occurs in the speeches genres of FRNACO 14 times (accounting for 73.68% of its occurrences in this sub-corpus), occurs in the speeches of FREUCO only twice (8.33% of its occurrences here). This locution therefore seems to be more characteristic of European Union administrative language as a whole, while within this discourse it is very much more frequent in written genres, whereas in the national French discourse it is less common on the whole, but where it does occur, it is more common in speech genres. The concordance lines for this locution confirm this assessment, and suggest a reason. In FREUCO, and in particular in the Official Journal genre (ojlfr), 'prendre part à' is part of the set formula: 'Le président ne prend pas part au vote', and tends to come towards the end of the text. In the speeches in FRNACO, the locution collocates weakly with the adjective 'active', but does not appear to be restricted in its usage.

'En détail' is another locution which appears from these statistics to function in very different ways in the two discourses. Fifty per cent (that is, nine) of its occurrences in FREUCO are in the considerably smaller speech mode, while in FRNACO it appears only twice in total and not at all in speeches. Since the figures are so low, this is not perhaps surprising, but the disparity between sub-corpora suggests a difference in usage, perhaps that it should be considered a fixed phrase or formula in EU language, as in the case of 'prendre part à' above. A concordance reveals no fixed pattern, however, although there is a strong tendency for the locution to collocate with words in the semantic field of examination: 'analyser', 'examiner', 'étudier', 'présenter'.

This suggests that some locutions are more discourse-based, and others more genre-based. FRNACO has slightly fewer locutions which show a strong tendency towards one mode over another: it will be remembered that FRNACO had a smaller number of locution tokens than FREUCO, and since the Assemblée Nationale debates genre has been disregarded in these calculations, the figure is smaller still. Despite these lower percentages, the rough ordering of locutions remains globally the same between the two sub-corpora.

It is also interesting to look at those locutions which are much more frequently used in written genres. The following are those (again with a total frequency of at least 20 occurrences in the whole corpus) which appear in the written mode of either of the two sub-corpora with a frequency of at least 90% (a locution which was evenly spread between the two modes would have a proportion of around 82% in the sub-corpus in question). Again the asterisk in the second table indicates those which appear in both tables.

Table 5.9: Locutions typical of FREUCO written texts

Locution	Occurrences in written genres	% of occurrences in written genres
Sous réserve de	102	100.00
Faire état de	16	100.00
Faire foi	16	100.00
A usage	15	100.00
A défaut de	15	100.00
A distance	14	100.00
Etre en droit de	13	100.00
Prendre acte de qqch	106	99.07
A compter de	148	98.67
En vertu de	282	98.26
Au plus tard	95	96.94
En temps utile	25	96.15
Dans la mesure du possible	22	95.65
Prendre (bonne) note	61	93.85
Mettre un terme à	15	93.75
Autant que possible	14	93.33
Sans délai	27	93.10
Pour le compte de	13	92.86
Entrer / Etre en vigueur	335	92.80
Prendre à sa (en) charge	24	92.31
Avoir lieu (de)	243	91.70
Avoir trait à	33	91.67
Prendre part à	22	91.67
Rendre compte	20	90.91
Faire usage de	20	90.91
Dans le cadre de	893	90.75
Entre autres	56	90.32

Table 5.10: Locutions typical of FRNACO written texts

Locution	Occurrences in written genres	% of occurrences in written genres[66]
* A défaut de	43	100.00
* Au plus tard	33	100.00
* Pour le compte de	14	100.00
Par la suite	12	100.00
* Faire foi	10	100.00

66 Compared with the speeches and written genres of FRNACO as a whole, but not including 'ancrs'.

Mettre en lumière	9	100.00
* Entre autres	7	100.00
Donner suite à (qqch)	4	100.00
* Prendre (bonne) note	2	100.00
* En temps utile	2	100.00
En détail	2	100.00
De sorte que	1	100.00
* Sous réserve de	89	98.89
* A compter de	146	97.99
* En vertu de	44	97.78
* A usage	21	95.45
Avoir droit à	45	93.75
* Faire état de	28	93.33
*Dans la mesure du possible	13	92.86
En tout	12	92.31
Dans la mesure de (où)	44	91.67
Faire valoir	22	91.67
* Entrer / Etre en vigueur	72	91.14
* A distance	50	90.91

Once again, a large number of the locutions appear in both lists (15 locutions), and either very low frequencies of occurrence or a proportion only slightly below the 90% cut-off point can account for some apparent discrepancies. A few locutions show interesting differences between the two corpora, however. 'En détail' and 'prendre part à' (both discussed above) are significant in the written part of one sub-corpus and the speech genres of the other. These two locutions appear therefore not to be bound by the mode of discourse; more influential for their usage is the discourse (EU or national).

A number of locutions therefore differ in usage according to mode. The following locutions, on the other hand, are distributed between speeches and written genres in proportions almost exactly that predicted by chance (a proportion of 16-24% in speech genres, equivalent to 76-84% in written genres). It might be surmised that their usage is defined more at the level of either discourse or register than mode.

FREUCO: en cause, en tout état de cause, faire appel à, avoir droit à, tirer parti de

FRNACO: en cause, prendre à sa (en) charge, être en mesure de, tout au (du) long de, d'ores et déja, prendre acte de qqch, en fait, faire le point, avoir trait à, être à même de, au détriment de, de premier plan, faire usage de, tirer profit de qqch

There is very little overlap between these two lists. This is partly due to the narrow band of percentage proportions allowed, and partly due to low frequencies of occurrence of certain locutions. In some cases also it suggests that discourse (EU or national) has a greater role to play than mode.

5.4 Distribution: conclusion

It seems therefore that different locutions are restricted in their usage at different levels. Some seem particularly common in the administrative register as a whole. Given the use of Rey and Chantreau's dictionary, with its literary and journalistic source material, as the starting point for this analysis, of course virtually none of the locutions is unique to the administrative register, but it is clear that some are used in different ways in this register from the language as a whole: this is the case with locutions which originated in legal contexts, but which have been adopted by the general language and often used in a metaphorical sense. Some, on the other hand, seem closely linked with one discourse (as represented by the two sub-corpora), some to a particular group of genres (e.g. speeches, legal texts), and some to an individual genre (e.g. Commission speeches, rather than Parliament speeches). Yet others will almost inevitably appear to be restricted to individual texts, without being tied to one of the above categories, but with a medium-sized corpus it is impossible to make generalisations on the textual level.

6. A case-study by genre: *Conclusions de la Présidence*

With a different corpus design, it would be possible to compare the use of locutions across two broadly equivalent genres. Given the aims of the administrative corpus design, and the fact that the two contexts are very different in terms of their history, present-day function and sphere of influence, it is difficult to find direct equivalents. The two sub-corpora are equivalent in that they both aim to sample a wide range of the types of document available. It is proposed here, therefore, to investigate the role of locutions in the Presidency Conclusions of the European Council genre of FREUCO ('pc98fr'). The corpus contains the conclusions, or summarized reports, from the European Councils which took place between December 1997 and June 1999.[67] European Councils are summit meetings which bring together the Heads of State or Government of the member states and the President of the European Commission, held in the member state which holds the Presidency of the Council, in order to discuss the general direction of the Union rather than specific everyday issues.

This genre is discussed by Straehle et al. (1999), in an analysis of the metaphor of 'struggle' as applied to the issue of unemployment, and compared in this research with the genre of Commissioners' speeches. They show that the differences between the two genres can be attributed to their different purposes and

---

67 This period covers the European Councils in Luxembourg (Luxembourg Presidency), Cardiff (UK), Vienna (Austrian), Berlin and Cologne (German Presidency)

audiences, Presidency Conclusions being "internal organizational discourse", directed in the first instance towards other organisations and governments, and Commissioners' speeches being external discourse. However, the distinction is not totally clear-cut since the understanding of both requires some inside knowledge of how the institutions work and both are ultimately available to a more general public than their initial audiences (cf. 1999, p. 96). Given the aim of Presidency Conclusions, to give instructions to politicians and officials, Straehle et al. are not surprised that "the foe-like characteristics of an opponent (i.e. the personification of unemployment) are minimally emphasized" (1999, p. 89). In the speeches, on the other hand, unemployment is presented as a problem to be solved (cf. also Chapter 6).

The Presidency Conclusions genre of FREUCO is 74,171 words in size, and accounts for just under 7% of the sub-corpus. A total of 615 locutions from the *Dictionnaire* occur in this genre: the average number of locutions per thousand words is therefore 8.29, which is the third highest proportion for a genre of this sub-corpus. As regards locution types, 104 are used in the genre, 43 of these only once. Many of these can be seen to reflect the genre's concern with the progress and development in the European Union, such as: 'poser les jalons' ('prepare the ground', for a project etc.), 'prendre son élan' ('gather speed', 'take a run up'), 'comme par le passé' ('as formerly'), 'clé de voûte' ('keystone'), 'mettre en chantier' ('undertake', e.g. a project), 'aller de l'avant' ('forge ahead'), 'à court terme' ('short-term'), 'faire le bilan de' ('take stock of'), 'parer à toute éventualité' ('prepare for all eventualities'). A number of others are concerned with the beginnings and endings of projects, their deadlines and intermediate stages - these include: 'toucher à sa fin' ('come to an end'), 'de bonne heure' ('early'), 'sous peu' ('soon'), 'au plus tôt' ('as soon as possible'), 'coup d'envoi' ('kick-off', 'start').

The most frequent locution in the genre, as in the complete corpus, is 'dans le cadre de', which occurs 124 times in the Presidency Conclusions. It collocates here with such nouns as 'processus', 'stratégie', 'politique', 'programme', 'dialogue', 'initiatives', 'Agenda' (as in 'Agenda 2000').[68] A number of locutions occur much more frequently in the genre than their relative proportions in the sub-corpus would lead one to expect. One of these is 'prendre acte de (qqch)' ('to note something', or 'record something formally'). The subject of the verb is almost always the European Council itself, and the object, most commonly, 'un rapport', but also 'des travaux' and 'l'intention de la Commission'. The Commissioners' speech genre contains no examples of this locution. 'Prendre

68 'Agenda 2000' is a study presented by Jacques Santer to the European Parliament in July 1997, described as a "detailed strategy for strengthening and widening the Union in the early years of the 21st century" (Bainbridge 1998, p. 8). It was accepted for further negociations at the Luxembourg European Council in December 1997.

(bonne) note' ('take note') also occurs more frequently than might be expected in the Conclusions. Again the European Council is most frequently the subject of the verb, and the phrase serves to present its view on a topic discussed or reported on in the course of the summit. The locution occurs only four times in the Commissioners' speech genre, of which two occurrences refer to the Cardiff European Council.

'En temps utile' ('in due course', esp. within a set deadline) is used of projects and measures relating to the development of the European Union. It comes as no surprise that this locution should be used in texts which report on the general directions of the Union. It appears only once in the speeches, and is used here in a less specific sense: discovering in due course (i.e. when all the facts come to light and not necessarily within a set deadline) which agricultural policy is best for the Union.

7. A case-study by locution: 'A long / moyen / court terme'

Finally, as a further approach, this section considers three variant forms of a single locution, and investigates in more detail their place and use in the administrative corpus. These locutions are 'à long terme', 'à moyen terme' and 'à court terme' (in the long / medium / short term). These were felt to be intuitively interesting, especially as regards the differences in usage, both among the three, and between the two sub-corpora: one might wonder, for example, whether the EU lexicalises its long term goals and plans differently from the national French administration.

It is clear from concordance lists of these locutions that there is a range of related locutions, such as 'sur le long terme', 'en long terme', '[solution/accord etc.] de long terme'. It is also notable that the three locutions, or any two of them, often combine in actual usage to indicate vagueness of reference or wideness of scope. For example, the complex locution 'à moyen et/ou (à) long terme' is quite frequent, and a number of other variants, such as 'à court, moyen et long terme', 'à court et à long terme' and 'à long et (à) moyen terme' also appear. There is a not unexpected strong tendency towards the order 'court', 'moyen', 'long', with the the nearer future considered first. Rather than count each of these as an instance of two or three locutions at once, and thereby inflate the figures for each, it was decided to count each only once, as an instance of the last locution in the combination: thus 'à court et à long terme' was taken to be an instance of 'à long terme'. It seems inevitable that findings will be skewed in some way.

'A long terme' is the most frequent of the three locutions (and the fourteenth most frequent of all the locutions in the corpus), with 165 occurrences, of which 134 are in FREUCO and 31 in FRNACO. 'A moyen terme' is the second most frequent, with 107 instances, 79 in FREUCO and 28 in FRNACO. 'A court terme' is least frequent (although still the fortieth most frequent locution in the whole corpus), with a total of 57 instances, 37 in FREUCO and 20 in FRNACO. European Union discourse, at least as represented by the corpus, has quantitatively greater recourse to these particular locutions than French national discourse. Looking at the corpus on the whole, 'à long terme' is used in 26 genre categories (out of 37), 'à moyen terme' in 23, with about a fifth of all occurrences in the European Central Bank speech genre (ecbfr), and 'à court terme' in 17, of which also about a fifth of all occurrences are in this same genre. A total of only 10, close to one in four, genres contain instances of all three locutions. This is surprising since it might be expected that the same type of text will use all three more consistently, as all are found in texts which set out projects for the future and guidelines as to the direction the Union might take.

In the corpus as a whole (FRADCO), there is a small amount of overlap between the collocates of each of the three locutions:

'à long terme':
moyen, taux, contrats, viabilité, court, politique, développement, perspective(s), effets, stabilité, stockage, création, économique(s)

'à moyen terme':
long, stabilité, budgétaire, perspectives, prix, programme, court, croissance, pacte, mesures, objectifs, politique, budget

'à court terme':
long, moyen, affectant, deséquilibres, écarts, heures, monétaire, œuvre

Each locution collocates with the other two. However, lists of decontextualised collocates reveal only part of the picture. 'A court terme' can be seen from a concordance to occur frequently with negative items. To put it differently, something which is only a short-term solution is not seen as very valuable, and things which are planned for the short term are often relatively negative, since a better solution in the long term often starts off as a regression compared with the original situation. There are texts which discuss the shrinking of the ozone layer in the short term, and a short-term imbalance in prices owing to such factors as price changes for raw materials. In the medium term, issues such as price stability and budgetary concerns appear most important. Long-term solutions are the ultimate goal because they lead to stability. At the same time, the wider context of the locution reveals problems that may arise in the long term which were not envisaged.

Looking at the collocates in each sub-corpus separately, the picture changes slightly:

'à long terme'
FREUCO: taux, moyen, contrats, viabilité, stabilité, stockage, clé, court, effets, économiques, commission, conseil, coopération
FRNACO: politique, cinq, moyen, équilibre

'à moyen terme'
FREUCO: stabilité, budgétaire, prix, croissance, programme, court, mesures, monétaire, pacte, politique, budget, communautaire, déficit, perspectives
FRNACO: court, formation, perspectives

'à court terme'
FREUCO: deséquilibres, monétaire
FRNACO: heures, supplémentaires

There are too few instances of 'à court terme' to enable generalisations to be drawn about the types of things which are envisaged or planned in the short term. In the medium term, it is the European Union discourse which is more concerned with budgetary issues and economic stability. The national French discourse appears more concerned with abstract plans, hopes, objectives and reform, although it too talks of medium-term economic issues. FRNACO has relatively few instances of 'à long terme' compared to FREUCO, but allowing for this quantitative difference, there seems to be little difference between the types of things which are planned or happen in the long term: employment issues, economic and financial issues, and political issues are all common.

8. The quantitative role of locutions in FRADCO

As with multiword sequences, it is difficult to give an accurate assessment of the proportion of the corpus which is made up of these locutions. Any attempt to calculate the proportion raises the issue of what exactly ought to be considered part of the locution, and the issue of variation within locutions. In addition, even if one were merely to calculate the mean number of words per locution based on the form of the locution as it appears in the *Dictionnaire*, there is also the issue of whether or not there is a correlation between the length of the locution and the number of tokens of that locution, as clearly it is the token count which is relevant here. A frequency-ordered list of locutions does suggest that there is a correlation, with the number of words in the locution increasing slightly as frequency decreases (that is to say, the more frequent locutions have an overall tendency to be shorter). Rosamund Moon too (1998a, p. 78) found a small corrrelation between frequency and length of the FEIs in her data: as frequency increases, the average number of words decreases. At the same time, however, the most frequent locution by far is above the mean. While this correlation may not be very revealing, therefore, it should not be completely overlooked.

In spite of all of these caveats, it is perhaps useful to make a rough estimate, in order to gauge the relative importance of the resources of general-language phraseological elements in the administrative corpus. Moon did not attempt to calculate this proportion, but estimated that between 4% and 5% of her corpus was made up of FEIs (1998a, p. 57). In the administrative corpus, there are 11,673 locution tokens. The overall average number of words per locution (based on types rather than tokens, and on the form of the locution in the *Dictionnaire*) is 3.39 words. Therefore, it can be calculated that around 39,600 words in the corpus are part of one of the locutions in the *Dictionnaire*. This represents around 1.87% of the total corpus. Of course, a larger proportion of the corpus will be made up of this type of locution, since, as was noted above, the *Dictionnaire* makes no pretensions to being exhaustive, and indeed a number of similar locutions were noted while searching for those contained in the dictionary. Thus, the disparity between the figure arrived at in this study and in Moon's could have resulted for a variety of reasons: the difficulty in arriving at a completely reliable estimate, or the fact that the focus here is on a smaller number of locutions and a smaller corpus: on the other hand, it may be a property of the register-specificity of this corpus.

9. Conclusions

The analysis carried out in this chapter has shown that a fairly small number of the locutions listed in Rey and Chantreau's *Dictionnaire des expressions et locutions* (1993) occur in the administrative corpus. Of these, the lower frequency locutions are of various types, including metaphorical, interpersonal and idiomatic: we cannot say that the register is entirely devoid of traditional idioms, although these play only a minor role, at least in quantitative terms, and their usage is concentrated in certain genres, notably speeches and press releases. Other locutions originated in legal or political contexts, and tend to be used in the corpus in their original, non-metaphorical sense. The higher frequency locutions tend to be grammatical in nature, and include complex prepositions, grammatical phrases, and discourse-structuring devices. These differ in their distribution between the two sub-corpora. The two discourses, of European Union French and national French administrative language, have been shown to draw on this phraseological resource to different extents and for subtly different purposes. Furthermore, the distribution of locutions differed both among genres, and also between the different modes covered by the corpus (written texts and those which have been written to be delivered orally). More detailed analyses were made of a particular genre, that of the Presidency Conclusions following European Council meetings, and of a set of three particular locutions, 'à long terme', 'à moyen terme' and 'à court terme'.

This approach clearly has shortcomings. By taking Rey and Chantreau's *Dictionnaire des expressions et locutions* as the source of locutions, discussion of such expressions has inevitably been limited to those contained in this dictionary:

an analysis of the corpus texts here reveals many more candidates for the status of a 'locution'. At the same time, the use of such a dictionary has the advantage of a ready-made list of prime candidates, and provided a point of contact with the general language, as it is represented by the collection of predominantly literary and journalistic texts used as the basis of the dictionary.

It is evident that more analysis could be carried out on this data. For example, a number of additional comparisons are possible: between other pairs of genres, between corpus genres and the comparator corpus. Also, more detailed analysis of individual locutions could prove insightful, and further investigation into the locutions employed by particular genres considered individually would certainly be enlightening. However, this analysis has contributed further to the picture of phraseology begun in Chapter 4, and indeed consolidated this picture. In terms of the phraseological resources of the general language to which the administrative register of French has recourse, the EU discourse can again be differentiated from its national counterpart. This is true at the level of the number and range of general language locutions employed, and at the level of the typical environment and function of individual sample locutions.

Chapter 6

The Phraseology of Keywords

My entire œuvre *seemed to be saturated in grease. I'd never realized I was so obsessed with the stuff.*

DAVID LODGE, SMALL WORLD: AN ACADEMIC ROMANCE

1. Introduction

Chapter 4 investigated phraseology which is the creation of those who use the particular discourse of administration; Chapter 5 examined the semantically and syntactically-defined phraseological resources of the general French which are employed by the administrative register. In each of these respects, the EU and national administrative discourses were found to differ. The sections of this chapter are connected by a focus on phraseological patterning which is the product of the corpus itself - that is to say, a statistical notion. The following sections are also linked through their concern with the collocational and phraseological patterning of individual words: administrative documents are not obsessed, like Frobisher in *Small World*, quoted after the title above, with grease, but some of the key words in the register, identified by computation rather than intuition, are just as surprising.

Chapter 2 discussed J. R. Firth's original notion of collocation and recent extensions to the concept, which, while they move beyond a strict notion of collocation, have produced many interesting and often unexpected findings, and have enabled collocation to become a central element in a more holistic conceptualisation of language. Michael Hoey has summarised the questions that can be asked of a word with regard to its patterning in text, and these are useful to bear in mind throughout this chapter:

> 1. What lexical patterns is it part of?
> 2. Is there any pattern of association of the word with other meanings?
> 3. What structure(s) does it appear in; i.e. what are its immediate colligations?
> 4. Is there any correlation between the word's uses/meanings and the structures in which it participates?
> 5. Is it associated with any (position in any) textual organisation; i.e. does it have any textual colligations? (Hoey 2000, p. 95)

Question one relates to the lexical environment of the word: that is to say, its collocations in Firth's own sense, and any idioms and terminological items of which it forms a part, whereas question two relates to the semantic environment of the word, including any discernible semantic prosody. While the theoretical distinction between the two questions is clear, in practice they are difficult to separate. With corpus evidence alone, it is not always straightforward to determine whether a word or phrase is indeed collocating with a meaning, or with a finite set of lexical items. Question three refers to the word's colligational or grammatical patterning, and question four to the relationship between pattern and meaning, following Hunston and Francis' demonstration that there is a strong correlation between the two (cf. 1999). Question five, finally, extends the examination to features of text and discourse.

Considered together, the questions investigate "actual words in habitual company" (Firth 1957c, p. 14): only question one, however, centres on the habitual lexical company of words. In the strict sense of the word, then, question one alone deals with collocation proper. The other four questions, however, seek to make additional features of the word's environment and phraseology more amenable to linguistic analysis. In this chapter, while the analysis is not restricted purely to question one, it is the lexical, i.e. collocational, environment of words which is the central focus.

The complete administrative corpus contains nearly 38,000 different word forms. Clearly, in order to analyse the patterning of individual words, a judicious selection is necessary. Each of the two main sections focuses on words which are 'key' by different definitions: a statistical definition and a sociological definition. Section 2 introduces the notion of statistical keywords, a concept which allows the corpus to speak for itself. Section 3 then deals with sociological keywords. The order taken here therefore parallels that taken in Chapters 4 and 5: in the first instance, the corpus provides the starting point for the analysis, and then areas which are likely to provide insights are targeted, from outside the corpus. The two sections further the analysis of Chapters 4 and 5, in seeking to differentiate the European Union and national discourses of administration through their phraseology: this is the descriptive goal of this study.

2. Statistical keywords

The statistical concept of keywords was developed by Mike Scott and a tool for their identification is part of WordSmith Tools:

> The purpose of this program is to locate and identify key words in a given text. To do so, it compares the words in the text with a reference set of words usually taken from a large corpus of text. Any word which is found to be outstanding in its frequency in the text is considered 'key'. (Scott 1999 - WordSmith Tools documentation)

This notion is closely mirrored in Michael Hoey's work on lexical patterns in text (cf. Hoey 1991). Keywords in Scott's sense, as the quotation above implies, need not be lexical words. Grammatical words can also appear as statistical keywords in a corpus, and very frequently do. Finally, while Scott's statistical keywords do not by definition differ in usage or collocational patterning among contexts, it transpires, however, that some do have strong patterns of collocation in the corpus, and that these can be different from their patterns in other registers, and can differ according to discourse or genre factors within the corpus. These are the focus of this section.

The Keywords facility of WordSmith Tools works by comparing wordlists compiled on the basis of the corpus in question and a specified reference corpus. There are therefore numerous possibilities for comparison using this method with FRADCO. It is possible to compare the two discourses with each other; the complete administrative corpus with* the comparator corpus; groups of related genres with others (such as speech genres with press releases); single genres with the whole corpus; or a single genre from one sub-corpus with the nearest equivalent genre in the other. Depending on the comparison made, different types of words in different proportions are shown to be key: names, nouns specific to the context, words which are part of formulae used in individual genres, adverbs and grammatical items.

Here I have concentrated on a comparison between, firstly, the complete administrative corpus and the comparator corpus (necessarily a tentative comparison), and secondly between the European Union and the French national halves of the administrative corpus. Reference is also made to the comparator corpus at certain points of the latter analysis, for example where the collocational behaviour of a particular word differs markedly between registers as well as between discourses. Appendix 5 contains keyword lists for three different comparisons: the complete administrative corpus (FRADCO) with reference to the comparator corpus; the EU sub-corpus (FREUCO) compared with the national sub-corpus (FRNACO) and, vice versa, FRNACO compared with FREUCO. For reasons of space, only the top 50 keywords for each are detailed.

It is notable that many of the keywords in the list for FREUCO compared with FRNACO also appear in the keyword list for the complete administrative corpus: this indicates that while a word may be key in the administrative corpus as compared to the 'general language', this may be due to a very high frequency of occurrence in a single part of the corpus, in this case the European Union discourse. Within the EU discourse, of course, the word may further owe its keyness to a single genre or group of genres. Comparing the three keyword lists in Appendix 5, it turns out that the following words are key in the register as a whole primarily because of their significance in FREUCO:

> article, Commission, membres, Conseil, européenne, Union, européen, directive, traité, paragraphe, communauté, règlement,

> mesures, euro, concernant, communautaire, conformément, UE, décision, présent, programme, membre, accord

Only one word, on the other hand, is key in the register primarily because of its significance in FRNACO: this is 'formation' ('training'). This shows once again that the European Union discourse has a higher proportion of words more or less specific to its context, and uses certain of these words very frequently. Below, also, are the words which are key in the administrative corpus as a whole, that is to say that their appearance in the keyword list of FRADCO against the comparator corpus is not due to their predominance in one or other discourse, but the two combined: these would seem therefore to have a special place in the administrative register as a whole. Many of these are grammatical words:

> des, l', la, dispositions, de, cadre, services,[69] les, coopération, mise, d', application, aux, développement, emploi, ou, conditions, procédure, du, niveau, notamment, accès, sécurité, information

In looking in more detail at a selection of these keywords below, each word is discussed in the context of the corpus or sub-corpus in which it is most key. The discussion of keywords in the full administrative corpus therefore concentrates on this final group of words.

2.1 Statistical keywords in FRADCO

If one looks at the keyword list for the administrative corpus compared with the more general comparator corpus, it can be seen that many of the top keywords do appear in the comparator corpus, although much less frequently. Indeed, there is only one word form in the top 50 keywords which does not appear at all in the comparator corpus: this is the abbreviation 'UE' (Union européenne). While the comparator corpus contains many references to the European Union, it does not abbreviate the name. These instances of 'UE' occur almost exclusively in the European Union part of the corpus (910 instances of the 912 in FRADCO): despite the fact that this abbreviation is so well-known, French national administrative texts tend to spell it out. Of the other keywords, some, primarily words concerning administrative institutions and legal instruments ('Commission', 'Conseil', 'dispositions', 'directive', 'traité', 'paragraphe', 'accord'), or words suggesting major policy areas or concerns ('emploi', 'développement', 'formation', 'sécurité', 'information') appear very infrequently compared to the administrative corpus, while others, often grammatical words, appear frequently in both corpora, but are still key in the administrative corpus as compared to the more general comparator corpus. Gledhill has pointed out that "Grammatical items appear to be excellent indicators of general phraseology, yet

69 The singular form 'service', however, is key in FRNACO.

they have not received as much attention in general lexicology or corpus linguistics as their lexical counterparts" (2000, p. 73). From the point of view of collocation, one can look in more detail at the words with the highest degree of 'keyness' (in FRADCO, these are both grammatical and lexical), and those whose keyness in a particular corpus may be counterintuitive.

Given the common appearance of 'état(s)' in the multiword sequences identified in Chapter 4, it is perhaps not surprising that its frequent collocate 'membre(s)' should appear in the keyword list. One might want to see, however, with what else 'membre' collocates in both the administrative register and the comparator corpus. In the latter, the keyword and its plural form occur overwhelmingly in the journalistic texts, although in the other parts of the comparator corpus it collocates with a number of organisations and bodies, such as 'Académie', 'Corps', 'Conseil d'état', 'Chambre', 'Institut' etc. In the corpus as a whole, it is to be found in the environment of a number of similar words, although mostly contemporary administrative bodies, such as 'comité', 'Conseil', 'bureau' and 'secrétariat'. It is only rarely used adjectivally, and when it is it collocates with 'état(s)', 'pays', and 'consommateurs'. In FRADCO on the other hand, just as 'état' collocates overwhelmingly with 'membre', so the reverse is true: three quarters of the instances of 'membre(s)' form part of 'état(s) membre(s)'. 'Pays membres' is much less frequent but does occur, often to refer to member states of organisations other than the European Union. As an adjective, it is also to be found with 'communes' (in FRNACO only), and very rarely 'habitants', 'candidats' and 'personnalité'. As a noun, it collocates in particular with numbers, the names of bodies and organisations and in apposition with the names of individuals (as in 'M. Bangemann, membre de la Commission').

Similarly, given the discussion in Chapter 5, it is not a surprise that 'cadre' is also to be found high in the keyword list. In FRADCO, it is part of the collocations 'dans le cadre de', 'dans un cadre + ADJ' and 'dans ce cadre': these account for around 70% of the instances of 'cadre'. In L1 position, the first word to the left of the node word, 'programme' ('programme-cadre' - 'framework programme'), 'nouveau' and 'accord' ('accord-cadre' - 'framework agreement') are the most frequent lexical items. In the comparator corpus, these collocations only account for 45% of the instances of 'cadre'. Another frequent collocation is 'hors cadre' ('seconded', 'detached' or 'unclassified'), especially in the expression 'préfet hors cadre'.

The fact of appearing in a keyword list for a particular corpus does not mean that a word is necessarily either specific to a particular context, or that it is used in a notably different way in that context. Some words merely occur in the corpus with a greater frequency than in the reference corpus against which it is compared. 'Niveau' ('level') is a case in point. In both the comparator corpus and the administrative corpus, it collocates with the same adjectives of degree: 'haut', 'bas' and 'élevé'. However, it is evident from the relative occurrences that things are referred to more in terms of rates and levels, whether rising or falling or being maintained over time, in the administrative corpus. The keyword is also very commonly followed by an adjective indicating the scope of an initiative, law, policy, etc., with such adjectives as 'européen', 'national', 'international', 'global', 'local', 'mondial'. This type of collocation is much less frequent in the comparator corpus, although some examples do exist. Much more typical of this corpus are instances of 'niveau' used to indicate a standard or level, as in 'niveau de vie' ('standard of living').

In the comparator corpus, 'coopération' occurs only in the journalistic texts. 'Coopération' may take place in various contexts, particularly economic, scientific, industrial and technological, and it may be international, bilateral or between specific areas ('Nord-Sud', 'entre le Nord et le Sud'), or individual nations ('américano-nippon', 'entre la France et la RFA'). Often only a single nation is mentioned explicitly, with France understood to be the other party. Cooperation is something desirable: 'la poursuite d'une coopération étroite', 'le maintien de bonnes relations de coopération', and something which one seeks to increase: 'accroître/élargir leur coopération'. France even has of course a 'Ministre de la coopération et du développement'. In the administrative corpus, there are a number of very frequent collocations, including 'accord(s) de coopération' and 'établissement public de coopération intercommunale'. Again, cooperation is presented as desirable: it has a positive prosody from its collocation with verbs like 'favoriser', 'intensifier', 'promouvoir', 'renforcer', 'stimuler' and 'améliorer'. As in the comparator corpus, the collocates of the keyword show that cooperation occurs in a wide range of areas: 'douanière', 'policière', 'scientifique', 'culturelle', 'judiciaire', 'au développement', and at various levels: 'régionale', 'intercommunale', 'internationale', between the European Union and other groups of nations.

There are a number of strong patterns of collocation in the environment of the keyword 'développement': it collocates, firstly, with words indicating the encouragement given to development in the administrative context: especially the verbs 'stimuler', 'promouvoir', 'favoriser' and the nouns 'coopération (au développement)', 'appui (au)', 'aide (politique au)'. Development is ideally 'durable' and 'harmonieux', and often presented as 'nouveau', which shows that it is considered from its starting point (an initiative taken or plans to concentrate on a particular area), rather than as a change in progress, although there is some reference to time frames, with the fixed expressions 'à long/moyen/court terme' often occurring in the environment of the keyword. There is also evidence of a large number of strategies, programmes and projects which have in view the development of certain areas of responsibility. Like 'coopération', development can be seen therefore to have a positive prosody. There is no reason why, for example, a doctor should not monitor the development of a disease, but neither corpus contains evidence of such negative usages. For a country to be 'en développement' comes across as positive, by emphasising the progress made towards development rather than the current underdevelopment.

In some cases, the keyness of a word with relation to the comparator corpus stems primarily from a small number of very frequent collocations. This is the case with 'information', over a third of the occurrences of which are accounted for by the collocations 'société de l'information', 'technologies de l'information' and 'système(s) de l'information'.

As was mentioned above, the keyword list for FRADCO contains grammatical as well as lexical words. All of these are key in the administrative corpus as a whole, that is to say that their appearance in the FRADCO keyword list is not due to their highly frequent occurrence in either of the sub-corpora individually. 'Des' is the most key grammatical word form in the corpus, with over 50,000 occurrences, as both the fusion of 'de' and the plural definite article, and the plural indefinite article. The definite article appears in the keyword list in five other forms: the feminine singular form 'la', the abbreviated form which precedes a vowel 'l'', the plural 'les' and its fused form when preceded by the preposition 'à': 'aux', and finally, 'du', the form produced by the fusion of 'de + le', and also a partitive article.

The coordinating conjunction 'ou' ('or') occurs around twice as frequently in FRADCO as in the similarly sized comparator corpus. A detailed analysis of the differences in usage of this individual word, which occurs nearly 8,500 times, in the two corpora, is beyond the scope of this study, where the aim is to give a more general picture. Let it suffice here to mention that 'ou' forms part of a number of repeated phrases in the administrative corpus, including 'Chefs d'état ou de gouvernement' and 'langues/cultures régionales ou minoritaires', and that in the comparator corpus its occurrence with the succeeding adverbs 'bien', 'même' and 'plutôt' ('or rather', 'or even') is notable compared with the administrative corpus in which these constructions are used very infrequently.

A number of other keywords can be placed more towards the grammatical end of the lexicogrammatical continuum, but are not purely grammatical words. 'Mise' owes its keyness to its part in a number of phrasal nouns: 'mise au point', 'mise à disposition', 'mise à jour' and especially 'mise en œuvre' and 'mise en place', which also occur in the comparator corpus but with lower frequencies. These appear to be one of the resources of the French language which the administrative register draws upon to the greatest extent. The adverb 'notamment' is also key in the administrative corpus: it is frequently followed by a set phrase indicating context, such as 'dans le cadre / domaine de', 'en ce qui concerne' and 'en matière de', and also by precise reference to an article of a piece of legislation, as in 'vu le traité instituant la Communauté européenne, et notamment son article 43' (from both the C and L Series of the *Journal Officiel*).

2.2 Statistical keywords in FREUCO

A large number of the top 50 keywords in FREUCO can be seen through intuition to have a particular importance in the European Union context (such as 'Bruxelles', 'Union', 'communauté' and its derived adjective 'communautaire', 'euro', 'Commission', 'traité'), or to have special meanings or specific reference in this context ('écus', 'Conseil', 'paragraphe' [in legislation]). Looking at the statistics too, the top key words in FREUCO have a greater combined frequency than those in FRNACO,[70] and these keywords are less likely to appear in the other sub-corpus.[71] The European Union keywords are on average more specific to their particular discourse than are the French national ones.

It is notable that there are no grammatical words in FREUCO's top 50 keywords: the most 'key' grammatical word is the feminine definite article 'la' in sixty-fourth place, which owes its keyness to the sheer frequency of reference to 'la Commission' in the EU sub-corpus. There are, however, a number of abbreviations: 'UE' ('Union européenne'); 'CEE' ('Communauté économique européenne', the EU's predecessor, formed by the Treaty of Rome); 'DN' ('document number': the English abbreviation is used in all language versions of documents); 'AOP' ('protection des appellations d'origine': all of the instances of this are to be found in a single text, a Commission press release approving an EU symbol for designations of origin and geographical indications for agricultural products); 'JO' ('Journal Officiel'); 'IP' (a handful of the occurrences of this refer to a computer's IP [i.e. Internet Protocol] address, but the vast majority form part of the document number of Commission press releases); and 'AFF' ('affaires': all of the instances of this occur in the Bulletin of the European Court of Justice documents, where it occurs as part of the reference number of particular cases). Apart from 'JO', which is used in the French national sub-corpus to refer to the French *Journal Officiel*, all of these abbreviations are very infrequent, or even in some cases non-existent, in FRNACO.

Many of the keywords form part of legal formulae: 'considérant', used as a recital giving factual information in a treaty; 'concernant', introducing the area of interest of a directive etc., such as in 'la directive 94/67/CE concernant l'incinération des déchets dangereux'; 'conformément', translated in the European Communities Glossary (1990) as 'as provided for in...' or 'in accordance with...', a previous piece of legislation, agreement or procedure;

---

70 66,459 occurrences compared with 55,349 in the FRNACO keyword list.

71 The combined occurrences of FREUCO's top 50 keywords in FRNACO is 13,425, whereas the combined occurrences of FRNACO's top 50 keywords in FREUCO is 21,036.

'instituant', 'establishing', particularly in 'traité instituant la Communauté européenne'; and 'statuant', 'acting', particularly in 'le Conseil, statuant à l'unanimité' ('acting unanimously'), 'statuant à la majorité qualifiée' ('acting by a qualified majority'), and 'statuant conformément à la procédure visée à l'article # [number]'.

The two sub-corpora have very similar patterns of collocation for the keyword 'marché' ('market'). These include: 'marché' followed by an adjective of a nation or group of nations (e.g. 'marché britannique', 'marché européen'), 'marché commun', 'marché communautaire', 'marché unique', 'marché intérieur', and particular market areas, 'de l'emploi' and more commonly 'du travail' and such collocations as 'marché monétaire / financier / des transports'. Surprisingly, the comparator corpus contains nearly three times as many instances of 'marché' as FRNACO. This is entirely due to the journalistic texts once again, where collocations like those listed above are common. In the other registers the form 'marché' is more frequently the past participle of the verb 'marcher', except in the expression 'bon marché'.

For 'mesures' also, the patterns of collocation are similar over the two sub-corpora, although the EU sub-corpus uses the word around two and a half times as frequently as the national sub-corpus. In both corpora, 'mesures' are talked about in groups: 'une série de mesures', 'une campagne de mesures', 'un ensemble de mesures'; but in the national sub-corpus also there is a strong tendency to talk about individual measures, especially in the formulae: 'le Conseil des Ministres a adopté les mesures individuelles suivantes' and 'ont été adoptées diverses mesures d'ordre individuel relatives à...'. Two principal verbs collocate with the keyword: 'prendre' and 'adopter'. The latter, 'adopter des mesures' ('introduce measures') and 'adopter une mesure', including all forms of the verb, has a strong tendency to occur towards the end of individual texts where it implies agreement, while 'prendre une/des mesure(s)' is distributed evenly throughout the texts and implies action taken. Measures appear to be 'adoptées' particularly in summaries, even when they have been 'prises' throughout the text.

2.3 Statistical keywords in FRNACO

Turning to the equivalent keyword list for the French national sub-corpus compared with the EU sub-corpus, a glance at the list suggests that a larger proportion of the keywords are not specific to the discourse in question, although many turn out to be used in distinct ways or with specific meanings in the discourse. However, despite the words themselves appearing to be more general in usage, there are still of course a number of words key in FRNACO which do not occur at all in FREUCO, referring as they do to organisations and bodies which are particular to the French context: these are 'gendarmerie', 'sénat', 'intercommunale', 'interministéri+', covering all forms of the adjective 'interministériel'.[72] Alongside a number of words which clearly have an importance in administrative language, whether in a French context particularly or more generally, such as 'loi',[73] 'ministère', 'ministre', 'décret', 'département(s)', there are many word of more general reference, including 'France', 'français(e)', 'femmes', 'ville', 'art', 'enfant', 'temps', 'parents', 'heures', 'travail' and 'continue'.[74] While in FREUCO there are a number of abbreviations among the statistical keywords, in FRNACO's top 50 keywords there is only one abbreviation: this is 'M.', standing for the title 'Monsieur'.

It is notable that there are a number of more grammatical words among the keywords of this sub-corpus. In addition to the third person singular form of the verb 'être', which occurs around 40% more frequently in FRNACO than FREUCO (see also Chapter 7), there are a number of personal pronouns: 'vous', 'on', 'il' and 'nous'; and the first person plural possessive adjective 'notre'. This is in part due to the inclusion of a transcribed meeting of the Assemblée Nationale, but even disregarding the presence of this text in the corpus, there is a significant difference in this regard between the two sub-corpora. The national sub-corpus appears also to appeal more, using 'vous', to the reader or audience of a text. First person plural possessive adjectives, especially in 'notre pays', 'notre patrimoine', 'notre culture', 'notre objectif commun', and even 'notre France', in FRNACO appeal to the reader or listener's sense of national pride, inviting cooperation and a sense of common purpose.

Here a number of the lexical keywords are discussed in more detail. First of all, it is notable that there are several keywords referring to people, grouped according to natural or socially-imposed criteria: 'femmes', 'familles', 'parents', 'enfant'[75] and 'élèves'.

---

72 WordList in WordSmith Tools is set to truncate word forms with more than 14 characters.

73 It may appear surprising that 'loi' should be by such a long way the most key word-form in FRNACO, given that laws are clearly important in both contexts. This is explained by the fact that the European Union does not use the word 'loi' for its legislative acts, but rather 'règlement', 'directive' and 'décision', depending on the applicability of the piece of legislation (see also footnotes in Appendix 1).

74 'Continue' owes its presence in the keyword list primarily to its use as an adjective in the collocation 'formation continue' ('life-long learning').

75 The plural form 'enfants' is less key in FRNACO. The singular form in FRNACO is key because of its use in such expressions as 'à tout enfant' (as in 'information accessible à tout enfant'), 'le droit de l'enfant', 'les besoins de l'enfant', where the singular is used collectively. This usage is extremely rare in FREUCO.

'Femmes' in both sub-corpora are mentioned primarily with respect to rights and careers: 'droits des femmes', 'égalité (des chances) entre les femmes et les hommes / entre les hommes et les femmes', 'les femmes dans la vie professionnelle / dans la fonction publique / dans les emplois'. In addition, in FREUCO there is much reference to violence towards women, among other 'vulnerable' groups, whereas in FRNACO nearly a quarter of the instances of 'femmes' appear in a co-text which makes direct reference to figures, proportions, and changes in these: 'les femmes représentent 57%', 'le nombre de femmes a doublé / est particulièrement élevé', 'la proportion d'hommes et de femmes...', 'le taux des femmes'. Taken together, the examples show a keenness to report cases, in administration or in business, where proportions or numbers of women employees have reached or exceeded a level of equality. The national French sub-corpus also gives evidence of 'femmes' qualifying another noun: 'les femmes cadres', 'les femmes candidats' and 'les femmes fonctionnaires', which do not occur at all in FREUCO.

Michael Stubbs finds in his data that the keyword 'family' occurs in collocations which indicate an important change in social structure, such as 'single-parent families'. 'Familles' is statistically important in FRNACO, with 430 occurrences, but is very infrequent in FREUCO, with only 19 occurrences, 17 of which appear in Commission Press Releases. While in FREUCO the families referred to are almost exclusively outside Europe, in troubled areas such as Bosnia, Afghanistan and the Balkans, in FRNACO, the families tend to be French. In both sub-corpora, however, there is a strong prosody of 'aid' in the environment of the keyword. The European Union documents' concern is with the repatriation of families, the reunification of people (such as refugees) with their families, and food aid to families in need. In FRNACO, while such concerns are present, the majority of examples bear on financial aid ('allocations familiales', 'soutien' and 'transferts financiers vers les familles') to poorer French families ('les familles les plus défavorisées/démunies/pauvres/modestes/qui ont le plus de difficultés'). Families are also shown to be important for the part they play in education: this is another role which does not appear in FREUCO.

'Parents', similarly, are infrequently mentioned in FREUCO (only 16 occurrences, in only 6 different documents, compared with 299 occurrences in FRNACO). Here, they are most commonly considered in relation to 'enseignants' or 'éducateurs', for the role they have to play in a child's education. In FRNACO there are clear patterns: 'parents' collocates frequently with 'enfants' (and 'bébés'), and with 'élèves', with parents having an important role to play from birth, through school, when 'parents' appears in the collocation 'parents d'élèves' (usually translated simply as 'parents' in English, with their role in the child's education not lexicalised), and beyond, when there may be 'une rupture avec [les] parents'. Throughout, they have a level of responsibility towards their children, which is highlighted repeatedly in the concordances.

It is perhaps not surprising that 'enfant' should also be infrequent in FREUCO: here it occurs only 5 times, compared with 290 in FRNACO. While it is impossible to indicate any typical collocates on the basis of a handful of occurrences, it can be seen that the keyword appears to occur in the context of rights and the protection provided in law for children. This is true also for FRNACO, which, despite many more occurrences of 'enfant', has few frequently repeated expressions containing the keyword, and few frequent collocates. The most common environment of the word concerns children's rights: 'l'enfant a droit à la protection de la loi / à la liberté d'expression / à l'éducation'. 'Élèves', on the other hand, understandably, occurs primarily in the context of education, in FREUCO referring to school pupils, and in FRNACO referring in addition to pupils and former pupils of 'conservatoires' and 'l'ÉNA'.

Finally, it is revealing to take a closer look at a couple of very general, unrelated, words which appear in the keyword list. These are 'ville' and 'temps' (usually meaning 'time', but used in many set expressions). 'Ville' in FREUCO is used only 24 times, a third of which are references to the European City of Culture ('capitale européenne de la culture'). Of the other instances, several refer to 'la ville de demain', a common theme in the context of urban transport systems and the protection of the environment. The others tend to be references to particular towns: 'la ville de Bonn / Vienne / Saint-Petersburg / Rennes' etc. In the French national context, which has nearly twenty times as many occurrences of the keyword, there is evidence of 'la politique de la ville', with its main concerns for employment, safety and education, carried out by means of detailed 'contrats de ville', being a much more important level of concern, and this is not due just to the existence of a 'Ministre délégué à la ville' and a 'Délégation interministérielle à la ville'. Towns are important in many respects, for example from the point of view of public transport (particularly with the annual 'journée "en ville sans ma voiture?"'), and even information technology, with the introduction of various urban intranet systems. 'Ville' also occurs, as in FREUCO, as a collocate of individual towns: 'la ville d'Issy-les-Moulineaux / Besançon / Saint-Etienne'.

The reason for the keyness of such a common word as 'temps' in FRNACO, where it occurs 1,190 times, over twice its frequency in FREUCO, is revealing. Both sub-corpora contain instances of the keyword in such expressions as 'ces derniers temps', 'entre-temps', 'en même temps', 'dans un premier temps', 'en temps voulu', 'la plupart du temps', as well as part of the lexical item 'emploi du temps'. The principal difference between the two discourses appears to be merely one of frequency of occurrence. While both the EU and the French national sides of the corpus use 'temps' very frequently in a number of expressions relating to work and employment, this is a more common concern of FRNACO. These expressions include: 'le temps de travail', and a number of expansions, 'directive sur le temps de travail', 'aménagement du temps de travail', 'réduction du temps de travail', and several common expressions also related to working hours: 'à temps partiel' and 'à temps complet / plein', all of which are very frequent in both corpora.

3. Sociological keywords

Sociological keywords are noted as a source of useful linguistic information by J. R. Firth in *The Technique of Semantics* (1935). Here, Firth reveals that "research into the detailed contextual distribution of sociologically important words, what one might call *focal* or *pivotal* words, is only just beginning" (Firth 1935, p. 10, the emphasis is Firth's). He goes on to indicate types of word which are linguistically interesting:

> The study of such words as *work, labour, trade, employ, occupy, play, leisure, time, hours, means, self-respect* in all their derivatives and compounds in sociologically significant contexts during the last twenty years would be quite enlightening. So would the study of words particularly associated with the dress, occupations, and ambitions of women, or the language of advertising, especially of quackery, entertainments, food, drink, or of political movements and propaganda. (*ibid*., p. 13)

Raymond Williams, in his well-known work on *Keywords* (1976, 1988) put some of Firth's ideas into practice,[76] although with a focus that was more social than linguistic, and more diachronic than synchronic. He explains that his interest was sparked by the realisation that the word 'culture' is important in the two separate domains of art and society. This led him to investigate other words which he also found to be key in more than one field (1976, p. 12). *Keywords* contains short essays on more than a hundred words, from 'aesthetic' to 'work'. His discussion of 'bureaucracy', for example, traces the different uses and connotations of the word from its origin in French to its contemporary importance. Mike Scott has explained the difference between his own statistical notion and Williams': for Williams a keyword is significant at the level of the context of culture, which Scott terms level 9 in his schema. Scott's keywords, on the other hand, are significant at level 6, the level of the text (Scott 1997b, p. 246 footnote).

Michael Stubbs has recently applied corpus linguistics to the study of English keywords, illustrating how such analysis could be carried out with the aid of computer technology, and with particular reference to collocation. He claims that:

> To talk repeatedly of education in terms of *falling standards* or *trendy teachers*, or to talk of employment in terms of *job losses, cheap*

---

76 Stubbs (1996, p. 166) claims, however, that Williams was not familiar with Firth's work.

> *labour* or *unemployment blackspots*, is to maintain familiar and limited sets of categories and metaphors for talking and thinking about the social world. Since such repeated collocations are simply used, as part of our habitual ways of talking, their connotations are not made explicit, are difficult to question and can seem merely natural. (Stubbs 1996, p. 194)

Stubbs discusses around forty keywords himself, in particular words concerning issues in contemporary society: these include 'class', 'work', 'labour', 'unemployment', 'care', 'national', 'Scottish', 'intellectual' and 'public' (see also Hunston 1999a, Piper 1999, Sealey 1999, Musolff 1996 for similar work).

The notion of sociological keywords is familiar in French research too, although there is no direct equivalent of Raymond Williams' *Keywords* for French. Benveniste (1966) contains a chapter-length discussion of the word 'civilisation', and he notes that "Toute l'histoire de la pensée moderne et les principaux achèvements de la culture intellectuelle dans le monde occidental sont liés à la création et au maniement de quelques dizaines de mots essentiels" (Benveniste 1966, p. 336). In the context of lexicology, Georges Matoré initiated 'la lexicologie' in 1953 (cf. Matoré 1953, 1988, and discussion in Picoche 1992, Posner 1997, Wise 1997). Matoré describes his work as "un examen conjugué du vocabulaire et de la civilisation dont ce vocabulaire est l'expression" (Matoré 1988, p. 14), and as such he identifies keywords which designate an important idea or notion in a particular age, such as feudal times, the Renaissance and the classical age.

Thody and Evans' *Faux Amis and Key Words* (1985) is perhaps the closest equivalent to Raymond Williams' *Keywords*, although entries are shorter and focus on contemporary usage rather than diachronic change. As the title suggests, they emphasise the relation between *faux amis*, often cognate forms, and keywords, as many of the entries have been selected on the basis of their surface similarity to English words.

This section takes a number of keywords, selected for their importance in the context of administration, and investigates their phraseology. Given the nature of keywords, in particular the fact that they are used in more than one context, one might expect their usage not to be dominated by a few very frequent patterns or collocations. Although the focus is primarily on their lexical environment, and where relevant, patterns of association with features of meaning, some attention is also lent to other features of the immediate environment of the word where this is noteworthy. In carrying out the analysis, patterns of distribution within the corpus are taken into consideration, especially between the European Union and national texts, but also highlighting strong genre biases. Cautious comparisons are also drawn with the more general comparator corpus. Space unfortunately requires that we must limit ourselves to two sets of keywords – keywords related to the notion of 'society' and keywords in the particular area of 'employment'. Distinctive patterning between the two discourses can also be found for words in such areas as development and change, and culture.

3.1 Society

The first group of related keywords are all concerned with society. It is interesting to see how the two discourses conceive of the areas within their administration, and the collocational differences and similarities between discourses. The keywords discussed here are 'communauté', 'société', 'régional', 'civilisation', 'tradition', and the triplet 'nation', 'pays' and 'état'.

3.1.1 'Communauté'

'Communauté' and its plural form occur a total of 2,694 times in FRADCO, with around two thirds of these occurrences in the European Union sub-corpus. This can be explained principally by the high frequency of references to 'la Communauté européenne' itself. Within FRNACO it is particularly frequent in the Assemblée Nationale draft legislation genre, and in the speeches. In FREUCO also it is most frequent in genres of a legal nature, such as the treaties, the Official Journal genres, and the bulletin of the European Court of Justice.

Both Williams and Stubbs deal with the English keyword 'community'. Williams points out that "it seems never to be used unfavourably, and never to be given any positive opposing or distinguishing term" (1988, p. 76). Stubbs contradicts this, citing the example of 'community charge' which in the late 1980s in the United Kingdom acquired a negative prosody. Other common collocations from his data, however, such as 'community values', emphasise the predominantly positive prosody of the word. Neither 'charge' nor 'values' collocates with 'community' in an English equivalent of FREUCO. It is not surprising that the collocation 'community charge' does not occur, given both the time frame of the corpus and its supranational character.

Many of the most frequent collocates in the two sub-corpora are in fact part of multiword sequences as discussed in Chapter 4. These are easy to locate using the 'Collocate' facility of WordSmith Tools, which ranks the most frequent collocates in each position around the node word (L1, R3 etc). Those frequent collocates which appear exclusively or almost exclusively in a single position in relation to the keyword are often part of a multiword sequence. For the keyword 'communauté' these include 'traité instituant la communauté européenne' (the formal name of the Treaty of Rome) and 'publication au journal officiel des communautés européennes'.

As regards discourse-based differences in the collocations which 'communauté' enters into, the word appears in very different contexts in the two sub-corpora. In FREUCO, the most frequent lexical collocates are: 'européenne' and its plural form, 'traité', 'instituant' (see above), 'membres' (usually as part of 'états membres'), 'article' and 'Commission'. In FRNACO, on the other hand, the adjective 'européenne' is only the thirty-first most frequent collocate, coming below such lexical items as 'communes' ('la communauté des communes'), 'urbaine(s)', 'Conseil', 'nouvelle', 'internationales' and 'villes' ('la communauté des villes'). These collocates are all fairly rare in FREUCO: where 'communes' only collocates with 'communauté' three times, and 'urbaine' does not collocate with it at all.

The comparator corpus contains nearly four hundred occurrences of the keyword, all but seven of which appear in journalistic texts, and here often in the context of the European Community. 'Communauté' also collocates with a number of adjectives denoting particular groups of society, such as 'juive', 'musulmane', 'religieuse', 'chiite', 'islamique', and 'scientifique', 'économique' and 'financière'.

'Communauté' differs considerably in its collocational patterns according to context. Its important role in European Union discourse means that it is particularly frequent in this discourse, especially in genres of a legal nature which commonly refer to treaties and institutions and also contain frequently repeated multiword sequences and formulae. In FREUCO, reference is made much less commonly to the European Community, but rather to groups smaller than nations, such as towns, working together. The comparator corpus, in addition to a large number of references to the European Community in the journalistic texts, uses the keyword with a variety of adjectives to designate groups with common interests, whether religious, social or economic, or adjectives of nationality

3.1.2 'Société'

Raymond Williams (1988) notes that 'society' in English refers both to the body of institutions and relationships within which large groups of people live, and also to the conditions in which such institutions and relationships are formed. Both of these meanings are represented in the French administrative corpus. 'Société' and its plural are slightly more frequent in FREUCO than FRNACO (759 occurrences as compared with 537). There is a certain amount of overlap in the most frequent collocates of the keyword: in FREUCO, the top lexical collocates are 'information' (in 'société de l'information'), 'gestion' (also in R2 position, that is, the second word to the right of the node), 'civile' and 'européenne'; in FRNACO on the other hand, the top collocates betray the texts' concern with French society specifically: in addition to 'information', and 'civile', which are important in both sub-corpora, the most frequent collocates are 'notre', 'France' and 'française'. It is rarely part of the phrase 'société anonyme' spelt out fully (there are only six instances), but there are thirty-three examples of the acronym 'S.A.', twenty-nine in FREUCO, overwhelmingly in the Bulletin of the Court of Justice and Commission Press Release genres, in the context of legal cases between private companies and the Commission. Otherwise, there is no strong bias as regards genre tendencies for the keyword.

3.1.3 'Régional'

For Williams, the context of the English word 'regional' tends to polarise: it can have either a positive or a negative semantic prosody, but is rarely neutral. In such collocations as 'regional accent', he claims it implies something subordinate or inferior, whereas in relation to cuisine or architecture, for example, it represents a valuable distinctive counter-movement. In the administrative corpus, as indeed in the comparator corpus, the keyword is used exclusively in a positive or neutral sense. Unlike 'communauté' and 'société' above, 'régional' and its inflected forms appear roughly twice as frequently in the French national sub-corpus as in the EU sub-corpus, and within the national sub-corpus they are particularly frequent in reports and speeches. The most frequent collocates in FRNACO are closer to those of the comparator corpus than the EU sub-corpus: these include 'conseil' ('Conseil régional') and 'conseiller'. 'Conseil' as a collocate appears only once in the whole of the EU sub-corpus. In addition, FRNACO places a strong emphasis on 'langues régionales' (often in the context of the promotion or teaching of regional and minority languages, not explicitly regarded as inferior, just previously overlooked), 'cultures régionales', and 'développement régional', in the light of the decentralisation of the 1980s. The EU sub-corpus, on the other hand, lexicalises 'régional' as one of the levels at which processes, such as 'intégration économique', 'coopération' and 'développement', happen. Frequent clusters include 'à finalité régionale' and 'au niveau régional'.

3.1.4 'Civilisation'

Benveniste's discussion of 'civilisation', as was mentioned above, concentrates on the description of the word from a diachronic perspective. Williams also traces the changing meanings of the word. He comments that in modern English, the word "attracts some defining adjective" (Williams 1988, p. 59) and has become relatively neutral, although it retains a certain normative quality: he lists such collocations as 'Western civilization', 'modern civilization', and 'industrial civilization'. Comparing this with its use in current administrative language, the word occurs only 40 times in the administrative corpus, 6 times in FREUCO and 34 times in FRNACO, especially in the speech genres. Fourteen of the instances are of the plural form 'civilisations'. Apart from three instances in the EU sub-corpus of 'civilisation européenne', which does not occur as a collocation in FRNACO, and one each in FRNACO of 'civilisation moderne', 'civilisation omeyyade' and 'civilisation occidentale', the word does not attract defining adjectives in the corpus. The comparator corpus contains a much higher proportion of 'civilisation' with a defining adjective or 'de + noun' fulfilling the same function. These include: 'civilisation(s)' 'chinoise', 'occidentale', 'de Byzance', 'de l'Europe', 'humaine', 'indo-iranienne', 'françaises', 'ancestrale', 'des Africains', 'urbaine'. Only 'civilisation occidentale' occurs more than once, which suggests that while 'civilisation' followed by an adjective is a common pattern in this corpus, there is no evidence of there being a bias towards individual adjectives. It appears in the environment of a meaning rather than entering into a pattern with a limited set of lexical items.

The equivalent English EU corpus contains only four instances of 'civilisation' (or 'civilization') or the plural form: all four cases occurring in parallel translation. That is, the French word is in all cases translated here by the English cognate. The other two instances of 'civilisation' in FREUCO are in the Commission Speeches genre, which do not have parallel versions in French, and this figure is too low to give any insights.

3.1.5 'Tradition'

'Tradition' / 'traditions', like 'régional' above, is much more frequent in the French national sub-corpus, especially in the speech genres. In this sub-corpus the keyword has a more consistently positive prosody, which collocates such as 'valeurs', 'ancienne' and 'patrimoine' support. There is, as is to be expected, much reference to specifically French tradition and heritage. The corpus also contains examples of 'tradition' with its related meaning of 'practice', such as 'une tradition de tolérance', 'une tradition d'échanges', where the prosody appears more neutral. This is a common use of the keyword in the EU sub-corpus too, where the most frequent lexical collocates are 'membres', and 'résultent' (in the sequence 'sauvegarde des droits de l'homme et des libertés fondamentales et tels qu'ils résultent de traditions constitutionnelles des États membres'). There are few repeated collocations, since 'tradition' occurs only 26 times in the EU sub-corpus, but individual collocations taken together show a neutral prosody for the word: these include 'une tradition d'autogestion', 'tradition de coopération transfrontalière', 'tradition de recherche en biologie moléculaire' and 'tradition démocratique'. Where the EU sub-corpus uses 'tradition' in the sense of cultural heritage, the reference is usually to traditions at a particular level (local, national), but the nation in question is not specified.

The comparator corpus uses the keyword more than twice as often as the national sub-corpus; by far the majority of instances occur in journalism. Once again, however, there are very few repeated lexical collocates: the only three in the top 50 collocates are 'pays', 'respect' and 'Dieu'. It is more informative to look at the semantic groupings of the collocates: particularly common in this corpus are adjectives of origin: 'viennoise', 'montmartroise', 'portugaise', 'françaises', 'occidentales'; of political adhesion: 'les gouvernements à tradition populiste', 'républicaine', 'absolutiste', 'colbertiste'; and of religious belief: 'spirituelle', 'chrétienne', 'catholique', 'pluriséculaire' and 'coranique'.

3.1.6 'Nation' / 'pays' / 'état'

Finally, this section looks at a number of overlapping synonyms, all items which may translate 'country', but each with different emphasis or status. Concordances were drawn up for each of 'nation', 'pays' and 'état' in the comparator corpus and the two sub-corpora of FRADCO, and also for the three English equivalents 'nation', 'country' and 'state' in the English EU corpus.

Stubbs has analysed the English word 'nation'. He finds that it collocates with adjectives revealing the categories in which nations are discussed, such as 'industrialized' and 'wealthiest'. 'Nationalist', on the other hand, has a strongly negative prosody. This is true also of the administrative register - there are very few instances of 'nationaliste(s)' in the corpus, which in itself is perhaps telling, but the collocates of those that do occur include 'xénophobe', 'fièvre' and 'sentiments exacerbés'. Williams discusses 'country' as a keyword, and finds that it has a more positive association than either 'nation' or 'state', perhaps in part because of its dual meaning of a native land and its rural areas. He claims that: "*Country* habitually includes the people who live in it, while *nation* is more abstract and *state* carries a sense of the structure of power." (1988, p. 81). The collocational patterns around the three more or less equivalent French words, 'nation', 'pays' and 'état', reveal that there are roughly parallel distinctions made in French, although there are differences between the more general comparator corpus and the administrative corpus compiled for this study.

Each of the two sub-corpora uses all of the three keywords to different extents. 'Nation', which occurs around 440 times in the administrative corpus, is around twice as frequent in the national French side of the corpus; 'pays', which occurs over 3,000 times in total, is around twice as frequent in the European Union sub-corpus; and in the case of 'état', by far the most frequent of the three keywords with over 8,000 occurrences, almost 70% of these occurrences are in the EU side of the corpus. It is revealing to make both a register-based comparison (that is, between the comparator corpus and the administrative corpus) and a discourse-based comparison (between the two halves of the administrative corpus).

'Nation' in the comparator corpus collocates signficantly with very few lexical words, and, when it does, this is often to form names of entities. The most frequent lexical collocate is 'Unies' (in 'Nations Unies'); also frequent as collocates are 'Assemblée' and 'générale' (in the longer 'Assemblée générale des Nations Unies'), and 'état' in 'état-nation' ('nation state'). 'Grande' is the most frequent adjectival collocate, occurring most often in Biblical texts; others include 'peuple', 'notre' and 'monde'. In the administrative corpus, the most frequent collocate is also 'Unies', and most of the other most important collocates also contribute to form names of organisations and instruments in the UN: 'secrétaire général des Nations Unies', 'la Charte des Nations Unies', 'la convention des Nations Unies'.

If the two sub-corpora are analysed separately, subtler differences become evident: while reference to the United Nations accounts for the majority of instances of the keyword in both sub-corpora, slightly less frequent collocates, or groups of collocates, reveal discourse-based differences. In the EU sub-corpus, most of the remainder occur in the context of the discussion of cooperation ('Elle rapproche les nations de la Communauté', 'paix entre les nations', 'le concert des nations', 'réconciliation des nations'). In FRNACO, on the other hand, only 30% of the instances of 'nation' are in the context of the United Nations. 'État-nation' is also a common pairing. In addition, there are several references to connections between the military and the nation: 'resserrer les liens Armée-Nation', 'rapprocher l'armée et la nation', 'relations entre la nation et son armée', 'relations entre les militaires et la nation'; and of war: 'les certitudes qui attendent chaque nation en temps de guerre'. Around a fifth of the instances where 'nation' is not part of 'Nations Unies' contain some reference to the army, to arms, or, less commonly, to war. A nation, the corpus suggests, is conceived in terms of its relation to other nations. It is therefore an abstract entity, in French as well as in English, as Williams suggested. This does not imply that a nation is always an indefinite notion in the administrative corpus. Whereas in the European Union sub-corpus all but one instance of the keyword is in the plural form,[77] in FRNACO nearly three-quarters of the instances are of the singular form, and over half of these are capitalised and refer to the French nation specifically, as do many of the non-capitalised instances. It is therefore not surprising that a number of the most frequent collocates also relate to the home nation: 'France', 'français', 'notre' and 'nos deux'.

'Pays' occurs 3,065 times in the complete administrative corpus, and 2,093 times in the comparator corpus. It contributes in both corpora, as is to be expected, to a number of names of countries and regions: 'Pays Basque', 'Pays de Galles', 'Pays Bas', and in the Bible texts of the comparator corpus 'Pays de Canaan'. There are also a number of collocations more particular to the administrative register, in both the administrative corpus and the journalism texts of the comparator corpus: 'les pays candidats', 'les pays de l'Union', 'les pays ACP' ('African, Caribbean and Pacific States'), 'les Pays de l'ASEAN' ('Association of South-East Asian Nations') and especially in the EU sub-corpus, 'les pays tiers' ('third countries'), that is to say, countries which are not members of the Union or other organisation in question, or countries which are not contracting parties to a treaty or agreement.

---

77 This instance, in fact, is indefinite: 'chaque nation intéressée est invitée à se joindre...'.

Disregarding compound names and very common collocations, the most frequent individual collocates in the comparator corpus are 'notre', 'monde', 'deux' (in L1 position), and 'développement'. It is more informative to look at the concordances themselves, where groups of related nouns stand out clearly. 'Pays' collocates frequently with adjectives and 'de + noun' functioning as adjectives, as Williams found for 'nation', such as 'industrialisés', 'nordiques', 'de l'Est', 'africains francophones', 'développés', 'pauvres', 'arabes'. The collocates and collocational patterns of 'pays' in each of the two sub-corpora are very different: they appear to be more dependent on discourse than on register or genre. The European Union sub-corpus is dominated by frequent collocates which combine with the keyword to create semantic units, such as those listed above. Apart from cases where 'pays' forms part of the name of one of the members of the European Union, the word is mostly used for non-member countries, both collectively and non-specifically in the collocations 'pays tiers', 'pays candidats', 'pays associés' etc., which all stress the relation between the Union as a whole and these outsiders, and individually: 'les pays de l'Asie', 'les pays de l'Amérique', 'les pays orientales'. Often, reference is to the inhabitants of a particular country: 'ressortissants' (nationals) come from 'pays', if outside the EU, or 'états membres', if one of the members of the Union. However, there are no instances of collocation with 'nation' (within a window of five words each side of the node).

The concordance produced for the national sub-corpus is much less dominated by reference to particular countries and groups of countries. It is clear from the list of frequent collocates that the corpus is of texts at a national level, as France features highly: 'notre', 'nos (deux)', 'France', although often in cooperation with other countries: 'nos deux pays', especially in speech genres. There is however still a great deal of comparison with the, especially economic, development of other countries.

'État',[78] finally, is by far the most frequent of the three keywords investigated here. This is, however, due in large part to the frequency of a few very common phrases which form semantic units in which 'état' is one of the component words. This is true for both the comparator corpus and the administrative corpus. These include: 'les États-Unis', 'secrétaire d'État', 'chef d'État', 'Conseil d'État', 'état-nation', and, originating in the EU context but present in both corpora, 'État Membre'. This last expression accounts for almost two-thirds of the instances of 'état' in the EU sub-corpus, but occurs as the R1 collocate, that is the collocate immediately to the right of the node word, only seven times in the national sub-corpus. In both sub-corpora, 'état' occurs almost always capitalised and referring

78 Concordances of 'état' are based only on instances of the keyword with its sense of a nation under one government, and not with the meaning of 'condition'.

to a particular state or a group of states, in the French national sub-corpus, of course, this is normally France. In each of the comparator corpus and the administrative corpus, Williams' statement that 'state' carries a sense of the structures of power rings true for the French 'état'. All of its frequent collocates concern the administrative and governmental context. For the comparator corpus, principally the journalistic texts, these are: 'Unis', 'major' ('état-major' - 'administrative staff'), 'ministre', 'secrétaire', 'chef', 'Conseil', 'France' and 'deux'. For the EU sub-corpus these are: 'Commission', 'membre(s)', 'Unis', 'Conseil', 'article', 'secrétaire' and 'européenne'; and for the national sub-corpus: 'secrétaire', 'mer' (usually in 'le secrétaire d'état d'outre-mer'), 'Conseil', 'publique', 'entre', 'décret', 'réforme' and 'fonction'.

3.2 Employment

We can also investigate the collocational patterning around related keywords in a single policy area. Employment has been a major area of policy in the European Union throughout the late 1980s and 1990s, following the increase in long-term unemployment in the 1980s. The Treaty of Amsterdam, formally signed in 1997, expanded the legal basis for employment policy in the Union. This section begins, therefore, by looking at 'emploi' and 'chômage' ('employment' / 'unemployment'), and then taking a look at 'travail' ('work').

3.2.1 'Emploi' and 'chômage'

Michael Stubbs has found that the English keyword 'employment' collocates with words which indicate a legal use (e.g. 'contract', 'discrimination', 'law', 'legislation', 'terminate'), and with statistical expressions (e.g. 'fluctuations', 'gainful', 'temporary', 'figures'). The collocates of 'unemployment', on the other hand, show that unemployment applies to areas or populations rather than individual people. It collocates notably with references to groups of people and areas and with quantitative expressions, and also forms part of a large number of fixed expressions.

Straehle et al. (1999) have carried out a qualitative analysis on a corpus of English EU Presidency Conclusions and Commissioners' speeches of the conceptualisation of unemployment. They show that in the European Union, unemployment is conceptualised as both a fight and a problem and that these can be subsumed under the conceptual metaphor of a struggle. They conclude that the speeches, which represent an external genre, that is, one directed to the public outside the European Union institutions, treat employment more abstractly than do the Presidency Conclusions, an example of what Straehle describes as an internal genre. Employment is conceptualised as a common enemy which affects institutions and citizens alike. This conceptualisation also has an effect on the collocational patterns of 'chômage'. A look at the typical collocates of both 'emploi' and 'chômage' in the administrative corpus and the comparator corpus highlights more general register differences.

The French 'emploi' also appears as a statistical keyword, the 32nd most key, of FRADCO. 'Chômage' does not appear at all: that is to say that it is not key in the administrative corpus in comparison with the comparator corpus. Of course, given that the corpus is not semantically tagged, the only way to discriminate between 'emploi' in the sense here ('employment' or 'job') and in its sense of 'use' is by manual intervention. Concordances were drawn up for 'chômage' and for 'emploi' in its sense of 'employment' or 'job' only: instances of the word with other senses have been discarded.

Looking first of all, however, at relative quantities, there is a striking difference between 'emploi' and 'chômage', namely that the former is around two and a half times more frequent in the comparator corpus (roughly 350 occurrences of 'emploi' to 130 of 'chômage'), and a massive thirteen times more frequent in the administrative corpus (over 2600 compared with just over 200), although both words are more or less evenly spread between the two sub-corpora. These figures suggest that issues of employment are very important in administrative discourse, both at supranational and national levels, and that it tends here to be framed in positive terms.

By far the majority of instances of 'emploi' in the comparator corpus occur in the journalistic texts. There are a number of fixed phrases, which this corpus shares with the administrative corpus: 'le bassin d'emploi' ('labour market area'), 'les demandeurs d'emploi' ('job seekers'), 'les sans-emploi' ('the unemployed'), which generally indicate negative phenomena. Other frequent lexical collocates are 'formation', 'travail', 'professionnelle' (feminine because of its collocation with 'formation'), 'ministre', 'création', 'mille' and 'nombre'. These latter show that the keyword collocates frequently with figures and statistics.

Similarly, all but one of the instances of 'chômage' in the comparator corpus occur in the journalistic texts. Unemployment comes across as having a strongly negative prosody in this register, collocating with such words as 'fléau', 'endémique', 'gâchis', 'pauvreté', 'violer' and 'aggraver' among many others. It is something which people and areas have very little choice about: 'ils se sont mis au chômage', 'il faudra faire face au chômage'; and something which governments must struggle against ('lutter contre'). Like 'emploi', the word is often found in the company of expressions of rates and levels (numbers, percentages, 'faible', 'bas') and words indicating change in rate ('augmentation', 'diminution'), and expressions of time period (months, years). These findings are similar to those of Michael Stubbs for his corpus of journalism, fiction, non-fiction and conversation.

The importance of the issue of employment in administrative language is shown by the frequent appearance of 'emploi' in the administrative corpus as part of the names of ministries and policies: 'ministre de l'emploi et de la solidarité', 'pacte européen pour l'emploi', 'stratégie européenne pour l'emploi' and 'le secteur emploi'. As in the comparator corpus, the keyword collocates frequently with percentages, rates and figures. It is often, however, considered in a positive light: although the situation may be less than ideal, the lexical collocates of 'emploi' show that it is usually discussed in terms of what a concerted effort may bring for the future: 'en faveur de', 'croissance', 'création', 'durable', 'possibilités', 'favoriser'. The national sub-corpus in particular talks frequently of measures to improve young people's employment opportunities.

'Chômage' in the administrative corpus appears to be something of a taboo word. It occurs only 211 times in total, evenly split between the two sub-corpora, and never as part of a policy name, unlike 'emploi'. In addition, it is most commonly found in speech genres. Concordances reveal that unemployment is much more frequently lexicalised positively, as employment, especially in the case of names of guidelines, strategies and bodies. This is reminiscent of George Orwell's *Nineteen Eighty-Four* where the Ministry of Peace concerned itself with war, the Ministry of Love maintained law and order and the Ministry of Plenty dealt with the less than plentiful economic situation.

Where the word does occur, concordance lines show that 'chômage' is frequently embedded in a noun phrase and presented as given information in most contexts: it is 'un problème', 'un lancinant problème', 'un fardeau', 'un fléau'. While 'chômage' is commonly grammaticalised as an actor (e.g. 'des jeunes adultes touchés par le chômage'), it is rarely the grammatical subject (although there are examples of this: 'le chômage est source de tensions'). Once again, it is also discussed in terms of rates and levels, and changes in level are noteworthy. The fixed expression 'taux de chômage' accounts for over thirty of the instances of the keyword. The collocates considered out of context suggest a positive picture ('réduction', 'réduire', 'baisse', 'diminution'): however, it is more often the case that the documents are talking about a hypothetical case of unemployment levels going down, or low levels in other countries, in previous decades, etc., than actually commenting on current low or promising levels of unemployment in Europe or France. High unemployment is presented as a given, with the actual level often not stated but understood to be high.

Most notably, unemployment is presented as something which must be struggled against, with 'combattre' and especially 'lutter' ('to struggle') being common collocates. It 'threatens' and 'hits' groups and people, and people must face it, tackle it and take action to stop it. As Straehle et al. (1999) found, there is clear evidence of unemployment being conceptualised as a problem, not just in Presidency Conclusions and speeches, but across genres. Collocationally, 'lutte' and 'lutter' are particularly common. A concordance of this word in the comparator corpus and the administrative corpus reveals that it is overwhelmingly found immediately before 'contre' or in the construction 'lutte anti-+noun', most commonly referring to a struggle against socially-constructed or man-made evils: 'la fraude', 'la drogue', 'l'apartheid', 'l'exclusion sociale', 'l'immigration clandestine', 'la toxicomanie', 'le blanchiment des capitaux', 'le dopage', 'la pollution', 'l'effet de serre' etc. The struggle is only rarely directed against naturally-occurring phenomena, such as 'certaines encéphalopathies'. There are very few positive instances, where the struggle is *for* a cause: fewer than thirty out of nearly a thousand, and of these the most common is 'la lutte pour l'emploi': one might wonder whether the apparent desire to avoid the word 'chômage' in the administrative register has led writers to go against the expected prosody associated with 'lutte'. The prosody of 'chômage' appears to be stronger than that of 'lutte'.

3.2.2 'Travail'

In light of the discussion above of 'emploi' and 'chômage', it is interesting for comparative purposes to look at related keywords in order to see how these are used in the two discourses and in the comparator corpus. Stubbs discusses the English words 'job', labour' and 'work'. Both 'job' and 'labour', he finds, have many negative collocates, in the latter case suggesting low-prestige and low-paid professions. He also finds that the various forms of the lemma 'work' have very different collocates: 'working' tends to occur in fixed phrases, 'work' occurs in compound nouns, and 'worker' in noun-noun phrases (such as 'factory worker'). The French 'travail' can translate all three of these English words. A concordance was made for 'travail*', truncating the node in order to retrieve all forms of the lemma. The basic noun form 'travail' turned out to be by far the most common in both the comparator corpus and the administrative corpus, although it was proportionally more frequent in the latter, and especially in FRNACO, which accounted for two-thirds of the occurrences in this corpus. The two corpora share many fixed expressions: 'groupe de travail' ('working party' or less commonly 'working group'), 'temps de travail', 'marché de travail', 'conditions de travail', and expressions indicating the amount of time worked: 'travail à temps partiel', 'temporaire'. In addition, the keyword is used in many more such expressions in the administrative corpus, often in the context of legislation, including 'le travail en équipe', 'le travail non déclaré', 'contrat de travail', 'heures de travail', 'durée (hebdomadaire) du travail', 'journée de travail', 'lieu de travail', 'code de travail'. It is also often to be found in particular constructions: 'le travail accompli par...', 'le travail de la Commission / du Conseil / parlementaire' and 'le travail interministériel'.

'Travailleur(s)' in the comparator corpus appears almost exclusively in the journalistic texts once again. Only a handful of the instances, all of which occur in the comparator corpus, are of the adjective, meaning 'hard-working'. Its usage in the comparator corpus appears to owe a lot to administrative language. In both corpora, 'travailleurs' are spoken about in terms of categories: 'certaines catégories de travailleur', 'travailleurs migrants / handicapés / à temps partiel / de sexe masculin / de sexe féminin / (non) salariés / (non) mobiles. Different categories of worker are shown to have different needs. In addition, workers are very often the beneficiaries of legislation or measures: 'droits des travailleurs', 'une protection appropriée', 'des périodes équivalentes de repos compensateur', 'droits à pension complémentaire', 'droits sociaux fondamentaux', 'sécurité', 'allocations d'assurance' and 'protection sociale'.

4. Conclusion

This chapter has furthered the descriptive aim of this study. A statistical notion of keyness has shown that different words are key in each discourse, although these keywords may be used in different ways. Lexically, the EU discourse appears to be more distinctive: this is not surprising as it describes new concepts within a fairly new administrative framework, even although this owes a lot to the French administrative framework. Phraseologically too, both statistical and sociological keywords are used in distinctive ways in the two discourses. The two contexts view issues from different ideological standpoints. While the focus is on the phraseological differences between the EU and the national discourses, it is important also to appreciate these differences in their proper light. Discoursal differences are only one element of language variety within the administrative register: language also varies according to factors of genre and type of genre. On the most general level, too, comparison with the more general corpus of French has suggested that the administrative register can itself be clearly differentiated from other registers of French. While the comparator corpus used here is not large or heterogeneous enough to provide conclusive evidence, there does appear to be a lot of similarity between the administrative documents and the journalistic texts in terms of collocational patterning. In the case of the majority of the sociological keywords examined, the word appears only rarely in the remainder of the comparator corpus, and when it does this is often with a different meaning.

Chapter 7

Language Change, Language Contact and Translation

1. The role of language change

Chapters 4, 5 and 6 have all shown that there are phraseological differences among parts of the administrative corpus. The analysis compared the administrative register as a whole with other registers of French, and looked within the corpus to individual genres and groups of genres. There are phraseological differences to be found in each of these cases: it is important not to overlook factors of register and genre, which highlight the multidimensional nature of language variety. There are also, however, phraseological distinctions to be made between the EU discourse of French and its national counterpart. These differences are clear in the patterning of formulae, the use of phraseological items from the general language, and extend to grammatical words as well as central lexical items.

In other words, the discourses of EU and national French administrative language in their current forms can be distinguished not only by their lexis and features of grammar, but also in terms of their characteristic phraseology. This was the descriptive goal of this study, to describe the French EU discourse in relation to the current state of the register from which it developed. This raises further questions. While it is not possible to come to firm conclusions on the basis of the corpus compiled here and within the scope of this study, this chapter aims to indicate two further areas of study which may be able to provide an explanation for the current states of the discourses.

The first question which might be asked is how this difference has come about. Is it the case that the two discourses were originally closer, and have come to differ over the last fifty years? Has the EU discourse diverged dramatically from its national counterpart? Alternatively, has the EU discourse remained more faithful to the register from which it has inherited many of its concepts and linguistic patterning?

Some of these questions would require an additional corpus to be compiled of the earliest EEC, and ECSC, documents. With such a corpus, it would be possible directly to compare the EU discourse of the late 1990s with that of its infancy. In the absence of such a corpus, however, we must turn to other sources of linguistic information for comparison.

1.1 The phraseology of key verbs in FRADCO

Chapter 1 mentioned Robert Catherine's (1947) work on administrative French. This section returns to this study, in order to give the study a diachronic perspective. Catherine's study dates from the years immediately preceding early supranational developments, such as the European Coal and Steel Community (ECSC), which led to the European Economic Community (EEC) in 1957. It can be taken therefore to represent the register of national French administrative language around the time when Europe was looking to France for its administrative framework.

Chapter 1 also discussed René Georgin's (1973) research into a later state of the same register. Georgin's study cannot give an insight into the EU discourse: what it can do, however, is to provide a picture of the national discourse roughly halfway between the language which fed into the EU discourse, just before the time of the accession of the United Kingdom, Ireland and Denmark, and its state as represented by the national half of the corpus compiled here.

Both Catherine and Georgin's studies contain a discussion of verbs and verb phrases or frequent verb-complement pairings in the register. These are, according to Georgin, "les verbes et locutions verbales qui reviennent le plus souvent dans les textes administratifs" (1973, p. 275). More recently, Altenberg too has highlighted the centrality of verbs in communication, and for offering prime conditions for collocational patterning (1993, p. 227). Verbs are therefore an ideal locus for comparison. The complement given, by Georgin in particular, is not always a particular collocate, but occasionally a hyperonym, or superordinate: in the case of 'se référer à un texte', for example, 'texte' is replaced by any of 'articles', 'conclusions', 'règlements' etc. in FRADCO, and presumably stands for similar hyponyms of 'texte' in Georgin's source documents.

Appendices 6 and 7 list the verbs in question in both Catherine and Georgin's studies respectively, with their frequent complements, or typical environment. Given the frequency of nominalisation in the administrative register, the nominalised form of each verb, where appropriate, was also used as a node for the purposes of making a concordance. The next two columns in each Appendix indicate the number of instances of the verb-complement pairing in each of FREUCO and FRNACO. The final column gives the most typical environments or complements of the verb in the complete administrative corpus (FRADCO). There is a high degree of overlap in the verbs in the two lists: in order to avoid repetition, Appendix 7 indicates the typical environment of the verb in FRADCO only when this is not already listed in Appendix 6. However, there is less overlap in the complements and typical environment detailed by the two researchers: Appendix 7 therefore indicates the occurrences of the pairing in each of the sub-corpora even where the verb itself appears also in Appendix 6. Here each of the lists is dealt with separately, in order that any changes which may be accounted for by the intervening time might be noted.

Robert Catherine's research details the phraseological environment for a total of 218 French verbs. Six of these verbs do not occur at all FRADCO, and a dozen others occur so infrequently that it is impossible to make any generalisations regarding their typical patterning in the register. Catherine indicates a total of 348 verb-complement pairings: several pairings are listed for a number of common verbs such as 'être', 'faire', 'porter' and 'tenir'. Of these pairings, only 120, just under a third, occur in both sub-corpora of FRADCO, while 165 occur in neither. This immediately suggests that the language represented by the corpus has changed fairly dramatically from the state of the register described by Catherine. His research, however, while based on authentic texts, is not based on a corpus as such, and it is quite likely that his focus was on pairings which are intuitively salient, but not necessarily the most frequent or typical.

Comparing the use of these 'locutions verbales' in the two sub-corpora, it can be seen that FREUCO contains examples of 147 pairings, or 42%. FRNACO contains 155 types of pairing, or 45%. This is only a small difference, but does not contradict the finding of Chapter 5 that FREUCO has recourse to fewer types of general language locution, or, to take the opposite perspective, that the national sub-corpus contains more phraseological variety. This is supported by the finding that only 27 pairings occur in FREUCO but not FRNACO, while 35 pairings are specific to the national side of the administrative corpus.

It is the figure for the respective number of tokens of these verb-complement pairs which is most striking. FREUCO contains a total of 3,014 instances of pairs, compared with only 1,967 in FRNACO: that is, just over 60% of the total number of tokens appear in FREUCO. As with the general language locutions in Chapter 5, this is due to a large number of occurrences of a few types, in particular 'adopter une résolution', 'arrêter une disposition', 'conférer des droits', 'décider de', 'émettre un avis', 'être conforme à', 'être en mesure de', 'informer de', 'il vous incombe de', 'prendre acte de', 'prendre en considération', and 'tenir compte de', which the EU sub-corpus draws on significantly more than the national sub-corpus. There are also cases where FRNACO draws on a particular pair more than FREUCO: examples of this include 'constater un fait', 'convenir avec', 'donner lieu à', 'exercer une fonction', 'insister sur', 'modifier un projet', 'organiser un service', and 'promulguer une loi'.

With the exception of a dozen or so verb-complement pairs, the examples picked out by René Georgin also do not appear to be central to the administrative register as represented by FRADCO. As with Catherine, however, without access to the documents which Georgin used as his source material, it is impossible to say whether this is due to a biased range of source material (for example including only certain genres), or changes in the register over time. There is a total of 64 verbs, and 116 verb-complement pairs given. Of the 116 pairings, 47 do not appear in the administrative corpus at all. Forty-five pairings appear in both sub-corpora. A total of 60 pairings appear in FREUCO, and 54 in FRNACO. This difference is small, but counterintuitive. It suggests that FREUCO resembles the register which Georgin was describing more closely than does the national discourse. Might this represent a general trend, whereby the EU discourse is drawing more and more on the French national administrative discourse as the number of languages which could exert an influence is growing? It is as if the EU discourse is an exaggeration, and not simply a conservative retention of the original register.

As regards tokens, FREUCO contains a total of 1,297 instances of Georgin's verb-complement pairings, while FRNACO contains only 690. This is the statistic where on the face of it the two sub-corpora differ most: however, this discrepancy is for the most part due to a couple of pairings which are highly frequent in FREUCO: 'être en mesure', '[il vous] incombe de', 'investir des capitaux' and, especially, 'tenir compte de'. Once again, therefore, the EU sub-corpus shows less variety but more dependency on phraseological elements.

1.2 Core verbs - case studies

Appendices 6 and 7 contain an indication of the most typical phraseological environment for each of the verbs highlighted by Catherine or Georgin as central to the administrative register. It is difficult to do more than sketch a verb's use in a register. This section therefore looks in more detail at some of the most central verbs, to see how they are used in the administrative register, and in the two discourses separately. Different word forms turn out to collocate differently: in this case therefore, an unlemmatised corpus highlights variation in phraseological patterning more clearly than a lemmatised corpus would. The downside, however, is that additional manual analysis is required to eliminate the homonyms of some word forms, for example, to exclude instances of a capitalised 'A' which are in fact the preposition 'à' devoid of its accent, but retaining those instances where it is the third person singular present tense of 'avoir'.

1.2.1 'Avoir'

The verb 'avoir' has 42 different word forms, of which 29 occur in FRNACO.[79] In total, there are 20,238 instances of the different forms of the verb in the corpus.

79 Those which do not occur are the second person singular present tense 'as', past historic forms 'eus', 'eûmes' and 'eûtes', future tense 'auras', conditional 'auriez', present subjunctive 'aie' and 'aies', and all of the imperfect subjunctive forms except for the third person singular 'eût'.

These are distributed fairly evenly across the two sub-corpora (9,894 instances in FREUCO and 10,344 in FRNACO). FRNACO, however, contains a wider range of word forms, all 29 of those which occur in the complete corpus. FREUCO contains no instances of past historic 'eut' and 'eurent', future tense 'aurai' and present subjunctive 'ayez'. The third person singular of the present tense, 'a', is the most common form in both sub-corpora, with over five thousand instances in each: this however includes examples where the verb is used as an auxiliary in a compound tense. Contrary to the frequently-heard contention that the past historic tense is used in writing but more rarely in spoken French, there are only nine instances of this tense, of which seven occur in the speech genres of FRNACO. These are fairly formal speeches, of course, where the past historic is not out of place, but it remains true that the past historic is rarely used in the more formal written genres, even reports which do commonly discuss past events.

There is not space here to set out the typical phraseological environments of all forms of the verb, but the most striking, in FREUCO or FRNACO specifically, or the administrative register more generally, are as follows:

<u>avoir</u>

FREUCO:	'défaut d'avoir transposé, dans le délai prévu, la directive...'
FRNACO:	'après avoir consulté / examiné...'
Both:	'avoir accès à...'
	'avoir lieu'
	'[pouvoir] avoir un effet'

<u>eu</u>

FREUCO:	'eu égard aux [conclusions]'
FRNACO:	'[décision] a eu pour effet de...'
Both:	'réunion / forum / débat / négociations qui a / ont eu lieu'
	'j'ai eu l'occasion de...'

<u>ayant</u>

FREUCO:	'[politique] ayant trait à la défense'
	'décisions ayant des effets / implications dans le domaine de...'
	'points ayant fait l'objet d'un débat'
FRNACO:	'départements ayant répondu au questionnaire'
	'ayant pour objet de...'
	'ayant opté pour les dispositions [prévues]'
Both:	'en ayant recours à'

<u>ai</u> (predominantly an auxiliary)

FREUCO:	'j'ai décidé de...'
FRNACO:	'j'ai souhaité que...' (especially in speech genres)
	'j'ai le sentiment que...'
Both:	'Comme je l'ai indiqué...'

a (predominantly an auxiliary verb)

FREUCO:	'la Commission / le Conseil a...' (i.e. institutions as actor in the clause. EU institutions appear as the actor much more frequently than do national institutions in FRNACO)
	'Monsieur l'avocat général, [nom] a présenté ses conclusions à l'audience' (in Court of Justice bulletins)
FRNACO:	'la France a... / le gouvernement a...'
	'le Conseil des ministres a adopté les mesures individuelles suivantes...'
	'Président de la République a réuni le Conseil des Ministres au Palais de l'Elysée...'
Both:	's'il y a lieu'
	'[nom] a souligné que...'

ont (including the perfect tense)

FREUCO:	'les États membres ont décidé / adopté...'
FRNACO:	'l'Assemblée nationale et le Sénat ont adopté...'
	'En outre, ont été adoptées diverses mesures d'ordre individuel...'
Both:	'[discussions] qui ont eu lieu à...'

aura (including the future perfect)

FREUCO:	'l'euro aura des conséquences...'
	'texte aura été mis au point...'
	'aura un impact important'
Both:	'[colloque etc] aura lieu'

1.2.2 'Être'

'Être' is almost twice as frequent in the corpus as 'avoir', with a total of 40,258 instances of the verb. This includes forms of 'être' as an auxiliary in compound tenses and the passive voice. As regards its distribution between sub-corpora, there is a small bias towards the national sub-corpus, which contains 22,176 instances, compared with only 18,082 in FREUCO. As for 'avoir', FRNACO contains a wider range of word forms than FREUCO: 34 different forms compared with only 29.[80] The most common form is the third person singular of

80 There are no instances at all in the complete corpus of the second person plural past historic 'fûtes', future tense 'seras', and the imperfect subjunctive forms 'fusse', 'fusses', 'fussions' and 'fussiez'. In addition to these, FRNACO does not contain examples of the second person conditional 'seriez'. FREUCO has no instances of the present tense 'es',

the present tense, 'est': nearly 60% of all instances of this form occur in FRNACO (cf. below for some of the most common phraseological environments which account for this discrepancy). The imperfect subjunctive is rare in both sub-corpora, but both third person forms do occur. The past historic is also uncommon, and especially so in FREUCO, where it occurs only 19 times, and only in its third person singular and plural forms. Again, this tense is more commonly to be found in spoken genres, both the formal speeches, and even the transcribed Assemblée Nationale debates. The typical phraseological environment of the most common verb forms are as follows:

être

FREUCO:	'une attention particulière doit être portée à...'
	'Ces mesures doivent être compatible avec le présent traité'
	'les variables doivent être transmises [sous forme brute]'
FRNACO:	'[...] est loin d'être [négligeable / une réalité]'
	'Nul ne peut être [soumis à / obligé de...]'
Both:	'une décision devant être prise à la majorité qualifiée'
	'la signature et / ou la date devraient être encadrées...'

étant

FREUCO:	'Étant donné que...' (rare in FRNACO)
FRNACO:	'Cela étant, ... [il faut]'
Both:	'Tout en étant'

suis (predominantly in speech genres)

FRNACO:	'je suis convaincu que...'
	'je suis frappé...'
Both:	'Je suis de ceux qui...'
	'Je suis heureux de [vous saluer / vous retrouver nombreux]

est

FREUCO:	'la Cour de Justice est compétente pour statuer...'
	'l'article est modifié comme suit: [...]'
FRNACO:	'l'article [no.] est ainsi modifié / rédigé'
	'[...] est au cœur de...'
	'la parole est à [nom]'
	'[article] est complété par une phrase ainsi rédigé...'
	'Il est inséré, après l'article [no.]'
Both:	'[loi / article] est applicable [dans les territoires]'
	'il est essentiel pour [...] de [...]'
	'C'est pourquoi...'

---

imperfect 'étiez', past historic 'fus' and 'fûmes', future 'serez', and present subjunctive 'sois'.

<u>sont</u>

FREUCO:	'les votes contraires ou abstentions sont indiqués'
	'les crédits annuels sont autorisés'
	'si elles ne sont pas conformes à l'avis émis par le comité'
FRNACO:	'les peines encourues par les personnes morales sont: [+ list]'
	'les mots [...] sont remplacés par les mots [...]' (in legal genres)
	'les mots [...] sont supprimés'
Both:	'[les résultats] sont les suivants [...]'
	'[les dispositions] sont applicables à [...]'

<u>sera</u>

FREUCO:	'la position commune sera adoptée'
	'l'accent sera mis sur [...]'
FRNACO:	'le présent arrêté sera publié au Journal Officiel'
	'la présente loi sera exécutée comme loi de l'Etat'
	'[...] sera mis en place'
Both:	'la décision sera prise / arrêtée / mise en œuvre'
	'une attention / un accent particulier/ière sera accordé(e)'

<u>serait</u>

FRNACO:	'Il serait souhaitable que...'
	'[...] serait de nature à [...]'
	'ne serait-ce que parce que...'

<u>soit</u>

FREUCO:	'[...] peut demander que le Conseil européen soit saisi de la question'
	'soit de sa propre initiative, soit...'
FRNACO:	'soit + number' (e.g. '42 sur 105 directeurs, soit 40% de l'effectif')
Both:	'Quoi qu'il en soit...'

1.2.3 'Faire'

There is a total of 4,632 instances of the verb 'faire', in 24 different forms.[81] Almost 60% of these instances appear in FRNACO (2,657, compared with 1,975

81 Examples of the noun 'fait' and of 'tout à fait' and 'en fait' have been removed from this total. The forms are 'faire', 'fait' (both past participle and third person singular present tense), 'faisant', all forms of the present tense, the imperfect 'faisait', 'faisions', 'faisaient', the past historic 'fit' and 'firent', all forms of the future tense except for 'feras', conditional 'ferait' and 'feraient', present subjunctive 'fasse', 'fassions', 'fassiez', and 'fassent'. The imperfect subjunctive does not occur in either sub-corpus.

in FREUCO). The only form for which FREUCO contains significantly more instances than FRNACO is the present participle ‘faisant’ (see below). The verb forms are involved in an especially large number of typical phraseological elements:

faire

FREUCO:	‘faire constater que...’ (especially in the sequence: ‘la Commission des Communautés européennes a introduit un recours visant à faire constater que...’)
	‘faire rapport à [au Conseil européen]’
FRNACO:	‘faire de la formation continue un outil privilégié’
	‘faire évoluer [la situation]’
	‘faire partie de...’
Both:	‘faire adopter [une loi]’
	‘faire appel à’
	‘faire avancer’
	‘faire bénéficier’
	‘faire connaître’
	‘faire des propositions’
	‘faire en sorte de... / que...’
	‘faire face à [aux conséquences / défis]’
	‘faire l’objet de [un traitement / de discussions]’
	‘faire le bilan de...’
	‘faire le point sur...’
	‘faire part de [difficultés / propositions]’
	‘faire preuve de’
	‘faire progresser [les droits / les choses]’
	‘faire respecter les règles’
	‘faire valoir [les intérêts]’
	‘savoir-faire’ (in a particular area, e.g. ‘technologique’ / ‘culinaire’)

faisant

FREUCO:	‘Ce faisant, [le Conseil tient compte des conséquences / elle [la Commission] signale en particulier toute irrégularité]’
	‘faisant partie [d’un groupe]’
Both:	‘faisant foi’ (e.g. ‘le cachet de la poste faisant foi’)
	‘faisant l’objet de [un dumping / une dérogation]’

fait

Both:	‘Fait à Bruxelles / Paris [+ date]’ (Journal Officiel genres of both sub-corpora - found at the end of a legal text)
	‘fait état de...’
	‘fait l’objet [d’un avis / un débat / une évaluation]’
	‘[nom] a fait observer que...’

'[...] fait partie [intégrante] de'

faisons
FRNACO: 'Faisons un [autre] rêve... Imaginons...' (in reports)

font
FREUCO: '[les dispositions] ne font pas obstacle [à l'adoption de...]'
'[En vertu des traités d'adhésion] font également foi les versions du présent traité en langue [anglaise et allemande]'

fera
FREUCO: 'la Commission fera des propositions...'
'la Commission fera rapport à...'
'[sujets] feront l'objet de [un débat / un travail / des discussions]'
FRNACO: '[...] fera l'objet d'une étude...'

1.2.4 'Tenir'

There is a total of 1,671 instances of the verb 'tenir' in the administrative corpus, covering sixteen word forms.[82] FREUCO contains almost 60% of these tokens: 983 instances. The most frequent form of the verb is the past participle, 'tenu(e/s/es)': its predominance is due to occurrences of the locution 'compte tenu de'. In fact, variations of 'tenir compte de' account for half of the instances of the verb, and the environments in which the verb is found are highly patterned. The forms of the verb typically occur as follows:

tenant
FRNACO: 'en tenant dûment compte'
Both: 'en tenant compte de'

tenir
FREUCO: 'Afin de tenir compte de...'
'[...] qui doit se tenir [+ date]'
Both: 'pour tenir compte de'
'sans tenir compte [du vote du représentant]'

tenu (including inflected forms)

---

82 These are 'tenir', 'tenu' (includinginflected forms), 'tenant', 'tiens', 'tient', 'tenons', 'tiennent', 'tenais', 'tenait', 'tenaient', 'tiendrai', 'tiendra', 'tiendront', 'tiendrait', 'tiendraient' and 'tienne'. FREUCO contains no instances of 'tenait' and 'tiendraient', and FRNACO has no examples of 'tiendrai'.

Both: 'Compte tenu du fait que...'
'Compte tenu des [ressources]'
'[Conférence etc.] s'est tenue à [location]'
'j'ai tenu à exprimer [l'importance de...]'

<u>tiens</u>
FREUCO: 'je tiens à souligner ici...'
FRNACO: 'je tiens à rendre hommage à ...'

<u>tient</u>
FREUCO: 'la Commission tient le plus grand compte de l'avis émis par [...]'
'le Conseil tient compte des conséquences éventuelles...'
FRNACO: '[...] tient une place importante'
Both: '[la mission] tient à souligner...'

1.2.5 'Venir'

Sixteen word-form types of the verb 'venir' occur in the administrative corpus.[83] There is a total of 731 instances of the verb, but a bias towards the national sub-corpus: 202 instances in FREUCO and 529 in FRNACO. These include examples of 'venir' in the senses of both 'to have just', and 'to come to'. Many of the forms do not occur frequently enough for patterns to be discerned. Phraseological patterning around the more common word forms is as follows:

<u>venir</u>
FRNACO: 'au cours des années à venir'
Both: 'dans les années à venir'
'dans les mois à venir'
'négociations à venir'

<u>venu</u>
Both: 'le moment est venu'
'le moment venu'
'le temps est venu'

<u>viennent</u>
FRNACO: '[dans les] années qui viennent'
'[trois] ans qui viennent'

83 These are: 'venir', 'venu' (including inflected forms), 'venant', 'viens', 'vient', 'venons', 'venez', 'viennent', 'venait', 'venaient', 'viendrai', 'viendra', 'viendront', 'viendrait', 'viendraient', 'vienne'. All occur in FRNACO, and all except 'viendrai' in FREUCO.

	'les jours qui viennent'
	'les semaines qui viennent'
Both:	'viennent renforcer' (e.g. 'diverses mesures viennent renforcer les droits des victimes')
	'viennent s'ajouter à...'

<u>viens</u> (especially in speech genres of both discourses)

FREUCO:	'... que je viens de décrire'
FRNACO:	'j'en viens maintenant à'
	'je viens de mentionner'
Both:	'je viens d'évoquer'

<u>vient</u>

FREUCO:	'Vient ensuite [la marché des obligations en yen]' (i.e. 'Vient' at head of sentence, cf. discussion of Georgin 1973 in Section 6.3. of Chapter 1)
FRNACO:	'[nom] vient de rendre publics les résultats...'
Both:	'[la Commission etc.] vient d'adopter...'

1.3 Conclusion

The analysis in this section, while it is limited to a comparison with two, non corpus-based studies, suggests that the EU discourse may be closer in some respects than the national discourse to the administrative French of the 1940s. This, if accurate, is counterintuitive. It might be expected, rather, that the EU discourse, given the new context of text production from which it developed, and the influence of other languages, might have differentiated itself more.

2. The multilingual context

The picture which has been built up from the analysis in Chapters 4, 5 and 6 is of an EU discourse which can be differentiated phraseologically from its national administrative counterpart. Perhaps surprisingly, the EU discourse appears to have changed less over time than the national discourse. To what factors should we turn, therefore, to explain these differences?

As Chapter 1 made clear, there are a number of important differences between the contexts in which the EU and national discourses are used: most crucially, the national discourse has a much longer history, and is based on a deeply-embedded national culture; the EU discourse is produced in a multilingual environment, and many documents undergo a process of translation. We might therefore look to the influence of other languages on the EU discourse in order to explain its current state. French and English are now by a substantial proportion the most commonly used languages of document production and internal communication in the EU:

what, then, has been the effect of English-French language contact through the period of existence of the EU, both before and after the accession of Britain and Ireland to the Union? English is not of course the only language with which French has been in contact through bilingual speakers in the administration: German, Italian and Dutch have also been official languages since 1957. A case may be made for all of these to have influenced EU French: Italian as the most closely related typologically; German as a close contender to be the most common language in the EU administration after French in the early days; and Dutch, given the location of EU institutions in Brussels. Another volume could be written for each of these cases. This section attempts merely to outline by means of examples some of the ways in which corpus methodology might be used to investigate the influence of English on EU French.

2.1 Language contact with English

Given the predominance of both languages, it might be expected that English will have had an influence on the phraseology of EU French. The analysis carried out thus far has not, however, been able to give specific evidence of such influence. In order to test the hypothesis that contact with English has not had a notable effect on the French EU discourse, it is necessary to focus on areas of the latter where the influence of English is most likely to have manifested itself. We are dealing here, however, as so often in corpus methodology, with 'black swan' data, in the sense described by Karl Popper (cf. 1959): regardless of the amount of evidence that can be gathered which points to a non-existent or minimal linguistic influence from English, this is not sufficient to prove that this is not a significant factor. One single example confirming such an influence, a black swan, however, will falsify the hypothesis.

One place where we might expect to see an imprint of language contact is in the phraseological environment of words which have been borrowed by one language from another. We saw in Chapter 1 that French has contributed greatly, semantically and lexically, to EU language generally. Tables 1.1 and 1.2 in Chapter 1 listed Eurospeak items which originated in French, and French terminological items used in English EU language, respectively. Have these words come to be used differently in French EU discourse compared with the national administrative discourse because of their central place in Eurospeak? If so, can the influence on their change be attributed to contact with one particular language more than others? The phraseological environments of these items in FREUCO may be compared with their use in FRNACO, an equivalent English EU corpus,[84] and an English comparator corpus (such as the BNC Sampler).

---

84 For this purpose, I compiled a corpus of English EU texts. This is partly a parallel corpus, where the texts from FREUCO are available in English

Influence from English may be suggested by words in FREUCO which bear a closer phraseological resemblance to their use in these two English corpora than to their use in FRNACO.

'Acquis' is one such example: it occurs 167 times in FREUCO,[85] in a number of common patterns including 'acquis de Schengen', 'acquis communautaire', 'acquis de l'Union', 'acquis environnemental', signifying the set of legal decisions taken in a certain area, or the complete set of legislation which a member state must adopt on accession to the Union. Even in French the word quite frequently appears in inverted commas, which suggests that it has not been fully integrated, and that its usage in EU discourse differs from that in other varieties of the French language. This is indeed the case: while it occurs 62 times in FRNACO, its phraseological patterning is very different here. There are a couple of occurrences of 'acquis communautaire', referring to the EU context, but there are fewer common patterns. Those that can be identified refer to an employment context: 'acquis de la formation', '[validation des] acquis professionnels'. The examples of 'acquis' in the French comparator corpus, all 23 of which occur in the journalism register, display few patterns, but 'acquis sociaux' can be identified. This collocation occurs only once in FRNACO. The English EU corpus does contain instances of 'acquis', both in the parallel texts and in the genre of Commission speeches. Except for the more frequent use of inverted commas, around either 'acquis' alone or 'acquis communautaire' as a collocation, there is no discernible difference here in the phraseological patterning of the word in English and French. It is impossible, therefore, to claim an effect of language contact in this case: rather the word appears to owe its typical patterning to semantic and pragmatic factors alone.

'Subsidiarité' / 'subsidiarity' is a similar case. It occurs in both FREUCO and FRNACO, but much more frequently in the former (115 times, compared with only 8). It occurs more commonly in the collocation 'principe de subsidiarité', in both sub-corpora, and also as 'principle of subsidiarity' (and less commonly 'subsidiarity principle') in the English EU corpus. Language contact appears to have resulted in French phraseology being adopted in English.

'Comitologie' / 'comitology', far from being a locus of phraseological change, appears from the evidence of the corpus to be going out of use. It occurs only 10 times in FREUCO, and of these 6 instances are in inverted commas. Bainbridge has indicated (1998, and see Chapter 1, Table 1.1) that 'comitology' is not yet assimilated into English: the corpus supports this. It occurs only once in the English EU corpus, in the sentence 'This is the area sometimes known as

---

(e.g. Official Journal documents), and partly comparable (e.g. speeches, which are not typically translated in full).

85 This total is of occurrences of the noun 'acquis' only, not the past participle of the verb 'acquérir'.

"comitology"'. More commonly, the French 'comitologie' is translated by 'committee procedures'. Indeed, there are instances where 'committee procedures' equates to 'procédure du comité' in FREUCO: although there are not enough instances to be certain, it appears that if English is in the process of influencing French phraseology in this case.

Secondly, we might investigate the converse situation, that is to say words of English origin in the French EU discourse, and especially words which do not also occur in FRNACO. It is not only these items themselves which are of interest, but also any phraseological 'baggage' they may have brought with them to French. By means of a WordList comparison, English words which appear frequently in FREUCO were identified, that is words which appear in both the English EU corpus and FREUCO. Some of the words which WordList identifies as appearing in both corpora are of course cognate forms which belong to both French and English (such as 'surveillance' and 'occasion'). Others appear to be English words, but are not: 'best' for example turns out to be the acronym standing for the name of a task force ('Business Environment Simplification Task Force'), and as such is always capitalised. Others still are indeed English words, but turn out rarely to be used except in titles and names (including 'Council' which is only used in the names of particular councils, 'new' which occurs in the place names 'New York' and 'New Holland', and 'speech' which is only used before the document number of a Commission speech to identify its genre). A couple of words, however, look promising.

The English word 'task' appears 41 times in FREUCO, as part of the collocation 'task force' (or hyphenated 'task-force') in all instances but one (where it is part of 'task group'). Only twice is it in inverted commas. The compound seems to be integrated into the French EU discourse, but has apparently not yet extended further: it does not occur in FRNACO, the French comparator corpus, or as an entry in *Le Petit Robert*. There is no evidence, however, of any phraseological baggage from English having been borrowed along with the word: apart from the one instance of 'task group' (which occurs in a Commission speech, that is to say a document originally written in French), its uses show little variation. It is generally followed by the name of the task force in question, as is the practice in French. Indeed, the name of the 'task force' is even found in following position in English: 'proposals as recommended by the Task Force "Educational Software and Multimedia"'. Again, phraseological influence appears to be in the direction of French to English, rather than English to French.

In the case of the adjective 'crucial', the evidence of the corpus suggests that typical English constructions, such as 'it is crucial to...' and 'of crucial importance' have been carried over into the French EU discourse, in 'il est crucial de' and 'd'une importance cruciale'. Neither of these constructions appears in the FRNACO or the French comparator corpus, but they are common in FREUCO, and both English corpora.

A further place to look for the effects on EU French of language contact is internationalisms, in the sense of Musolff (1996). These are “Terms that look or sound similar in different languages and are recognizable as etymologically ‘related’ expressions, such as ‘democracy’, ‘constitution’, ‘capitalism’”, but which

> often carry different meaning aspects in their different realizations in various languages, and thus can add to problems of cross-national communication, as their outward similarity seems to suggest the existence of a ‘common ground’ for understanding which does not in fact exist. (Musolff 1996, p. 16)

If it could be shown that such terms differ even subtly in their usage in FREUCO from FRNACO and the French comparator corpus, then there may be a case for arguing the influence of English: this could be supported by collocational analysis of the terms in the English EU corpus and the BNC Sampler.

Related to internationalisms, but of more general significance are *faux amis*, or false cognates. These are words or expressions in more than one language which have the same form but are semantically different. If it can be shown that such false cognates, while differing in their propositional meaning in the English and French comparator corpora, bear a closer relationship to each other in the English and French EU corpora, then it may be possible to argue for the influence of English on French through contact in their respective EU discourses.

It is outside the scope of this research to carry out such an investigation. Initial attempts, however, on such common *faux amis* as ‘demand ‘/ ‘demander’, ‘achieve’ / ‘achever’, ‘sensible’ / ‘sensible’, ‘eventual’ / ‘éventuel’ do not suggest that this is a particularly fruitful area for the influence of the phraseological patterning of English on French. ‘Éventuel’ in FREUCO occurs in a number of frequent patterns, and in all cases is used in the sense of ‘possible’: ‘en vue de l’intégration éventuelle de l’UEO dans l’Union’, ‘le Conseil tient compte des conséquences éventuelles d’une telle suspension...’ and ‘éventuelles adhésions’. In the English EU corpus, on the other hand, the cognate ‘eventual’ is used to indicate both ‘happening at the end of a period of time’ and ‘possible’: it occurs only four times. In the instance ‘reduction and eventual elimination of pollution’, it is used to mean ‘at the end of a (long) period of time’, and in the instances ‘enables member states to respond to eventual agricultural concerns’, ‘in order to address eventual new needs’, and ‘Project aimed at the eventual return home of 20 women refugees’ it is used in a sense identical to the French sense of ‘possible’, ‘hypothetical’. This final example is a translation of the French ‘éventuel’ in ‘Projet visant au retour éventuel de 20 femmes réfugiées’. The BNC Sampler corpus, however, contains 19 instances of the word, of which 17 are clearly of the former sense, with collocates which indicate this: ‘eventual winners', '94 of his eventual 134 not out [in cricket]', 'loss of the means of livelihood and eventual pauperization', etc. Two examples are ambiguous, and both occur in the 'world affairs' texts: 'thinking of any eventual cooperation between his party and Party B' and 'Ankara's eligibility for eventual membership of the EC'. If anything, then, it is French which is exerting a certain influence over English in the EU domain, not the converse.

Faux amis are usually described in purely semantic terms, but since, according to Firth, a word's meaning is its function in context, there is no reason why the concept of *faux amis* should be restricted to propositional meaning. Words which are semantically very close may still differ wildly in their collocational patterning, especially across registers or discourses as this research has aimed to demonstrate with relation to administrative language.[86] The translation scholar Peter Newmark makes this point:

> 'native' translators are inexperienced and unaware that interference from the source or a third language may go beyond a few conventional *faux amis* (like *troubler, demander*), to clauses, phrases, technical terms, metaphors, word order and most collocations. (Newmark 1991, p. 23)

It may be useful to extend the notion of *faux amis* to identical word forms which differ in their usage, and therefore their meaning, across registers or discourses. That is to say, the concept of collocationally false friends can be useful when considered intralingually as well as interlingually.

Since it does not go beyond isolated examples, this suggestion can only be tentative and cannot make a claim for or against specific influence from English. Even if a case can be made for the influence of English on EU French which goes beyond the patterning of a few key words, however, this cannot explain all of the apparent phraseological differences between the EU and national discourses. Chapter 4 found that the EU discourse relied more than the national discourse on repeated sequences of words. Chapter 5, similarly, showed that the EU discourse has more recourse to locutions of French in terms of tokens: that is to say, while it shows less variety in this respect, overall it evidences a greater reliance on such semantic and syntactic phraseological resources. We might conclude from these two chapters that the EU discourse is more restricted than the national register: this is not to say that it does not have further resources, but simply that it appears not to rely on the resources open to it as fully as the national discourse. Section 1 of this chapter similarly suggested that while both discourses have evolved over

---

86 Cf. also Partington (1998), on 'true' and false friends in English and Italian, and Tognini-Bonelli (1996) who approaches the subject from the level of the unit of meaning, postulating a database of comparable units of meaning in English and Italian.

the last fifty years or so, the EU discourse of French has remained truer to its origins in the administrative French of the middle of the century. This may be shown to be due to the influence of a particular language: if this is not the case, where, then, should we turn to explain this finding?

2.2 The effects of translation

If the phraseological differences which can be seen between the EU and national discourses in the late 1990s are not the result of contact with individual languages, then perhaps they are the result of the effects of the translation process itself. Mona Baker, in her work based on the Translational English Corpus has noted as one of the features of translated text, in any language, its conservatism, or 'normalisation', which she defines as "the tendency to conform to patterns and practices which are typical of the target language, even to the point of exaggerating them" (1996, p. 176). This may explain the apparent lack of variety in EU discourse which Chapters 4 and 5 both suggested, for multiword sequences and locutions. A further contributing factor might be the practice in the EU institutions of relying on previously translated documents in order to speed up the translation process. Another feature which Mona Baker finds to be typical of translated text is what she terms 'levelling out', or "the tendency of translated text to gravitate around the centre of any continuum rather than move towards the fringes [which] simply means that we can expect to find less variation among individual texts in a translation corpus than among those in a corpus of original texts" (*ibid.*, p. 177). This also appears to be relevant here. We are left with something of a paradox: while the language contact situation suggests variety, through the influence of other languages, the translation process suggests there will be a degree of conservatism, and a relatively high level of repetition. The result of both of these factors is a unique context of production for European Union documents.

Chapter 8

Concluding Remarks

A number of conclusions can be drawn on the basis of the analysis carried out. First of all, it should be noted that the EU and French national discourses, as represented by the FREUCO and FRNACO sub-corpora, have a large degree of phraseological similarity. While the differences between the two discourses have been the principal focus and as such require more discussion, it is important to begin by recognising the high level of similarity. This supports the notion of a register of administration, as described in neo-Firthian research; that is to say that the administrative register can be differentiated from other registers of French and the general language by its phraseology and collocational patterning.

Chapter 4 demonstrated that while the multiword repeated sequences which occur in both of the sub-corpora are limited in number and tend to be short and grammatical in nature, they provide a point of contact between the two discourses, and highlight the underlying aims of these two varieties of administrative language; the transmission and often the explanation of complex subject matter to a general public. The administrative speech genres, of both discourses, also contain fewer multiword sequences: this difference may be attributable to the different mode of production. The limited range of registers in the comparator corpus and the relatively small quantity of text from each register makes it impossible to confirm the suggestion that the administrative register employs formulae or multiword sequences more than other registers.

With regard to the role of locutions in the register, Chapter 5 provided a phraseological point of contact between the administrative register and the general language. Once again there is a degree of similarity between the discourses in terms of the types of locution employed. As regards the phraseological patterning around keywords, Chapter 6 highlighted the differences between discourses, but also revealed a unity between the two discourses when these are set against the comparator corpus. A large number of statistical keywords are key in the administrative register because of their combined significance in both discourses: many of these are grammatical or function words, which shows that the two discourses have correspondences which go far beyond lexical items. A fundamental degree of similarity can also be seen in the collocational patterning of individual statistical and sociological keywords, which appear in similar phraseological environments in both sub-corpora, although relative frequencies differ, and may be contrasted with their usages in the comparator corpus.

A second main conclusion, however, is that despite this degree of similarity with the national discourse, the European Union discourse can indeed be differentiated with respect to the various types of collocational and phraseological patterning investigated here. Despite its origins predominantly in French administrative language and the French administrative framework, the EU discourse can be said now to have a recognisable phraseological identity, something which will not come as a surprise to anyone who has encountered the variety. This gives hope to John Gaffney's suggestion that "the legitimacy of the European Union depends upon the emergence of a European-level political discourse" (Gaffney 1999, p. 199). At the phraseological level at least, this appears already to be the case.

Differences can also be seen at both the macro level of the whole discourse and at the micro level of individual genres and groups of genres. In consistently showing differentiation at the levels of register, discourse and genre, the analysis here breaks down a monolithic notion of administrative French, and demonstrates that despite the common overriding function of administrative language, this has different manifestations in the EU and national contexts, and also in different genres within these discourses. This endorses work done by corpus linguists on other registers and other languages.

The overall picture from the different stages of analysis carried out in Chapters 4 to 7 is revealing. In some regards, the EU discourse appears to be quite conservative as compared with the national discourse, and more highly patterned, having recourse to phraseological resources more frequently. There seems, therefore, to be linguistic justification for the popular perception of the discourse as conservative. In other respects, it differentiates itself noticeably from its national counterpart, proving itself to be more distinctive, compared with the general language. While many differences can be explained with reference to semantic or pragmatic factors, others go much deeper, to the phraseological patterning of words located at the grammatical end of the lexicogrammatical continuum, including pronouns and core verbs.

The EU corpus is more dependent on repeated identical multiword sequences. Generally, it is the shorter sequences which appear in both sub-corpora, and semantic and pragmatic factors can be seen to have large part to play in longer sequences. The EU discourse can also be seen, however, to be more distinctive in this regard: it contains a greater number than the national discourse of types of formulae specific to it.

This picture is consolidated by the analysis of phraseological elements in the form of locutions adopted from the general language. The EU discourse is more dependent on traditional locutions of French as regards tokens, but employs fewer types of locution. The register is not devoid of traditional idioms, but these are infrequent and more typical of spoken genres than written ones.

The statistical keywords of the EU part of the corpus may be seen to be more distinctive than those of the national administrative register. A much larger number of keywords are key in the complete administrative corpus because of their significance in the EU sub-corpus. With regard to sociological keywords, while it is impossible to evaluate the extent of difference, discourse and genre do have an effect on the patterns surrounding these.

Also, in considering the verb-complement patterns highlighted by Catherine and Georgin as typical of the register of administrative language, once again the EU discourse demonstrates a greater reliance on such patterning in terms of tokens, but again reveals less variety. As a result of differently biased source data and semantic and pragmatic changes in the administrative context over time, however, neither sub-corpus shows a very strong reliance on this patterning.

The global consistency of the picture of the EU discourse which is built up over the course of Chapters 4 to 7 demonstrates that the notion of phraseology employed here is a workable concept and a useful point of entry for register and discourse analysis. There is value in the investigation of a range of different types of collocation and phraseological patterning: this highlights the multiple factors at work, and the semantic subtleties which are possible despite strong patterns in the data. The approach taken here has drawn on traditional notions of phraseological units, in the form of locutions and set formulae, and corpus-based notions of collocation as a process by which both lexical and grammatical words adopt typical linguistic environments, themselves both lexical and grammatical in nature, to present a picture of the phraseologies of EU and national French administrative language. The fact that there are distinctive patterns of phraseology shows administrators' and translators' consciousness of the particular phraseological resources of the genre, register and discourse which combine to define texts. In the same way that a narrow notion of collocation closes off potentially fertile avenues for research, and creates exceptions to rules which demand an explanation in linguistic terms, so a highly specific definition of phraseology may act as a blinker to the ways in which real language works. While research must be focused for it to contribute usefully to linguistic description, we must not lose sight of the wider picture: in this case the complexity of languages and registers, and the massive potential for choice even in a register which is perceived (rightly, it seems) to be highly formulaic.

All of the types of phraseological investigation here point to an EU discourse which is phraseologically conservative. It has regular recourse to multiword sequences, and makes frequent use of a limited number of locutions from the general language. Statistical and sociological keywords also form part of repeated phraseological resources. Undoubtedly, this is the combined effect of a number of factors. To explain fully the current state of divergence of the EU and national discourses would require a diachronic analysis of their development over the last fifty years, which is beyond the scope of this study. Initial comparison was made, however, with the French register of administration to which both discourses can be traced. This analysis found, perhaps counter-intuitively, that the EU discourse appears to be more faithful to its origins than the national discourse is. This raises further questions regarding the external influences on both discourses. Contact with English, while it has arguably had an influence on EU French, is not able to explain the apparent conservatism of the discourse.

Rather, various factors are likely to have contributed to the differentiation of EU French, regardless of whether it is fair to call it 'conservative'. These include the multilingual context of document production, the language contact situation, and, in particular, the role of translation in the EU institutions. Recent work on translated texts using corpus methodology (Baker 1996; Laviosa 2002) has shown such conservatism or 'normalisation' to be characteristic of such texts. It seems likely therefore that it is the translation process itself, a process which is so central to the workings of the EU and right at the heart of its ideology, which has contributed most to the distinctive nature of the French language as it is spoken and written in this context. Although not all of the corpus texts here are the result of translation into French, many are the product of a non-native drafter, and even those written originally in French by a native speaker may owe a proportion of their wording to precedents translated or drafted by a speaker of another official language of the EU. This does not imply that texts will show the traces of a particular language: rather it is the translation itself which has an influence on the language. The paradoxical result is that while a meeting place for many languages may suggest linguistic variety, the translation process leads to conservatism and levelling out. Comparison with the discourses of similar institutional bodies, such as the United Nations or NATO would show to what extent the phraseological character of European Union documents is distinctive.

Two types of diachronic study present a natural next step for corpus research into EU administrative French. First, it would be revealing to take a step back in time to the origins and early manifestations of the EU, to investigate the discourse in its nascent state, either the earliest EU documents, or indeed the language of its predecessors: the post-war planning system of the European Coal and Steel Community, established in 1951, and Euratom, established on the same day as the signing of the Treaty of Rome in 1957. Second, it will be exciting to see the effect that the accession of new member states is currently having on the balance of the EU and the nature of its associated language varieties.

References

Aarts, J. and W. Meijs (eds.) (1984), *Corpus Linguistics: Recent developments in the use of computer corpora in English Language Research*. Amsterdam: Rodopi.

Aarts, J. and W. Meijs (eds.) (1986), *Corpus Linguistics II: New Studies in the Analysis and Exploitation of Computer Corpora.* Amsterdam: Rodopi.

Aarts, J. and W. Meijs (eds.) (1990), *Theory and Practice in Corpus Linguistics*. Amsterdam: Rodopi.

Aarts, J., P. de Haan and N. Oostdijk (eds.) (1993), *English Language Corpora: Design, Analysis and Exploitation*. Amsterdam: Rodopi.

Aijmer, K. and B. Altenberg (eds.) (1991), *English Corpus Linguistics: Studies in Honour of Jan Svartvik*. London: Longman.

Altenberg, B. (1993), 'Recurrent verb-complement constructions in the London-Lund Corpus'. In Aarts et al. (1993), 227-246.

Altenberg, B. (1998), 'On the phraseology of spoken English: the evidence of recurrent word-combinations'. In A. P. Cowie (ed.) (1998), 101-122.

Altenberg, B. and M. Eeg-Olofsson (1990), 'Phraseology in spoken English: presentation of a project'. In J. Aarts and W. Meijs (eds.) (1990), 1-26.

Anderman, G. and M. Rogers (eds.) (2005), *In and Out of English: For Better, For Worse?* Clevedon: Multilingual Matters.

Anttila, R. (1989), *Historical and Comparative Linguistics*. Amsterdam: John Benjamins.

Atkins, S., J. Clear, and N. Ostler (1992), 'Corpus design criteria'. *Literary and Linguistic Computing* 7(1): 1-16.

Atkinson, D. and D. Biber (1994), 'Register: a review of empirical research'. In D. Biber and E. Finegan (eds.) (1994), 351-385.

Auger, C. P. (1994), *Information Sources in Grey Literature*. (3rd Edition), London: Bowker-Saur Ltd.

Ayres-Bennett, W. (1996), *A History of the French Language Through Texts*. London: Routledge.

Bahns, J. (1993), 'Lexical collocations: a contrastive view'. *ELT Journal* 47(1): 56-63.

Bainbridge, T. (1998), *The Penguin Companion to European Union.* London: Penguin.

Baker, M. (1992), *In Other Words: A Coursebook on Translation.* London: Routledge.

Baker, M. (1993), 'Corpus linguistics and translation studies - implications and applications'. In Baker et al. (1993), 233-250.

Baker, M. (1996), 'Corpus-based translation studies: the challenges that lie ahead'. In H. Somers (ed.) (1996), 175-186.

Baker, M. (1999), 'The role of corpus in investigating the linguistic behaviour of professional translators'. *International Journal of Corpus Linguistics.* 4 (2): 281-298.

Baker, M., G. Francis and E. Tognini-Bonelli (eds.) (1993), *Text and Technology: In Honour of John Sinclair*. Amsterdam: John Benjamins.

Ball, R. (1997), *The French Speaking World: A Practical Introduction to Sociolinguistic Issues*. London: Routledge.

Banchoff, T. and M. P. Smith (eds.) (1999), *Legitimacy and the European Union: the contested polity*. London: Routledge.

Battye, A. and M.-A. Hintze (1992), *The French Language Today*. London: Routledge.

Battye, A., M.-A. Hintze, P. Rowlett (2000), *The French Language Today*. (2nd edition), London: Routledge.

Baudot, J. (1992), *Fréquences d'utilisation des mots en français écrit contemporain*. Montréal: Les Presses de l'Université de Montréal.

Bazell, C. E., J. C. Catford, M. A. K. Halliday and R. H. Robins (eds.) (1966), *In Memory of J. R. Firth*. London: Longmans, Green & Co. Ltd.

Beedham, C. (ed.) (1999), Langue *and* Parole *in Synchronic and Diachronic Perspective: Selected Proceedings of the XXXIst Annual Meeting of the* Societas Linguistica Europaea, *St. Andrews, 1998*. Amsterdam: Pergamon.

Benson, M., E. Benson and R. Ilson (1986), *The BBI Combinatory Dictionary of English*. Amsterdam: John Benjamins.

Benveniste, E. (1966), *Problèmes de linguistique générale*. Paris: Éditions Gallimard.

Bergounioux, G. (1996), 'Etude socio-linguistique sur Orléans (1966-1970)'. *Revue française de linguistique appliquée: Dossier Corpus: de leur constitution à leur exploitation.* Vol. 1 - 2 (décembre 1996): 87-88.

Berruto, G. (1987), *Sociolinguistica dell'Italiano Contemporaneo*. Rome: La Nuova Italia Scientifica.

Berruto, G., C. Bettoni, G. Francescato, A. Giacalone Ramat, C. Grassi, E. Radtke, G. Sanga, A. A. Sobrero and T. Telmon (1997), *Introduzione all'italiano contemporaneo*. 3rd Edition. Rome: Laterza.

Berry, M. (1977), *An Introduction to Systemic Linguistics: 2 Levels and Links*. London: Batsford.

Biber, D. (1985), 'Investigating macroscopic textual variation through multifeature/multidimensional analyses'. *Linguistics* 23: 337-360.

Biber, D. (1988), *Variation across speech and writing*. Cambridge: Cambridge University Press.

Biber, D. (1989), 'A typology of English texts'. *Linguistics* 27(1): 3-43.

Biber, D. (1990), 'Methodological Issues Regarding Corpus-based Analyses of Linguistic Variation'. *Literary and Linguistic Computing* 5(4): 257-269.

Biber, D. (1992), 'The multi-dimensional approach to linguistic analyses of genre variation: an overview of methodology and findings'. *Computers and the Humanities* 26(5-6): 331-345.

Biber, D. (1993a), 'Representativeness in corpus design'. *Literary and Linguistic Computing* 8(4): 243-57.

Biber, D. (1993b), 'Co-occurrence patterns among collocations: a tool for corpus-based lexical knowledge acquisition'. *Computational Linguistics* 19(3): 531-538.

Biber, D. (1994), 'An analytical framework for register studies.' In Biber and Finegan (eds.) (1994), 31-56.

Biber, D. (1996), 'Investigating language use through corpus-based analyses of association patterns'. *International Journal of Corpus Linguistics* 1(2): 171-197.

Biber, D. and S. Conrad (2001), 'Register variation: a corpus approach'. In Schiffrin et al. (2001), 175-196.

Biber, D. and E. Finegan (1986), 'An initial typology of English text types'. In J. Aarts and W. Meijs (eds.) (1986), 19-46.

Biber, D. and E. Finegan (1991), 'On the exploitation of computerized corpora in variation studies'. In K. Aijmer and B. Altenberg (eds.) (1991), 204-220.

Biber, D. and E. Finegan (eds.) (1994), *Sociolinguistic Perspectives on Register*. Oxford: Oxford University Press.

Biber, D., S. Conrad and R. Reppen (1994), 'Corpus-based approaches to issues in applied linguistics'. *Applied Linguistics* 15(2): 169-189.

Biber, D., S. Conrad and R. Reppen (eds.) (1998), *Corpus Linguistics: Investigating Language Structure and Use*. Cambridge: Cambridge University Press.

Biber, D., S. Johansson, G. Leech, S. Conrad and E. Finegan (1999), *Longman Grammar of Spoken and Written English*. London: Longman.

Blanche-Benveniste, C. (1996), 'De l'utilité du corpus linguistique'. *Revue française de linguistique appliquée: Dossier Corpus: de leur constitution à leur exploitation*. Vol. 1 - 2 (décembre 1996): 25-42.

Bronckart, J.-P. (1996), *Activité langagière, textes et discours*. Lausanne; Paris: Delachaux et Niestlé.

Brulard, I. (1997), 'Linguistic Policies'. In S. Perry (ed.) (1997), 191-207.

Brunot, F. (1905), *Histoire de la langue française des origines à 1900*. Tome I: *De l'époque latine à la Renaissance*. Paris: Armand Colin.

Brunot, F. (1906), *Histoire de la langue française des origines à 1900*. Tome II: *Le seizième siècle*. Paris: Armand Colin.

Brunot, F. (1917), *Histoire de la langue française des origines à 1900*. Tome V: *Le français en France et hors de France au XVIIe siècle*. Paris: Armand Colin.

Burton, F. and P. Carlen (1979), *Official Discourse: On discourse analysis, government publications, ideology and the state*. London: Routledge & Kegan Paul.

Butler, C. S. (1985a), *Computers in Linguistics*. Oxford: Blackwell.

Butler, C. S. (1985b), *Statistics in Linguistics*. Oxford: Blackwell.

Butler, C. S. (1997), 'Repeated word combinations in spoken and written text: some implications for Functional Grammar'. In Butler et al. (1997), 60-77.

Butler, C. S. (1998), 'Collocational frameworks in Spanish'. *International Journal of Corpus Linguistics* 3(1): 1-32.

Butler, C. S., J. H. Connolly, R. A. Gatward, R. M. Vismans (eds.) (1997), *A Fund of Ideas: Recent Developments in Functional Grammar.* Amsterdam: IFOTT, University of Amsterdam.

Bywater, I. (1909), *Aristotle on the Art of Poetry.* Oxford: Clarendon.

Caldas-Coulthard, C. R. and M. Coulthard (eds.) (1996), *Texts and Practices: Readings in Critical Discourse Analysis.* London: Routledge.

Campbell, C., H. Feigenbaum, R. Linden and H. Norpeth (1995), *Politics and Government in Europe Today.* (2nd Edition), Boston: Houghton Mifflin Company.

Caput, J.-P. (1975), *La langue française: histoire d'une institution.* (tome II, 1715-1974), Paris: Larousse.

Carter, R. and W. Nash (1990), *Seeing Through Language*. Oxford: Blackwell.

Casagrande, J. and W. J. Sullivan (1992), 'Causes of irreversibility in binomial idioms: a case study in English and French'. In *Proceedings of the XVth International Congress of Linguists.* Quebec, Université Laval 9-14 August 1992. Quebec: Les Presses de l'Université Laval. 358-360.

Catherine, R. (1947), *Le style administratif.* (1st edition) Paris: Albin Michel.

Catherine, R. (1985), *Le style administratif.* (5th edition) Paris: Albin Michel.

Čermák, F. (2001), 'Substance of idioms: perennial problems, lack of data or theory?' *International Journal of Lexicography* 14 (1): 1-20.

Charrow, V. R. (1982), 'Language in the bureaucracy'. In R. J. di Pietro (ed.) (1982), 173-188.

Christie, F. and J. R. Martin (eds.) (1997), *Genres and Institutions: Social Processes in the Workplace and School.* London: Cassell.

Clear, J. (1992), 'Corpus sampling'. In G. Leitner (ed.) (1992), 21-32.

Clear, J. (1993), 'From Firth principles - computational tools for the study of collocation'. In Baker et al. (1993), 271-292.

Clear, J., G. Fox, G. Francis, R. Krishnamurthy and R. Moon (1996), 'COBUILD: The state of the art'. *International Journal of Corpus Linguistics* 1(2): 303-314.

Coleman, J. A. and R. Crawshaw (eds.) (1994), *Discourse Variety in Contemporary French.* London: AFLS/CILT.

Corpas Pastor, G. (1996), *Manual de fraseología española.* Madrid: Editorial Gredos.

Corpas Pastor, G. (ed.) (2000), *Las Lenguas de Europa: estudios de Fraseología, Fraseografía y Traducción*. Granada: Editorial Comares.

Coulmas, F. (ed.) (1991a), *A Language Policy for the European Community.* Berlin, New York: Mouton de Gruyter.

Coulmas, F. (1991b), 'European integration and the idea of the national language: Ideological roots and economic consequences'. In F. Coulmas (ed.) (1991a), 1-43.

Couture, B. (ed.) (1986a), *Functional Approaches to Writing: Research Perspectives*. Norwood, NJ: Ablex.

Couture, B. (1986b), 'Bridging epistemologies and methodologies: research in written language function'. In B. Couture (ed.) (1986a), 1-10.

Couture, B. (1986c), 'Effective ideation in written text: a functional approach to clarity and exigence'. In B. Couture (ed.) (1986a), 69-92.

Cowie, A. P. (1978), 'The place of illustrative material and collocations in the design of a learner's dictionary'. In P. Strevens (ed.) (1978), 127-139.

Cowie, A. P. (ed.) (1998), *Phraseology: Theory, Analysis, and Applications*. Oxford: Clarendon Press.

Cowie, A. P. (1999), 'Phraseology and corpora: some implications for dictionary-making'. *International Journal of Lexicography*, 12 (4): 307-323.

Cruse, D. A. (1986), *Lexical Semantics*. Cambridge: Cambridge University Press.

Crystal, D. (1997), *The Cambridge Encyclopedia of Language*. (2nd Edition) Cambridge: Cambridge University Press.

Crystal, D. and D. Davy (1969), *Investigating English Style*. Harlow, Essex: Longman.

Davies, A. (1999), *An Introduction to Applied Linguistics: From Practice to Theory*. Edinburgh: Edinburgh University Press.

Deacon, T. (1997), *The Symbolic Species*. London: Allen Lane, Penguin.

Dees, A. (1980), *Atlas des formes et des constructions des chartes françaises du 13e siècle*. Tübingen: Max Niemeyer Verlag.

Dijk, T. A. van (1985), *Handbook of Discourse Analysis* Vols. 2, 4. London: Academic Press.

Dijk, T. A. van (2001), 'Critical discourse analysis'. In Schiffrin et al. (2001), 352-371.

Dorian, N. C. (1978), *East Sutherland Gaelic: The Dialect of the Brora, Golspie, and Embo Fishing Communities*. Dublin: Dublin Institute for Advanced Studies.

Drake, H. and J. Gaffney (eds.) (1996), *The Language of Leadership in Contemporary France*. Aldershot: Dartmouth.

Duggan, J. J. (1969), *A Concordance of the Chanson de Roland*. Ohio: Ohio State University Press.

Duggan, J. J. (1973), *The Song of Roland: Formulaic Style and Poetic Craft*. Berkeley and Los Angeles, California: University of California Press.

Eggins, S. (1994), *An Introduction to Systemic Functional Linguistics*. London: Pinter.

Ellis, J. (1966), 'On contextual meaning'. In Bazell et al. (1966), 79-95.

Ellis, J. and J. Ure (1969), 'Language Varieties: Register'. In A. R. Meetham (1969), 251-259.

Ellis, J. and J. Ure (1982), *Register Range and Change. International Journal of the Sociology of Language*. 35. Amsterdam: Mouton.

Engwall, G. (1996), 'Corpus de français établis en Suède'. In *Revue française de linguistique appliquée: Dossier Corpus: de leur constitution à leur exploitation*. Vol. 1 - 2 (décembre 1996): 89-90.

European Communities Glossary. French-English, 8th Edition (revised) (1990) Luxembourg: Office des publications officielles des Communautés européennes.

Fairclough, N. (1989), *Language and Power*. London: Longman.

Fernando, C. (1996), *Idioms and Idiomaticity*. Oxford: Oxford University Press.
Fillmore, C. J. (1992), '"Corpus linguistics" or "Computer-aided armchair linguistics"'. In J. Svartvik (ed.) (1992a), 35-60.
Finegan, E. and D. Biber (1994), 'Register and social dialect variation: an integrated approach.' In D. Biber and E. Finegan (eds.) (1994), 315-347.
Firth, J. R. (1935), 'The technique of semantics'. In J. R. Firth (1957a), 7-33.
Firth, J. R. (1948), 'The semantics of linguistic science'. In J. R. Firth (1957a), 139-147.
Firth, J. R. (1950), 'Personality and language in society'. In J. R. Firth (1957a), 177-189.
Firth, J. R. (1951a), 'Modes of meaning'. In J. R. Firth (1957a), 190-215.
Firth, J. R. (1951b), 'General linguistics and descriptive grammar'. In J. R. Firth (1957a), 216-228.
Firth, J. R. (1957a), *Papers in Linguistics: 1934-1951*. London: Oxford University Press.
Firth. J. R. (1957b), 'Ethnographic analysis and language with reference to Malinowski's views'. In R. Firth (ed.) (1957), 93-118.
Firth, J. R. (1957c), 'A synopsis of linguistic theory, 1930-1955'. *Studies in Linguistic Analysis.* Special Volume of the Philological Society. Oxford: Blackwell, 1-32.
Firth, J. R. (1964), *The Tongues of Men and Speech*. London: Oxford University Press.
Firth, R. (ed.) (1957), *Man and Culture: An Evaluation of the Work of Bronislaw Malinowski*. London: Routledge and Kegan Paul.
Flesch, C. (1998), 'Fight the Fog'. Speech given to the European Commission's Fight the FOG Campaign on 9 March 1998.
(http://europa.eu.int/comm/translation/en/ftfog/index/htm)
Foley, J. A. (ed.) (1996), *J. M. Sinclair on Lexis and Lexicography.* Singapore: UniPress.
Fontenelle, T. (1994), 'What on earth are collocations?' *English Today* Vol. 10, no. 4.: 42-48.
Fontenelle, T. (1999), 'English and multilingualism in the European Union'. *Zeitschrift für Anglistik und Amerikanistik* 47/2: 120-132.
Fowler, R. (1996), 'On critical linguistics'. In C. R. Caldas-Coulthard and M. Coulthard (eds.) (1996), 3-14.
Fowler, R., B. Hodge, G. Kress and T. Trew (1979), *Language and Control.* London: Routledge and Kegan Paul.
Francis, G. (1993), 'A corpus-driven approach to grammar - principles, methods and examples'. In Baker et al. (1993), 137-156.
Francis, G. and J. Sinclair (1994), ' 'I bet he drinks Carling Black Label': a riposte to Owen on corpus grammar'. *Applied Linguistics* 15(2): 190-200.
Francis, W. Nelson (1992), 'Language corpora B.C.'. In J. Svartvik (ed.) (1992a), 17-32.
Frey, C. and D. Latin (eds.) (1997), *Le corpus lexicographique.* Louvain-la-Neuve: Duculot, Département de De Boeck & Larcier.

Gaffney, J. (1993), 'Language and style in politics'. In C. Sanders (ed.) (1993), 185-198.

Gaffney, J. (1999), 'Political rhetoric and the legitimation of the European Union'. In T. Banchoff and M. P. Smith (eds.) (1999), 199-211.

Galonnier, B. (1997), 'Le discours juridique en France et en Angleterre. Convergences et spécificités.' *ASp* 15/18: 85-104.

Garside, R., G. Leech and A. McEnery (eds.) (1997), *Corpus Annotation: Linguistic Information from Computer Text Corpora*. London: Longman.

Gellerstam, M. (1992), 'Modern Swedish text corpora'. In J. Svartvik (ed.) (1992a), 149-163.

Gellerstam, M. (2005), 'Fingerprints in Translation'. In G. Anderman and M. Rogers (eds.) (2005), 201-213.

Georgin, R. (1973), *Le code du bon langage. Le langage de l'administration et des affaires*. Paris: Les Editions ESF.

Gerth, H. H. and C. Wright Mills (eds.) (1948), *From Max Weber: Essays in Sociology*. London: Routledge and Kegan Paul.

Giddens, A. (1984), *The Constitution of Society*. Cambridge: Polity Press.

Gitsaki, C. (1996), *The Development of ESL Collocational Knowledge*. Unpublished Ph.D. Thesis.

Gläser, R. (1992), 'Relations between phraseology and terminology in specialized language'. In *Proceedings of the XVth International Congress of Linguists*. Quebec, Université Laval 9-14 August 1992. Quebec: Les Presses de l'Université Laval. 195-197.

Gläser, R. (1998), 'The stylistic potential of phraseological units in the light of genre analysis'. In A. P. Cowie (ed.) (1998), 125-143.

Gledhill, C. (1995), 'Collocation and genre analysis. the phraseology of grammatical items in cancer research abstracts and articles'. *Zeitscrift für Anglistik und Amerikanistik* 43(1): 11-36.

Gledhill, C. (1997), 'Les collocations et la construction du savoir scientifique'. *ASp* 15/18: 85-104.

Gledhill, C. (1999), 'Towards a description of English and French phraseology'. In C. Beedham (ed.) (1999), 221-237.

Gledhill, C. (2000), *Collocations in Science Writing*. Tübingen: Gunter Narr Verlag.

Goffin, R. (1997), 'L'Eurolecte: le langage d'une Europe communautaire en devenir'. *Terminologie et Traduction* I, (1997): 63 - 73.

Gowers, E. (1973), *The Complete Plain Words.* (2nd revised edition by Sir Bruce Fraser), London: HMSO.

Granger, S. (1998), 'Prefabricated patterns in advanced EFL writing: collocations and formulae'. In A. P. Cowie (ed.) (1998), 145-160.

Greenbaum, S., G. Leech and J. Svartvik (eds.) (1979), *Studies in English Linguistics for Randolph Quirk*. London: Longman.

Gross, G. (1996), *Les expressions figées en français*. Gap; Paris: Ophrys.

Guiraud, P. (1961), *Les locutions françaises*. Paris: PUF.

Guyomarch, A., H. Machin and E. Ritchie (1998), *France in the European Union.* Basingstoke: Macmillan Press Ltd.

Habert, B., A. Nazarenko and A. Salem (1997), *Les linguistiques de corpus.* Paris: Armand Colin.

Hagège, C. (1994), *Le souffle de la langue: voies et destins des parlers d'Europe.* Paris: Editions Odile Jacob.

Halliday, M. A. K. (1961), 'Categories of the theory of grammar'. *Word* 17: 241-292.

Halliday, M. A. K. (1966a), 'Some notes on 'deep' grammar'. *Journal of Linguistics* 2 (1): 57-67.

Halliday, M. A. K. (1966b), 'Lexis as a linguistic level'. In C. E. Bazell, J. C. Catford, M. A. K. Halliday and R. H. Robins (eds.) (1966), 148-162.

Halliday, M. A. K. (1973), *Explorations in the Functions of Language.* London: Edward Arnold.

Halliday, M. A. K. (1978), *Language as Social Semiotic.* London: Edward Arnold.

Halliday, M. A. K. (1985), *An Introduction to Functional Grammar.* London: Edward Arnold.

Halliday, M. A. K. (1991), 'Corpus studies and probabilistic grammar'. In K. Aijmer and B. Altenberg (eds.) (1991), 30-43.

Halliday, M. A. K. (1992), 'Language as system and language as instance: the corpus as a theoretical construct'. In J. Svartvik (ed.) (1992a), 61-77.

Halliday, M. A. K. (1993), 'Quantitative studies and probabilities in grammar'. In M. Hoey (ed.) (1993), 1-25.

Halliday, M. A. K. (1994), *An Introduction to Functional Grammar.* (2nd Edition) London: Arnold.

Halliday, M. A. K. and R. P. Fawcett (eds.) (1987), *New Developments in Systemic Linguistics.* Vol. I Theory and Description. London and New York: Frances Pinter.

Halliday, M. A. K. and R. Hasan (1976), *Cohesion in English.* London: Longman.

Halliday, M. A. K., A. McIntosh and P. Strevens (1964), *The Linguistic Sciences and Language Teaching.* London: Longman.

Hansen, S. (2000), 'A contrastive analysis of multilingual corpora: a Functional model'. Paper given at 11th Euro-International Systemic Functional Linguistics Workshop, 19-22 July 2000, University of Glasgow.

Hasan, R. (1987), 'The grammarian's dream: lexis as most delicate grammar'. In M. A. K. Halliday and R. P. Fawcett (eds.) (1987), 184-211.

Hatim, B. and I. Mason (1990), *Discourse and the Translator.* London: Longman.

Heffer, C. and H. Sauntson (eds.) (2000), *Words in Context: a Tribute to John Sinclair on his Retirement.* Birmingham: University of Birmingham.

Heid, U. (1996), 'Using Lexical Functions for the extraction of collocations from dictionaries and corpora'. L. Wanner (ed.) (1996), 115-146.

Hill, T. (1958), 'Institutional linguistics'. *Orbis.* 7: 441-455.

Hockett, C. F. (1958), *A Course in Modern Linguistics.* New York: Macmillan.

Hockey, S. (2000), *Electronic Texts in the Humanities: Principles and Practice*. Oxford: Oxford University Press.

Hoey, M. (1991), *Patterns of Lexis in Text*. Oxford: Oxford University Press.

Hoey, M. (ed.) (1993), *Data, Description, Discourse: Papers on the English Language in Honour of John McH. Sinclair on his Sixtieth Birthday*. London: HarperCollins.

Hoey, M. (1997), 'From concordance to text structure: new uses for computer corpora'. In B. Lewandowska-Tomaszczyk and P. J. Melia (eds.) (1997), 2-23.

Hoey, M. (2000), 'About sixty: the collocations, colligations and semantic prosodies of a number'. In C. Heffer and H. Sauntson (eds.) (2000), 95-109.

Hornby, A. S. (1975), *Guide to Patterns and Usage in English*. 2nd Edition. (1st Ed. 1954) Oxford: Oxford University Press.

Householder, F. W. (1959), 'On linguistic primes'. *Word* 15: 231-239.

Howarth, P. A. (1996), *Phraseology in English Academic Writing*. Tübingen: Max Niemeyer Verlag.

Howarth, P. A. (1998), 'The phraseology of learners' academic writing'. In A. P. Cowie (ed.) (1998), 161-186.

Hudson, R. A. (1996), *Sociolinguistics*. (2nd Edition) Cambridge: Cambridge University Press.

Hunston, S. (1999a), 'Corpus evidence for disadvantage: issues in critical interpretation'. Paper given at BAAL/CUP Applied Linguistics Seminar, University of Reading - 22nd May 1999.

Hunston, S. (1999b), 'Local grammars: the future of corpus-driven grammar?' Paper presented at the 32nd BAAL Annual Meeting, Edinburgh, 16-18 September 1999.

Hunston, S. (2000a), 'Phraseology and the modal verb: a study of pattern and meaning'. In C. Heffer and H. Sauntson (eds.) (2000), 234-248.

Hunston, S. (2000b), 'Colligation, lexis, pattern, and text'. In M. Scott and G. Thompson (eds.) (2000), 13-33.

Hunston, S. and G. Francis (1998), 'Verbs observed: a corpus-driven pedagogic grammar'. *Applied Linguistics* 19(1): 45-72.

Hunston, S. and G. Francis (1999), *Pattern Grammar*. Amsterdam: John Benjamins.

Iedema, R. (1997), 'The language of administration: organizing human activity in formal institutions'. In F. Christie and J. R. Martin (eds.) (1997), 73-100.

Iglesias-Rábade, L. (2000), 'French phrasal power in late Middle English: some evidence concerning the verb *nime(n)/take(n)*'. In D. A. Trotter (ed.) (2000), 93-130.

Inkster, G. (1997), 'First catch your corpus: building a French undergraduate corpus from readily available textual resources'. In A. Wichmann et al. (eds.) (1997), 267-276.

Judge, A. (1993), 'French: a planned language?' In C. Sanders (ed.) (1993), 7-26.

Judge, A. and S. Judge (1998), 'The impact of European linguistic policies on French'. In Marley et al. (1998), 291-318.

Kennedy, G. (1998), *An Introduction to Corpus Linguistics*. London and New York: Longman.

Kenny, D. (1997a), '(Ab)normal translations: a German-English parallel corpus for investigating normalization in translation'. In B. Lewandowska-Tomaszczyk and P. J. Melia (eds.) (1997), 387-392.

Kenny, D. (1997b), 'Creatures of habit? What collocation can tell us about translation'. Poster presented at ACH-ALLC 97 Queen's University, Kingston, Ontario, 3-7 June 1997.

Kita, K., Y. Kato, T. Omoto and Y. Yano (1994), 'Automatically extracting collocations from corpora for language learning'. In A. Wilson and T. McEnery (eds.), (1994), 53-64.

Kjellmer, G. (1984), 'Some thoughts on collocational distinctiveness'. In J. Aarts and W. Meijs (eds.) (1984), 163-172.

Kjellmer, G. (1987), 'Aspects of English collocations'. In W. Meijs (ed.) (1987), 133-140.

Kjellmer, G. (1990), 'Patterns of collocability'. In J. Aarts and W. Meijs (eds.) (1990), 163-178.

Kjellmer, G. (1991), 'A mint of phrases'. In K. Aijmer and B. Altenberg (eds.) (1991), 111-127.

Kjellmer, G. (1994) *A Dictionary of English Collocations*. Oxford: Clarendon Press.

Knapp, A. and V. Wright (2001), *The Government and Politics of France*. (4th Edition), London and New York: Routledge.

Kretzschmar, W. A. and S. Tamasi (2001), 'Distributional Foundations for a Theory of Language Change'. Paper given at NWAVE 30, Raleigh (2001).

Krishnamurthy, R. (2000), 'Collocation: from *silly ass* to lexical sets'. In C. Heffer and H. Sauntson (eds.) (2000), 31-47.

Kytö, M., M. Rissanen and S. Wright (eds.) (1994), *Corpora Across the Centuries*. Amsterdam: Rodopi.

Labarrère, C. (1990), 'Langue française et administration'. *40 ans de défense de la langue française: 1952-1992*. November 1992. Edition électronique. (http://www.refer.mg/textinte/dlf/admini.htm)

Labov, W. (1972a), *Sociolinguistic Patterns*. Philadelphia: University of Pennsylvania Press.

Labov, W. (1972b), 'The study of language in its social context'. In W. Labov (1972a), 183-259.

Labov, W. (1994), *Principles of Linguistic Change: Volume 1: Internal Factors*. Oxford: Blackwell.

Larsen, H. (1997), *Foreign Policy and Discourse Analysis*. London: Routledge.

Lass, R. (1997), *Historical Linguistics and Language Change*. Cambridge: Cambridge University Press.

Laviosa, S. (2002), *Corpus-based Translation Studies*. Amsterdam: Rodopi.

Leech, G. (1991), 'The state of the art in corpus linguistics'. In K. Aijmer and B. Altenberg (eds.) (1991), 8-29.

Leech, G. (1993), 'Corpus annotation schemes'. *Literary and Linguistic Computing* 8(4): 275-81.

Leech, G. (1997a), 'Introducing corpus annotation'. In R. Garside et al. (eds.) (1997), 1-18.

Leech, G. (1997b), 'Grammatical tagging'. In R. Garside et al. (eds.) (1997), 19-33.

Leech, G. (1997c), 'Teaching and language corpora: a convergence'. In A. Wichmann et al. (eds.) (1997), 1-23.

Lehmann, W. P. (1992), *Historical Linguistics: An Introduction.* (3rd Edition), London and New York: Routledge.

Leitner, G. (ed.) (1992), *New Directions in English Language Corpora.* Berlin: Mouton de Gruyter.

Lewandowska-Tomaszczyk, B. and P. J. Melia (eds.) (1997), *PALC '97: Practical Applications in Language Corpora.* Lódz: Lódz University Press.

Lodge, D. (1984), *Small World: An Academic Romance.* London: Secker and Warburg.

Lodge, R. A. (ed.) (1985), *Le plus ancien registre de comptes des consuls de Montferrand en provençal auvergnat 1259-1272.* Clermont-Ferrand: La Française d'Edition et d'Imprimerie.

Lodge, R. A. (1993), *French: From Dialect to Standard.* London: Routledge.

Longe, V. U. (1985), 'Aspects of the textual features of officialese - the register of public administration'. *International Review of Applied Linguistics in Language Teaching* 23(4): 301-313.

Louw, B. (1993), 'Irony in the text or insincerity in the writer? The diagnostic potential of semantic prosodies'. In Baker et al. (1993), 157-176.

Louw, B. (2000), 'Contextual prosodic theory: bringing semantic prosodies to life'. In C. Heffer and H. Sauntson (eds.) (2000), 48-94.

Lyons, J. (1966), 'Firth's theory of meaning'. In Bazell et al. (1966), 288-302.

Makkai, A. (1972), *Idiom Structure In English.* The Hague: Mouton.

Makkai, A. (1992a), 'Summary of the first symposium on idioms'. In *Proceedings of the XVth International Congress of Linguists.* Quebec, Université Laval 9-14 August 1992. Quebec: Les Presses de l'Université Laval. 345-346.

Makkai, A. (1992b), 'Idiomaticity as the essence of language'. In *Proceedings of the XVth International Congress of Linguists.* Quebec, Université Laval 9-14 August 1992. Quebec: Les Presses de l'Université Laval. 361-363.

Malinowski, B. (1935), *Coral Gardens and their Magic.* Volume 2. *The Language of Magic and Gardening.* London: George Allen and Unwin.

Malinowski, B. (1949), 'The problem of meaning in primitive languages'. Supplement 1 in C. K. Ogden and I. A. Richards (1949), 296-336.

Marley, D., M.-A. Hintze and G. Parker (1998), *Linguistic Identities and Policies in France and the French-speaking World.* London: AFLS/CILT.

Martin, J. (1997), 'Du bon usage des corpus dans la recherche sur le discours spécifique'. *ASp* 15/18: 75-83.

Martin, J. R. (1997), 'Analysing genre: functional parameters'. In F. Christie and J. R. Martin (eds.) (1997), 3-39.

Matoré, G. (1953), *La méthode en lexicologie*. Paris: Didier.

Matoré, G. (1988), *Le vocabulaire et la société du XVIe siècle*. Paris: PUF.

McEnery, T. and A. Wilson (1996), *Corpus Linguistics*. Edinburgh: Edinburgh University Press.

McEnery, T. and A. Wilson (2001), *Corpus Linguistics*. 2nd Edition. Edinburgh: Edinburgh University Press.

McKenny, J. A. (1999), Message and bibliography posted on CORPORA list 04/08/99.

Meetham, A. R. (1969), *Encyclopaedia of Linguistics, Information and Control*. Oxford: Pergamon.

Meijs, W. (ed.) (1987), *Corpus Linguistics and Beyond: Proceedings of the Seventh International Conference on English Language Research on Computerized Corpora*. Amsterdam: Rodopi.

Mel'čuk, I. A. (1996), 'Lexical Functions: a tool for the description of lexical relations in a lexicon'. In L. Wanner (ed.) (1996), 37-102.

Mel'čuk, I. A. (1998), 'Collocations and lexical functions'. In A. P. Cowie (ed.) (1998), 23-53.

Meyer, I. and K. Mackintosh (1996), 'The corpus from a terminographer's viewpoint'. *International Journal of Corpus Linguistics* 1(2): 257-285.

Mitchell, T. F. (1971), 'Linguistic "Goings On": Collocations and other lexical matters arising on the syntagmatic record'. *Archivum Linguisticum N. S.* 2: 35-69.

Mitchell, T. F. (1975), *Principles of Firthian Linguistics*. London: Longman.

Moon, R. (1998a), *Fixed Expressions and Idioms in English*. Oxford: Clarendon Press.

Moon, R. (1998b), 'Frequencies and forms of phrasal lexemes in English'. In A. P. Cowie (ed.) (1998), 79-100.

Musacchio, M. T. (2005), 'The Influence of English on Italian: The Case of Translations of Economics Articles'. In G. Anderman and M. Rogers (eds.) (2005), 71-96.

Musolff, A. (1996), 'False friends borrowing the right words? Common terms and metaphors in European communication'. In A. Musolff, C. Schäffner and M. Townson (eds.) (1996), 15-30.

Musolff, A., C. Schäffner and M. Townson (eds.) (1996), *Conceiving of Europe: Diversity in Unity*. Aldershot: Dartmouth.

Nattinger, J. R. and J. DeCarrico (1992), *Lexical Phrases and Language Teaching*. Oxford: Oxford University Press.

Newmark, P. (1991), *About Translation*. Clevedon: Multilingual Matters Ltd.

Nunan, D. (1993), *Introducing Discourse Analysis*. London: Penguin.

Oakes, M. P. (1998), *Statistics for Corpus Linguistics*. Edinburgh: Edinburgh University Press.

Offord, M. (1990), *Varieties of Contemporary French*. Basingstoke: Macmillan.
Offord, M. (1994), 'Protecting the French language'. In Parry et al. (1994), 75-94.
Ogden, C. K. and I. A. Richards (1949), *The Meaning of Meaning: A Study of the Influence of Language Upon Thought and of the Science of Symbolism*. (10th Edition), London: Routledge & Kegan Paul Ltd.
Orwell, G. (1946), 'Politics and the English language'. In *Collected Essays: George Orwell* (1961), London: Secker and Warburg. 353-367.
Owen, C. (1993), 'Corpus-based grammar and the Heineken effect: lexicogrammatical description for language learners'. *Applied Linguistics* 14(2): 167-187.
Palmer, H. E. (1917), *The Scientific Study and Teaching of Languages*. London: George G. Harrap.
Palmer, H. E. and F. G. Blandford (1976), *A Grammar of Spoken English*. (3rd Edition 1969, first published 1924). Cambridge: Cambridge University Press.
Parry, M. M., W. V. Davies and R. A. M. Temple (eds.) (1994), *The Changing Voices of Europe: Social and Political changes and their linguistic repercussions, past, present and future*. Cardiff: University of Wales Press and Modern Humanities Research Association.
Partington, A. (1998), *Patterns and Meanings: Using Corpora for English Language Research and Teaching*. Amsterdam: John Benjamins.
Pawley, A. and F. H. Syder (1983), 'Two puzzles for linguistic theory: nativelike selection and nativelike fluency'. In J. C. Richards and R. W. Schmidt (eds.) (1983), 191-226.
Pearson, J. (1998), *Terms in Context*. Amsterdam: John Benjamins.
Perry, S. (ed.) (1997), *Aspects of Contemporary France*. London: Routledge.
Phillipson, R. (2003), *English-Only Europe? Challenging Language Policy*. London and New York: Routledge.
Picoche, J. (1992), *Précis de lexicologie française: l'étude et l'enseignement du vocabulaire*. Paris: Nathan.
Pietro, R. J. di (ed.) (1982), *Linguistics and the Professions*. Norwood, NJ: Ablex.
Pinker, S. (1999), *Words and Rules*. London: Weidenfeld and Nicolson.
Piper, A. (1999), 'Some have credit cards and others have giro cheques: a study of "individuals" and "people" learning under New Labour'. Paper given at BAAL/CUP Applied Linguistics Seminar, University of Reading - 22nd May 1999.
Popper, K. (1959), *The Logic of Scientific Discovery*. London: Hutchison.
Posner, R. (1997), *Linguistic Change in French*. Oxford: Clarendon Press.
Quirk, R., S. Greenbaum, G. Leech and J. Svartvik (1985), *A Comprehensive Grammar of the English Language*. London: Longman.
Renouf, A. (1987), 'Corpus development'. In J. M. Sinclair (ed.) (1987a), 1-40.
Renouf, A. (ed.) (1998), *Explorations in Corpus Linguistics*. Amsterdam: Rodopi.
Renouf, A. and J. M. Sinclair (1991), 'Collocational frameworks in English'. In K. Aijmer and B. Altenberg (eds.) (1991), 128-144.

Resche, C. (1997), 'Prolégomènes à la phraséologie comparée en langue de spécialité: exemple de l'anglais et du français de la finance'. *ASp* 15/18: 487-503.

Rey, A. and S. Chantreau (1993), *Dictionnaire des expressions et locutions*. (2nd edition), Paris: Robert.

Richards, J. C. and R. W. Schmidt (eds.) (1983), *Language and Communication*. London/New York: Longman.

Robins, R. H. (1961), 'John Rupert Firth'. *Language* 37 (2): 191-200.

Robins, R. H. (1967), *A Short History of Linguistics* (1st Edition), London and New York: Longman.

Robins, R. H. (1990), *A Short History of Linguistics* (3rd Edition), London and New York: Longman.

Romaine, S. (1994), *Language in Society: An Introduction to Sociolinguistics*. Oxford: Oxford University Press.

Rothwell, W. (2000), 'Aspects of lexis and morphosyntactical mixing in the languages of medieval England'. In D. A. Trotter (ed.) (2000), 213-232.

Ryan, A. and A. Wray (eds.) (1997), *Evolving Models of Language*. Clevedon: BAAL, Multilingual Matters.

Sanders, C. (ed.) (1993), *French Today: Language in its Social Context*. Cambridge: Cambridge University Press.

Sanders, C. (1994), 'Register and genre in French and English: notes towards contrastive research'. In J. A. Coleman and R. Crawshaw (eds.) (1994), 87-105.

Schaetzen, C. de (1996), 'Corpus et terminologie: constitution de corpus spécialisés pour la confection de dictionnaires'. *Revue française de linguistique appliquée: Dossier Corpus: de leur constitution à leur exploitation*. Vol. 1 - 2 (décembre 1996): 57-76.

Schäffner, C. (1997), 'Strategies of translating political texts'. In A. Trosborg (ed.) (1997a), 119-143.

Schäffner, C. (1999), 'Metaphor, politics, Europe, translation'. Paper given at Durham University - 23rd February 1999.

Schiffrin, D. (1994), *Approaches to Discourse*. Oxford: Blackwell.

Schiffrin, D., D. Tannen and H. E. Hamilton (eds.) (2001), *The Handbook of Discourse Analysis*. Oxford: Blackwell.

Scott, M. (1997a), 'PC Analysis of key words and key key words'. *System* 25 (2): 233-245.

Scott, M. (1997b), 'The right word in the right place'. *Arbeiten aus Anglistik und Amerikanistik* 22(2): 235-248.

Scott, M. (1999), *WordSmith Tools*. Version 3. Oxford: Oxford University Press.

Scott, M. (2000), 'Mapping key words to *problem* and *solution*'. In M. Scott and G. Thompson (eds.) (2000), 109-127.

Scott, M. and G. Thompson (eds.) (2000), *Patterns of Text: In Honour of Michael Hoey*. Amsterdam/Philadelphia: John Benjamins.

Sealey, A. (1999), 'Using the BNC to investigate linguistic representations of children'. Paper given at BAAL/CUP Applied Linguistics Seminar, University of Reading - 22nd May 1999.

Seidel, G. (1985), 'Political discourse analysis'. In T. A. van Dijk (1985), *Handbook of Discourse Analysis,* Vol. 4. London: Academic Press. 43-60.

Seleskovitch, D. and M. Lederer (1984), *Interpréter pour traduire.* Paris: Publications de la Sorbonne, Didier Érudition.

Sinclair, J. M. (1966), 'Beginning the study of lexis'. In Bazell et al. (1966), 410-430.

Sinclair, J. M. (1984), 'Naturalness in language'. In J. Aarts and W. Meijs (eds.) (1984), 203-210.

Sinclair, J. M. (ed.) (1987a), *Looking Up: An Account of the COBUILD Project in Lexical Computing and the Development of the Collins COBUILD English Language Dictionary*. London: Collins ELT.

Sinclair, J. M. (1987b), 'The nature of the evidence'. In J. M. Sinclair (ed.) (1987), 150-159.

Sinclair, J. M. (1987c), 'Grammar in the dictionary'. In J. M. Sinclair (ed.) (1987), 104-115.

Sinclair, J. M. (1987d), 'Collocation: a progress report'. In R. Steele and T> Threadgold (eds.) (1987), Volume II. 319-331.

Sinclair, J. M. (1987e), 'The dictionary of the future'. Reprinted in J. A. Foley (ed.) (1996), 121-136.

Sinclair, J. M. (1987f), 'The first Cobuild dictionary'. Reprinted in J. A. Foley (ed.) (1996), 137-152.

Sinclair, J. M. (1990), 'Progress in English computational lexicography'. Reprinted in J. A. Foley (ed.) (1996), 102-120.

Sinclair, J. M. (1991), *Corpus, Concordance, Collocation.* Oxford: Oxford University Press.

Sinclair, J. M. (1992), 'The automatic analysis of corpora'. In J. Svartvik (ed.) (1992a), 379-397.

Sinclair, J. M. (1996), 'The empty lexicon'. *International Journal of Corpus Linguistics* 1(1): 99-119.

Sinclair, J. M. (1997), 'Corpus evidence in language description'. In A. Wichmann et al. (eds.) (1997), 27-39.

Sinclair, J. M. (1998), 'The lexical item'. In E. Weigand (ed.) (1998), 1-24.

Sinclair, J. M. (2000a), 'The search for units of meaning'. In G. Corpas Pastor (ed.) 7-38.

Sinclair, J. M. (2000b), 'The deification of information'. In M. Scott and G. Thompson (eds.) (2000), 287-314.

Sinclair, J. and R. Carter (eds.) (2004), *Trust the Text: Language, Corpus and Discourse*. London: Routledge.

Sinclair, J. M. and S. Jones (1974), 'English lexical collocations - a study in computational linguistics'. Reprinted in J. A. Foley (ed.) (1996), 21-54.

Sinclair, J. M. and A. Renouf (1988), 'A lexical syllabus for language learning'. Reprinted in J. A. Foley (ed.) (1996), 72-92.

Sinclair, J. M., M. Hoey and G. Fox (eds.) (1993), *Techniques of Description: Spoken and Written Discourse*. London: Routledge.

Smith, J. M. H. (1992), *Province and Empire: Brittany and the Carolingians*. Cambridge: Cambridge University Press.

Somers, H. (ed.) (1996), *Terminology, LSP and Translation.* Amsterdam: John Benjamins.

Sperberg-McQueen, C. M. and L. Burnard (1995), 'The design of the TEI encoding scheme'. *Computers and the Humanities.* 29 (1): 17-39.

Sripicharn, P. (2000), 'Data-driven learning materials as a way of teaching lexis in context'. In C. Heffer and H. Sauntson (eds.) (2000), 169-178.

Steele, R. and T. Threadgold (eds.) (1987), *Language Topics: Essays in Honour of Michael Halliday*. Vols. I and II. Amsterdam: John Benjamins.

Stevens, A. (1996), *The Government and Politics of France.* 2nd Edition. Basingstoke: Macmillan.

Straehle, C., G. Weiss, R. Wodak, P. Muntigl and M. Sedlak (1999), 'Struggle as metaphor in European Union discourses on unemployment'. *Discourse and Society* 10(1): 67-99.

Strevens, P. (ed.) (1978), *In Honour of A. S. Hornby*. Oxford: Oxford University Press.

Stubbs, M. (1993), 'British traditions in text analysis - from Firth to Sinclair'. In Baker et al. (1993), 1-33.

Stubbs, M. (1995), 'Collocations and semantic profiles'. *Functions of Language* 2(1): 23-55.

Stubbs, M. (1996), *Text and Corpus Analysis*. Oxford: Blackwell.

Stubbs, M. (1997), 'Whorf's children: Critical comments on Critical Discourse Analysis (CDA)'. In A. Ryan and A. Wray (eds.) (1997), 100-116.

Stubbs, M. (1999), 'Society, education and language: the last 2000 (and the next 20?) years of language teaching'. Paper presented at the 32nd BAAL Annual Meeting, Edinburgh, 16-18 September 1999.

Stubbs, M. (2000), Using very large text collections to study semantic schemas: a research note'. In C. Heffer and H. Sauntson (eds.) (2000), 1-9.

Stubbs, M. (2001a), 'Computer-assisted text and corpus analysis: lexical cohesion and communicative competence'. In Schiffrin et al. (2001), 304-320.

Stubbs, M. (2001b), *Words and Phrases: Corpus Studies of Lexical Semantics*. Oxford: Blackwell.

Stubbs, M. and A. Gerbig (1993), 'Human and inhuman geography: on the computer-assisted analysis of long texts'. In M. Hoey (ed.) (1993), 64-85.

Svartvik, J. (ed.) (1992a), *Directions in Corpus Linguistics.* Proceedings of Nobel Symposium 82, Stockholm, 4-8 August 1991. Berlin: Mouton de Gruyter.

Svartvik, J. (1992b), 'Corpus linguistics comes of age'. In J. Svartvik (ed.) (1992a), 7-13.

Swales, J. M. (1990a), *Genre Analysis: English in Academic and Research Settings*. Cambridge: Cambridge University Press.

Swales, J. M. (1990b), 'Discourse analysis in professional contexts'. *Annual Review of Applied Linguistics* 11 (1990): 103-114.

Swales, J. M. (1998), *Other Floors, Other Voices: A Textography of a Small University Building.* Mahwah, N.J.: Lawrence Erlbaum.

Teubert, W. (1996), Editorial: *International Journal of Corpus Linguistics* 1(1): iii-x.

Thody, P. and H. Evans (1985), *Faux Amis and Key Words*. London: The Athlone Press.

Thomas, J. and M. Short (eds.) (1996), *Using Corpora for Language Research.* London and New York: Longman.

Thomason, S. G. (2001), *Language Contact: An Introduction*. Edinburgh: Edinburgh University Press.

Thompson, G. (1996), *Introducing Functional Grammar*. London: Arnold.

Tognini-Bonelli, E. (1996), *The Role of Corpus Evidence in Linguistic Theory and Description*. Ph.D. Thesis, Birmingham University.

Tognini-Bonelli, E. (2001), *Corpus Linguistics at Work.* Amsterdam: John Benjamins.

Trager, G. L. (1940), 'The Russian gender categories'. *Language* XVI: 300-307.

Tribble, C. (1998), 'Genres, keywords, teaching: towards a pedagogic account of the language of project proposals'. Paper presented at TALC 98.

Trosborg, A. (ed.) (1997a), *Text Typology and Translation.* Amsterdam: John Benjamins.

Trosborg, A. (1997b), 'Text typology: register, genre and text type'. In A. Trosborg, (ed.) (1997a), 3-23.

Trosborg, A. (1997c), 'Translating hybrid political texts'. In A. Trosborg (ed.) (1997a), 145-158.

Trotter, D. A. (ed.) (2000), *Multilingualism in Later Medieval Britain.* Cambridge: D. S. Brewer.

Trudgill, P. (1995), *Sociolinguistics: An Introduction to Language and Society.* (Revised Edition) London: Penguin.

Tucker, G. (2000), 'From theory to corpora and back to theory'. Paper given at 11th Euro-International Systemic Functional Linguistics Workshop, 19-22 July 2000, University of Glasgow.

Ventola, E. (1984), 'Orientation to social semiotics in foreign language teaching'. *Applied Linguistics* 5: 275-286.

Wagner, E. (2005), 'Translating and/or Editing – The Way Forward?' In G. Anderman and M. Rogers (eds.) (2005), 214-226.

Wagner, E., S. Bech and J. M. Martínez (2002), *Translating for the European Union Institutions.* Manchester: St. Jerome.

Walter, H. (1988), *Le français dans tous les sens*. Paris: Robert Laffont.

Wanner, L. (ed.) (1996), *Lexical Functions in Lexicography and Natural Language Processing*. Amsterdam/Philadelphia: John Benjamins.

Wardhaugh, R. (1986), *An Introduction to Sociolinguistics*. Oxford: Basil Blackwell.

Wardhaugh, R. (1987), *Languages in Competition: Dominance, Diversity and Decline*. Oxford: Basil Blackwell.

Weigand, E. (ed.) (1998), *Contrastive Lexical Semantics.* Amsterdam: John Benjamins.

Weinreich, U. (1953), *Languages in Contact: Findings and Problems*. New York: Publications of the Linguistic Circle of New York.

Wichmann, A., S. Fligelstone, T. McEnery and G. Knowles (eds.) (1997), *Teaching and Language Corpora*. London: Longman.

Williams, G. (1992), *Sociolinguistics: A Sociological Critique*. London: Routledge.

Williams, G. (1999), *French Discourse Analysis: the method of post-structuralism*. London: Routledge.

Williams, G. C. (1998), 'Collocational networks: interlocking patterns of lexis in a corpus of plant biology research articles'. *International Journal of Corpus Linguistics*. Vol. 3(1): 151-171.

Williams, G. C. (2001a), *Les réseaux collocationnels dans la construction et l'exploitation d'un corpus dans le cadre d'une communauté de discours scientifique*. Lille: Presses Universitaires de Septentrion.

Williams, G. C. (2001b), 'Sur les caratéristiques de la collocation'. *Tome 2. Actes de TALN*, Tours 2-5 juillet 2001. Université de Tours. 9-16.

Williams, R. (1976), *Keywords*. London: Croom Helm.

Williams, R. (1988), *Keywords: A Vocabulary of Culture and Society*. London: Fontana.

Wilson, A. and T. McEnery (eds.) (1994), *Corpora in Language Education and Research: A Selection of Papers from Talc94*. Lancaster: Lancaster University Unit for Computer Research on the English Language.

Wilson, J. (2001), 'Political discourse'. In Schiffrin et al. (2001), 398-415.

Wise, H. (1997), *The Vocabulary of Modern French: Origins, Structure and Function*. London: Routledge.

Witte, B. de (1991), 'The impact of European Community rules on linguistic policies of the Member States'. In F. Coulmas (ed.) (1991a), 163-177.

Wittgenstein, L. (1967), *Philosophical Investigations*. 3rd Edition. (trans. G. E. M. Anscombe) Oxford: Basil Blackwell.

Wouden, T. van der (1997), *Negative Contexts. Collocation, Polarity and Multiple Negation.* London: Routledge.

Wright, L. (2000), 'Bills, accounts, inventories: everyday trilingual activities in the business world of later medieval England'. In D. A. Trotter (ed.) (2000), 149-156.

Wright, V. (1989), *The Government and Politics of France.* (3rd Edition), London: Routledge.

Zipf, G. K. (1949), *Human Behaviour and the Principle of Least Effort.* New York: Hafner.

Appendix 1: Text Sources and Design of Administrative Corpus

All of the texts in the administrative corpus were drawn from the Internet between March and September 1999. The key sites used were as follows:

EU texts:

http://europa.eu.int
http://ue.eu.int
http://www.ecb.int
http://www.euro-ombudsman.eu.int
http://www.europarl.eu.int

French national texts:

http://www.adit.fr
http://www.premier-ministre.gouv.fr
http://www.assemblee-nat.fr
http://www.elysee.fr
http://www.ladocfrancaise.gouv.fr
http://www.legifrance.gouv.fr
http://www.senat.fr
http://www.justice.gouv.fr
http://www.plan.gouv.fr

Table A1.1: Outline of EU half of Administrative Corpus (FREUCO)

		Texts	Words
PRSP	Discours - Commission[87]	80	168,434
PASP	Discours - Parliament[88]	8	15,110
ECB	Discours - ECB[89]	3	12,737
PRIP	Comm. de presse - Commission[90]	250	177,761
PRPRES	Communiqué de presse - Council[91]	20	21,855
PRCES	Communiqué de presse - Ecosoc[92]	10	4,470
OMBPR	Comm. de presse - Ombudsman[93]	4	1,582
RG	Rapport Général - introductions[94]	2	5,129

87 Speeches by EU Commissioners

88 Speeches by the President of the European Parliament at various meetings and councils

89 Speeches by the European Central Bank to the public

90 Press releases issued by the European Commission

91 Press releases issued by the Council of Ministers of the European Union

92 Press releases issued by the Economic and Social Committee

93 Press releases from the European Ombudsman

OJL	Textes législatifs - JO (OJ L Series)[95]	40	135,445
COM	Documents COM (OJ C Series)[96]	20	56,631
TREAT	Traités[97]	3	107,645
CE	Session du Conseil Européen[98]	25	103,954
PC98	Concl. de la Présidence (Conseil)[99]	5	74,171
LB	Livres blancs[100]	3	43,545
PRCJE	Bulletin de la CJE[101]	5	43,498
PT	Programme de Travail[102]	3	35,864
PRMEMO	Memo - Commission[103]	20	35,210
PRPESC	PESC - Council[104]	40	11,592
PA97	Plans d'action[105]	2	10,756
		543	1,065,389

94 Introductions to General Reports on the activity of the European Union

95 Community legislation. The L Series of the Official Journal contains EU legislation. This includes: Regulations (binding in their entirety and directly applicable in all Member States), Directives (binding in the States to which they are addressed, their method of application left to national authorities), Decisions (binding on those to whom they are addressed), Recommendations and Opinions (with no binding force).

96 The C Series of the OJ (Communications) contains material other than actual legislation, including European Commission proposals for legislation.

97 Founding treaties: Amsterdam Treaty, Maastricht Treaty (consolidated), and Treaty of Rome (consolidated)

98 Meetings of various European Councils (e.g. on Agriculture, Budget, Culture etc.)

99 Presidency Conclusions from European Councils

100 White papers (proposals for Community action) and Green papers (communications on a specific policy area)

101 Bulletin of the European Court of Justice

102 Commission programme of work

103 Informal Commission documents providing background information on topics, primarily for journalists

104 Council of Ministers' statements in the framework of the External and Security Cooperation Policy (PESC)

105 Commission action plans

Table A1.2: Outline of French national half of Administrative Corpus (FRNACO)

		Texts	Words
SPPR	Discours - President[106]	30	52,113
SPPM	Discours - Premier Ministre[107]	30	71,734
SPM	Discours - Ministres[108]	30	74,255
CPCM	Communiqué - Conseil de Ministres[109]	40	47,788
CPPM	Communiqué de presse - PM[110]	60	15,946
CPM	Communiqué de presse - Ministères[111]	200	77,943
CPS	Communiqué de presse - Sénat[112]	30	31,869
RAPO	Rapports officiels[113]	10	195,596
RAPM	Rapports[114]	4	132,671
JO	Journal Officiel[115]	60	82,982
DP	Dossiers de Presse[116]	10	67,638

106 Speeches by the President of the French Republic, Jacques Chirac

107 Speeches by the Prime Minister, Lionel Jospin

108 Speeches from Ministries: Agriculture et Pêche; Culture et Communication; Défense; Economie, Finances et Budget; Education Nationale, Recherche et Technologie; Equipement, Transports et Logement; Intérieur; Jeunesse et Sports; Justice; PME, Commerce et Artisanat; Santé; Social; Télécommunications, Technologies de l'Information et Postes; Tourisme; Ville.

109 Press releases from the Conseil de Ministres

110 Press releases from the Premier Ministre

111 Press releases from the various Ministries: Aménagement du Territoire et de l'Environnement; Commerce Extérieur; Culture et Communication; Défense; Economie, Finances et Budget; Education Nationale, Recherche et Technologie; Emploi et Solidarité; Equipement, Transports et Logement; Industrie; Jeunesse et Sports; Outre-Mer; PME, Commerce et Artisanat; Santé; Social; Télécommunications, Technologies de l'Information et Postes; Tourisme; Ville.

112 Press releases from the Sénat

113 Official reports from experts to Ministers on a range of topics and issues

114 Reports from experts to Ministers on a range of topics and issues

115 Documents from the Official Journal, including Lois, Ordonnances, Décrets, Arrêtés and Circulaires

TFCONV	Textes fond. - Conventions[117]	1	8,444
TFCONS	Textes fond. - Constitution[118]	2	14,531
TFDH	Textes fond. - Droits de l'Homme[119]	2	8,350
ANCRs	Compte rendu (Ass. Nat.- transc.)[120]	1	50,355
ANCRw	Compte rendu (Commissions of the Ass. Nat.)[121]	20	46,315
ANPL	Assemblée Nationale projets de loi[122]	10	73,714
CGLM	Lettres de mission - Commissaire au plan[123]	3	3,920
		543	1,056,164

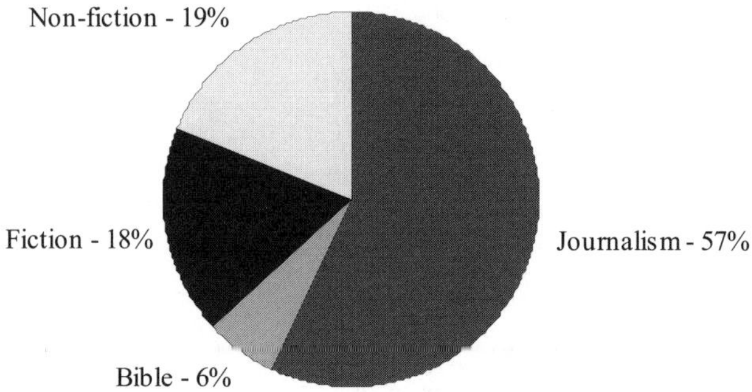

Figure A.1.1: Comparator Corpus – 2.25 million words

116 Dossiers on a range of topics, predominantly for the Press, emanating from various ministries

117 Convention relative aux droits de l'enfant

118 Constitutions

119 Déclaration des Droits de l'Homme, and Convention européenne des Droits de l'Homme

120 Transcription of National Assembly debates

121 Reports from various commissions of the Assemblée Nationale

122 Draft legislation from the Assemblée Nationale

123 Letters from Premier Ministre to Commissaire au Plan. Between 1946 to 1952, Jean Monnet was head of the Commissariat Général du Plan, before he left to run the European Coal and Steel Community.

Appendix 2: Locutions in FRADCO

Dans le cadre de...	1481
Tenir compte de...	895
Entrer/Être en vigueur	440
Avoir lieu (de)	408
Jouer un rôle	338
En vertu de	332
A compter de...	299
A l'égard de...	251
En cause	247
Prendre à sa (en) charge	194
Sous réserve de...	193
De plus en plus	189
Dans la mesure de (où)	181
A long terme	165
De (plein) droit	153
Faire face	146
Être en mesure de	139
En revanche	137
Au plus tard	132
Donner lieu à...	130
Bien sûr!	127
Tout au (du) long de	121
D'ores et déjà	118
Prendre acte de qqch	118
A moyen terme	107
A (ce) propos	97
Faire preuve de...	80
En tout état de cause	74
A l'heure	70
Entre autres	70
Faire appel à	70
A distance	69
Prendre (bonne) note	68
En fait	67
Avoir l'intention de...	66
Rendre hommage à(qc/qn)	64
Mettre en évidence	60
Mener à bien	59
A défaut de	58
A court terme	57
Avoir droit à	57
Faire le point	54
Rendre compte	54
Faire valoir	51
Faire part de qqch à qqn	49
Faire état de	46
Être en train de...	45
Sans délai	45
Tirer parti de...	45
Avoir trait à	43
Prendre part à...	43
Être loin de...	42
Il est vrai que...	41
Par la suite	40
Aller loin	39
A usage	37
Dans la mesure du possible	37
Plus ou moins	36
Être à même de...	35
Au détriment de	34
De premier plan	34
Ce faisant...	33
Mettre à profit	33
A son tour	32
Faire usage de	32
Vouloir dire	32
A côté de	31
Aux côtés de qqn	30
De sorte que	29
Donner suite à (qqch)	28
En quelque sorte	28
En temps utile	28
Faire le bilan de...	28
Pour le compte de	28
Au fil de...	27
Mettre un terme à	27
Faire foi	26
Prendre position	26
Aller de pair avec...	25
Faire suite à	25
A mon sens	24
Autant que possible	24
Dresser le bilan de...	24

Faire défaut	24
Sans réserve	24
Avoir raison	23
Être en droit de	22
Mettre en lumière	22
Premier pas	22
Suivre de près	22
Voir (le) jour	22
Au fur et à mesure	21
En tout	21
Il est (n'est pas) question de	21
Mettre à plat	21
Tirer profit de qqch	21
A juste titre	20
A peu près	20
En détail	20
Tout comme	20
De longue date	19
Rendre service (à qqn)	19
Avoir tendance à...	18
En retour	17
Sur le point de	17
A l'écart (de)	16
Aller dans le sens de qqn	16
Au premier chef	16
Dans l'ensemble	16
De concert	16
En retard	16
Entre temps	16
Faire entendre	15
A condition de...	14
A/sur (une) grande échelle	14
Au plus vite	14
Autrement dit	14
Être en jeu	14
Donner le signal de (qqch)	13
En connaissance de cause	13
Mettre à (l')exécution	13
Porter préjudice à qqn	13
Prendre la parole	13
Tenir à cœur	13
...de réserve	12
Aller de l'avant	12
Donner l'exemple	12
En honneur de (qqn ou qqch)	12
Mettre en chantier	12
Pour peu que...	12
A tout prix	11
Du reste	11
Mettre en pratique	11
Mettre en vigueur	11
Par comparaison (avec)	11
Sous le signe de...	11
Sur un pied de	11
Tout de suite	11
Dans une certaine mesure	10
Prendre place	10
Quand même!	10
A bref délai	9
Au plus tôt	9
En tout point/ en tous points	9
Être garant de qqch	9
Faire écho à	9
Pas du tout	9
Qui plus est	9
A l'usage de qqn	8
A vrai dire	8
De telle sorte que	8
Donner corps à qqch	8
En bonne voie	8
En gros	8
Faire ses preuves	8
Mettre en doute	8
Passer en revue	8
Prendre garde	8
Sous prétexte (de...)	8
A brève échéance	7
Au premier plan	7
Avoir tort	7
Bonne foi	7
Cela dit	7
Clé de voûte	7
De bout en bout	7
De premier (second, dernier) ordre	7
De toute urgence	7
En résumé	7

En somme	7
Faire (toute) la lumière sur qqch	7
Faire sien (sienne)	7
Premier plan	7
Se faire jour	7
A deux vitesses	6
A la rencontre (de...)	6
Au long de	6
Bonne volonté	6
Cas de force majeure	6
Comme il se doit	6
Comme par le passé	6
Coup d'envoi	6
Dans la ligne	6
De longue haleine	6
Donner à penser	6
Il y va de...	6
Mettre en jeu	6
Surveiller de près	6
(Être/entrer) en concurrence avec	5
A la portée de qqn	5
Après tout	5
Au courant	5
Avoir qualité pour...	5
Cas de figure	5
Coup d'État	5
Dans la foulée	5
Donner la préférence à...	5
En aucune manière	5
En douceur	5
En famille	5
En fin de compte	5
En instance	5
En masse	5
En revenir	5
En usage	5
Entrer en ligne de compte	5
Faire place à qqn	5
Faire son entrée	5
Jouer le jeu	5
Se rendre compte	5
Sous peu	5
Tenir à l'écart	5
A coup sûr	4
A huis clos	4
A tour de rôle	4
Arrière(-)pensée	4
Au bout du compte	4
Bel et bien	4
Courir le (un) risque	4
De bon (mauvais) augure	4
Donner raison à qqn	4
En comparaison de	4
En lieu et place de qqn	4
Être en possession	4
Faire fond sur...	4
Faire grief (à qqn de qqch)	4
Faire la différence	4
Faire les frais de...	4
Flagrant délit	4
Hors d'usage	4
Il/Cela va sans dire	4
Laisser à penser	4
Le cachet de la poste faisant foi	4
Mettre sur pied	4
Mode d'emploi	4
Ne rien avoir à voir avec (qqn,qqch)	4
Noyau dur	4
Par voie de conséquence	4
Prendre au sérieux	4
Prendre corps	4
Prendre ses précautions	4
Toutes choses égales d'ailleurs	4
(Re)mettre sur les rails	3
A bout de...	3
A condition que...	3
A la tâche	3
A proprement parler	3
Aller au devant de...	3
Au dernier, au plus haut point	3
Avoir force de loi	3
Avoir partie liée avec qqn	3
Avoir ses raisons	3
Bon vent!	3

Dans la course	3
De fortune	3
De plein fouet	3
Des bouts de ficelle	3
Du jour au lendemain	3
Du même coup	3
En retrait	3
Entre parenthèses	3
Être en passe de...	3
Être juge et partie	3
Faire date	3
Faire double emploi	3
Faire droit à	3
Faire office de	3
Faire son chemin	3
Fort des halles	3
Laisser passer	3
Les grandes occasions	3
Mauvaise foi	3
Mettre à mal qqn	3
Mettre en demeure	3
Mettre en question	3
Montrer du doigt	3
Nulle part	3
Occuper le devant de la scène	3
Passer outre (à qqch)	3
Passer sous silence	3
Point de repère	3
Porter un grand coup	3
Prendre racine	3
Prendre soin de...	3
Si j'ose dire...	3
Tourner la page	3
(Être) en reste	2
A chaud	2
A la pointe de...	2
A point nommé	2
A reculons	2
A tel point que...	2
Aller trop (un peu) loin	2
Au plus fort de...	2
Autant dire	2
Avoir gain de cause	2
Avoir la cote	2
Avoir le dernier mot	2
Avoir l'honneur de...	2
Avoir qqch à cœur	2
Avoir son mot à dire	2
Avoir/mettre un tigre dans le (son) moteur	2
Baisser la (sa) garde	2
Battre en brèche	2
Bonne (mauvaise) conscience	2
C'est bien le moins	2
C'est chose faite	2
C'est pas vrai!	2
Contre vents et marées	2
Coup de fouet	2
Coup de pouce	2
De circonstance	2
De côté	2
De plain-pied	2
De temps à autre	2
De temps en temps	2
De tous côtés	2
De tout temps	2
Dernier mot	2
Des hauts et des bas	2
Du coup	2
En catamini	2
En dernier recours	2
En mon âme et conscience	2
En prise (directe) avec	2
Entrer en jeu	2
Et pour cause	2
Être à la merci de	2
Être bon pour...	2
Être en position	2
Être en règle	2
Être en service	2
Être hors de question	2
Être laissé pour compte	2
Être maître de qqch	2
Faire cause commune	2
Faire échec à	2
Faire mal	2
Faire montre de	2
Faire un tour d'horizon	2

Gagner du terrain	2
Jeter le discrédit	2
Jusqu'à concurrence de...	2
Le petit écran	2
Mauvais coup	2
Mettre en service	2
Mot d'ordre	2
Ni plus ni moins	2
Ô combien!	2
Par dessus-tout	2
Par le menu	2
Passer la parole à qqn	2
Pour une fois	2
Prendre de court	2
Prendre des risques	2
Prendre en main	2
Prendre le parti de...	2
Prendre pied	2
Prendre son élan	2
Procès d'intention	2
Que sais-je (encore)?	2
Quelque part	2
Quoi qu'on dise	2
Remettre les compteurs à zéro	2
Rendre des comptes	2
Rideau de fer	2
Sans appel	2
Savoir gré à (qqn) de (qqch)	2
Se battre à armes égales	2
Souhaiter la bonne année	2
Sous la houlette de	2
Sous le couvert de...	2
Sur cet article	2
Tenir en laisse	2
Tenir qqn en haute (grande) estime	2
Tourner le dos à qqn	2
Tout au plus	2
Tout court	2
Tout est pour le mieux (...)	2
Trouver moyen de...	2
Venir à bout de qqch	2
Venir à l'esprit	2

(A) cent pour cent	1
(C'est) la moindre des choses	1
(Être) le dos au mur	1
...comme un(e) malade	1
A bout de souffle	1
A cela près	1
A cette heure	1
A cheval	1
A cor et à cris	1
A dessein	1
A double sens	1
A double tranchant	1
A la chaîne	1
A la clé	1
A la dérive	1
A la longue	1
A l'usage	1
A plus forte raison	1
A portée de la main	1
A première vue	1
A tout propos	1
A tout risque	1
Aller et venir	1
Aller sur le terrain	1
Aller un peu vite	1
Aller vite en besogne	1
Au (grand) complet	1
Au ban de...	1
Au pied de la lettre	1
Au reste	1
Autant que faire se peut	1
Aux abonnés absents	1
Avant la lettre	1
Avec armes et bagages	1
Avoir (une) bonne/ mauvaise presse	1
Avoir beau jeu de (pour)	1
Avoir deux poids et deux mesures	1
Avoir l'air	1
Avoir matière à	1
Avoir ses habitudes	1
Avoir toute latitude pour	1
Avoir voix au chapitre	1

Baisser les bras	1
Baptême du feu	1
Billet vert	1
Bon an, mal an	1
Bons offices	1
Brouiller les pistes	1
Ce n'est pas du luxe	1
Ce n'est pas la peine de...	1
Ce n'est pas une petite (mince) affaire	1
C'est (n'est pas) un cadeau	1
C'est (trop) commode	1
Clés en main	1
Contre nature	1
Coup d'accélérateur	1
Coup de grâce	1
Coup de main	1
Coup de poing	1
Crier victoire	1
Dans le désordre	1
Dans le principe	1
Dans les limbes	1
Dans tous les azimuts	1
De bon cœur	1
De bonne heure	1
De chair et de sang	1
De fraîche date	1
De près ou de loin	1
De prime abord	1
De quel droit?	1
De toute(s) sorte(s)	1
Demander des comptes	1
Déposer son bilan	1
Dernier cri	1
Descendre dans la rue	1
Donner acte à qqn	1
D'un seul coup	1
En (bon) père de famille	1
En bonne intelligence	1
En compagnie	1
En conscience	1
En cours de route	1
En dents de scie	1
En réserve	1
En temps normal	1
En vrac	1
Enfoncer une porte Ouverte	1
Engager le fer	1
État de choses	1
Être à (la) portée (de qqn)	1
Être à égalité (avec)	1
Être à la botte de qqn	1
Être à la veille de	1
Être au-dessous de la barre	1
Être de (tout) cœur avec qqn	1
Être de son temps	1
Être de taille à...	1
Être en action	1
Être en délicatesse avec qqn	1
Être en phase	1
Être en situation de...	1
Être fort de...	1
Être hors course	1
Être loin du compte	1
Être sur la mauvaise pente	1
Être sur la touche	1
Être sur ses gardes	1
Être/se mettre dans la peau de qqn	1
Faire avec	1
Faire bloc	1
Faire bon (mauvais) ménage avec	1
Faire carrière	1
Faire cas de...	1
Faire comme si	1
Faire connaissance (avec)	1
Faire du bruit	1
Faire école	1
Faire fausse route	1
Faire florès	1
Faire honneur à (qqch)	1
Faire la grève	1
Faire la navette	1
Faire la soudure	1
Faire le coup de poing	1
Faire le jeu de qqn	1

Faire le plein	1
Faire le tour de (qqch)	1
Faire l'éloge de qqn	1
Faire machine arrière	1
Faire œuvre de	1
Faire peine, de la peine à	1
Faire pencher la balance	1
Faire profession de...	1
Faire semblant	1
Faire ses premières armes	1
Faire un bout de chemin avec qqn	1
Faire violence à qqn	1
Fermer les yeux	1
Fermer sa porte à...	1
Force de dissuasion	1
Force des choses	1
Gros sous	1
Hors pair	1
Hors service	1
Il doit se retourner dans sa tombe	1
Il est grand temps de...	1
Il y a belle lurette	1
Je vous prie de croire (que...)	1
Jeter aux oubliettes	1
Jeter de l'huile sur le feu	1
Jouer au chat et à la souris	1
Jour J	1
La dernière ligne droite	1
La nouvelle vague	1
La politique de l'autruche	1
L'affaire est faite	1
Laisser (libre) cours à	1
Laisser à désirer	1
Laisser dire	1
Laisser le champ libre	1
Le jeu n'en vaut pas la chandelle	1
Le pire n'est pas toujours sûr	1
Le pourquoi et le comment	1
Le siècle des Lumières	1
Le troisième âge	1
Les quatre coins de...	1
Les règles de l'art	1
Marcher tout seul	1
Mauvaise volonté	1
Mettre à contribution	1
Mettre à la portée de (qqn)	1
Mettre à l'épreuve	1
Mettre au jour	1
Mettre des bâtons dans les roues	1
Mettre en pièces	1
Mettre en vedette	1
Mettre le cap sur...	1
Mettre les bouchées doubles	1
Oiseau de mauvais augure	1
On dirait...	1
On ne peut plus	1
Ouvrir la porte à...	1
Ouvrir le chemin	1
Ouvrir l'esprit	1
Parer à toute éventualité	1
Parler au cœur	1
Pas de si tôt	1
Passer à l'acte	1
Passer d'un extrême à l'autre	1
Payer de sa personne	1
Perdre du terrain	1
Perdre prise	1
Porter à faux	1
Porter au pinacle	1
Porter bonheur	1
Poser les jalons	1
Pour le meilleur et pour le pire	1
Pré carré	1
Prendre la place de	1
Prendre le taureau par les cornes	1
Prendre les devants	1
Prendre parti (pour, contre)	1
Prendre possession de...	1
Prendre qqch à cœur	1

Prendre qqn au dépourvu	1
Prendre rang	1
Prendre son plein essor	1
Prendre un bon (mauvais) tour	1
Prêter le flanc à	1
Quitter la place	1
Quoi de neuf?	1
Recevoir qqn cinq sur cinq	1
Réchauffer le cœur	1
Regarder d'un œil	1
Remonter à la surface	1
Renvoyer dos à dos	1
Rester à la traîne	1
Sans aller plus loin	1
Sans commune mesure (avec)	1
Sans compter que...	1
Sans crier gare	1
Sans plus	1
Se faire un nom	1
Se faire un plaisir à...	1
Se jeter à l'eau	1
Se rendre maître de qqch	1
Se tirer d'affaire	1
Second souffle	1
Serrer le cœur	1
Si tant est que	1
Sonner le glas (de qqch)	1
Souffler mot	1
Sur les barricades	1
Sur-le-champ	1
Tant qu'à faire	1
Tant soit peu	1
Tenir parole	1
Tirer au clair	1
Tirer des plans sur la comète	1
Toucher à sa fin	1
Tour de table	1
Tourner en dérision	1
Tout de go	1
Tout un chacun	1
Travailler d'arrache-pied	1
Un tant soit peu	1
Vivre de l'air du temps	1
Voir loin	1
Y perdre son latin	1

Appendix 3: Wordlists

Wordlist: FRADCO

Bytes	13,529,846
Tokens	2,121,553
Types	37,904
Type/Token Ratio	1.79
Standardised Type/Token Ratio	38.00
Ave. Word Length	4.91
Sentences	53,201
Sent. Length	35.37
sd. Sent. Length	55.65
Paragraphs	9,455
Para. length	114.60
sd. Para. length	779.50

Top 100 words by frequency

N	Word	Freq.	N	Word	Freq.
1	DE	124,136	26	OU	8,444
2	LA	78,257	27	ARTICLE	7,652
3	L	61,785	28	SONT	6,981
4	DES	53,486	29	COMMISSION	6,937
5	ET	52,525	30	CONSEIL	6,455
6	LES	49,462	31	PAS	6,366
7	À	44,389	32	PLUS	6,280
8	LE	44,287	33	QU	6,239
9	D	40,993	34	NE	5,884
10	EN	31,051	35	S	5,836
11	DU	29,470	36	ÊTRE	5,540
12	DANS	20,625	37	AVEC	5,475
13	UNE	19,392	38	CETTE	5,266
14	UN	18,795	39	N	5,095
15	POUR	17,383	40	CES	4,788
16	QUE	16,543	41	ONT	4,230
17	EST	15,955	42	SE	4,171
18	PAR	15,880	43	MEMBRES	4,060
19	AU	15,362	44	LEUR	3,892
20	SUR	13,329	45	EUROPÉENNE	3,796
21	A	13,246	46	ENTRE	3,710
22	QUI	12,041	47	ÉTÉ	3,519
23	IL	10,477	48	ELLE	3,391
24	AUX	9,574	49	AINSI	3,348
25	CE	8,595	50	NOUS	3,308

51	C	3,254	76	NOTAMMENT	2,219
52	UNION	3,202	77	DOIT	2,190
53	SON	3,190	78	MINISTRE	2,178
54	M	3,072	79	DEUX	2,154
55	PAYS	3,065	80	MESURES	2,147
56	EUROPÉEN	3,052	81	COMMUNAUTÉ	2,139
57	POLITIQUE	2,875	82	LEURS	2,136
58	COMME	2,666	83	FAIT	2,129
59	JE	2,666	84	TOUS	2,110
60	AUTRES	2,644	85	FORMATION	2,068
61	PEUT	2,605	86	DISPOSITIONS	2,065
62	ETAT	2,557	87	FRANCE	2,043
63	SES	2,497	88	LOI	2,032
64	MAIS	2,469	89	ÉTAT	2,024
65	MÊME	2,448	90	CONDITIONS	1,983
66	CADRE	2,416	91	ETATS	1,979
67	SERVICES	2,400	92	MARCHÉ	1,933
68	TRAVAIL	2,370	93	CAS	1,927
69	DÉVELOPPEMENT	2,349	94	ILS	1,914
70	MISE	2,326	95	AUSSI	1,901
71	Y	2,287	96	DONT	1,885
72	SA	2,274	97	EMPLOI	1,873
73	TOUT	2,249	98	COOPÉRATION	1,869
74	SI	2,226	99	ACTION	1,862
75	ÉTATS	2,219	100	ÉGALEMENT	1,859

<u>Wordlist: FREUCO</u>

Bytes	7,005,956
Tokens	1,065,389
Types	24,461
Type/Token Ratio	2.30
Standardised Type/Token Ratio	36.48
Ave. Word Length	4.95
Sentences	27,353
Sent. Length	34.79
sd. Sent. Length	61.76
Paragraphs	3,925
Para. length	120.92
sd. Para. length	577.77

Top 100 words by frequency

N	Word	Freq.	N	Word	Freq.
1	DE	60,204	29	OU	3,840
2	LA	41,417	30	MEMBRES	3,533
3	L	31,503	31	SONT	3,358
4	ET	26,786	32	EUROPÉENNE	3,214
5	DES	26,408	33	QU	3,105
6	LES	25,303	34	PAS	2,841
7	À	23,436	35	UNION	2,776
8	LE	22,732	36	EUROPÉEN	2,768
9	D	20,558	37	ÊTRE	2,711
10	EN	16,207	38	AVEC	2,604
11	DU	14,783	39	NE	2,601
12	DANS	10,887	40	PLUS	2,566
13	UNE	9,465	41	S	2,519
14	UN	9,379	42	CES	2,454
15	POUR	9,209	43	CETTE	2,383
16	QUE	8,813	44	N	2,285
17	AU	8,077	45	ÉTATS	2,158
18	PAR	7,739	46	ONT	2,078
19	SUR	7,413	47	PAYS	1,981
20	A	6,786	48	SE	1,954
21	EST	6,673	49	ENTRE	1,908
22	COMMISSION	6,010	50	ÉTÉ	1,832
23	QUI	5,753	51	LEUR	1,706
24	AUX	5,249	52	TRAITÉ	1,697
25	CONSEIL	4,987	53	COMMUNAUTÉ	1,693
26	ARTICLE	4,877	54	CADRE	1,620
27	CE	4,551	55	MARCHÉ	1,618
28	IL	4,340	56	ELLE	1,587

57	AUTRES	1,586	79	EURO	1,166
58	ÉTAT	1,569	80	NOTAMMENT	1,165
59	POLITIQUE	1,567	81	MATIÈRE	1,146
60	AINSI	1,564	82	DÉCISION	1,145
61	MESURES	1,537	83	COMME	1,139
62	ETATS	1,533	84	Y	1,136
63	SON	1,519	85	PRÉSENT	1,135
64	DIRECTIVE	1,491	86	SA	1,128
65	MEMBRE	1,482	87	EUROPE	1,125
66	C	1,462	88	CONCERNANT	1,124
67	MISE	1,326	89	NIVEAU	1,090
68	DISPOSITIONS	1,307	90	ÉGALEMENT	1,069
69	RÈGLEMENT	1,284	91	PARLEMENT	1,062
70	ACCORD	1,280	92	COMMUNAUTAIRE	1,060
71	ACTION	1,258	93	SI	1,060
72	SES	1,244	94	SERVICES	1,045
73	ÉCONOMIQUE	1,228	95	PROGRAMME	1,044
74	PARAGRAPHE	1,220	96	LEURS	1,037
75	PEUT	1,217	97	CAS	1,023
76	COOPÉRATION	1,215	98	DOIT	1,018
77	DÉVELOPPEMENT	1,211	99	TOUT	1,016
78	NOUS	1,171	100	CONDITIONS	1,004

Wordlist: FRNACO

Bytes	6,523,890
Tokens	1,056,164
Types	27,887
Type/Token Ratio	2.64
Standardised Type/Token Ratio	39.47
Ave. Word Length	4.88
Sentences	25,848
Sent. Length	35.98
sd. Sent. Length	48.34
Paragraphs	5,530
Para. length	110.12
sd. Para. length	895.54

Top 100 words by frequency

N	Word	Freq.	N	Word	Freq.
1	DE	63,932	29	PAS	3,525
2	LA	36,840	30	S	3,317
3	L	30,282	31	NE	3,283
4	DES	27,078	32	QU	3,134
5	ET	25,739	33	CETTE	2,883
6	LES	24,159	34	AVEC	2,871
7	LE	21,555	35	ÊTRE	2,829
8	À	20,953	36	N	2,810
9	D	20,435	37	ARTICLE	2,775
10	EN	14,844	38	CES	2,334
11	DU	14,687	39	SE	2,217
12	UNE	9,927	40	LEUR	2,186
13	DANS	9,738	41	ONT	2,152
14	UN	9,416	42	NOUS	2,137
15	EST	9,282	43	M	2,092
16	POUR	8,174	44	LOI	1,892
17	PAR	8,141	45	ETAT	1,849
18	QUE	7,730	46	ELLE	1,804
19	AU	7,285	47	ENTRE	1,802
20	A	6,460	48	C	1,792
21	QUI	6,288	49	AINSI	1,784
22	IL	6,137	50	JE	1,704
23	SUR	5,916	51	ÉTÉ	1,687
24	OU	4,604	52	FRANCE	1,685
25	AUX	4,325	53	MINISTRE	1,678
26	CE	4,044	54	SON	1,671
27	PLUS	3,714	55	MÊME	1,650
28	SONT	3,623	56	MAIS	1,616

57	TRAVAIL	1,590	79	AUSSI	1,134
58	FORMATION	1,552	80	TOUS	1,124
59	COMME	1,527	81	NOTRE	1,123
60	CONSEIL	1,468	82	LEURS	1,099
61	PEUT	1,388	83	SERVICE	1,098
62	NATIONALE	1,371	84	PREMIER	1,094
63	SERVICES	1,355	85	PAYS	1,084
64	VOUS	1,338	86	FAIRE	1,081
65	ON	1,318	87	ILS	1,071
66	POLITIQUE	1,308	88	AUTRES	1,058
67	SES	1,253	89	NOTAMMENT	1,054
68	TOUT	1,233	90	SERA	1,048
69	FAIT	1,216	91	PUBLIC	1,032
70	DEUX	1,212	92	SANS	1,024
71	TEMPS	1,190	93	GÉNÉRAL	1,006
72	DOIT	1,172	94	MISE	1,000
73	SI	1,166	95	GOUVERNEMENT	996
74	DONT	1,164	96	CONDITIONS	979
75	PRÉSIDENT	1,154	97	SOIT	959
76	Y	1,151	98	TRÈS	944
77	SA	1,146	99	ENSEMBLE	940
78	DÉVELOPPEMENT	1,138	100	COMMISSION	927

Wordlist: Comparator corpus

Bytes	13,201,977
Tokens	2,223,862
Types	68,392
Type/Token Ratio	3.08
Standardised Type/Token Ratio	43,94
Ave. Word Length	4.55
Sentences	93,202
Sent. Length	18.45
sd. Sent. Length	16.00
Paragraphs	53,573
Para. length	41.06
sd. Para. length	153.50

Top 100 words by frequency

N	Word	Freq.	N	Word	Freq.
1	DE	107,517	29	JE	10,127
2	LA	62,618	30	SE	10,064
3	LE	49,671	31	SUR	9,642
4	ET	47,803	32	S	9,357
5	L	47,282	33	ON	9,354
6	À	41,743	34	M	8,772
7	LES	39,106	35	NOUS	8,381
8	DES	32,853	36	MAIS	8,248
9	D	32,422	37	SON	7,824
10	IL	29,736	38	C	7,811
11	EN	28,972	39	AVEC	7,222
12	UN	26,582	40	ELLE	7,047
13	EST	25,628	41	LUI	6,475
14	QUE	23,717	42	VOUS	6,357
15	DU	23,432	43	COMME	6,235
16	UNE	21,181	44	CETTE	6,039
17	QUI	19,452	45	ILS	5,750
18	A	17,272	46	SONT	5,570
19	DANS	16,803	47	SA	5,510
20	PAS	14,445	48	TOUT	5,435
21	QU	14,414	49	AUX	5,374
22	POUR	14,341	50	MÊME	5,335
23	AU	13,813	51	SES	5,285
24	NE	13,720	52	Y	5,237
25	PAR	11,784	53	OU	4,917
26	CE	11,771	54	ÉTAIT	4,865
27	N	11,092	55	SI	4,717
28	PLUS	10,753	56	ÊTRE	4,470

57	CES	4,450
58	ONT	4,342
59	LEUR	4,321
60	MONDE	4,141
61	AVAIT	4,073
62	BIEN	3,974
63	FAIT	3,953
64	ÉTÉ	3,907
65	J	3,889
66	DIT	3,602
67	DEUX	3,588
68	OÙ	3,432
69	SANS	3,408
70	ME	3,084
71	PEUT	2,920
72	AUSSI	2,807
73	DONT	2,796
74	FAIRE	2,786
75	TOUS	2,766
76	APRÈS	2,594
77	ENTRE	2,588
78	ANS	2,559
79	ENCORE	2,466
80	AI	2,423
81	AUTRE	2,348
82	DEPUIS	2,256
83	FRANCE	2,252
84	HOMME	2,239
85	AUTRES	2,133
86	SOUS	2,127
87	MON	2,107
88	PAYS	2,093
89	NON	2,066
90	TRÈS	2,065
91	PAGE	2,054
92	LÀ	2,042
93	LEURS	2,016
94	QUAND	1,950
95	PEU	1,936
96	POINT	1,928
97	AVOIR	1,918
98	CONTRE	1,914
99	AINSI	1,896
100	MOINS	1,893

Appendix 4: Sequences common to FREUCO and FRNACO speech genres

	Freq.[124]
5-word sequences	
DANS LE DOMAINE DE LA	20
DANS LE CADRE DE LA	15
LA MISE EN ŒUVRE DE	10
4-word sequences	
DANS LE CADRE DE	51
MESDAMES ET MESSIEURS LES	35
EN CE QUI CONCERNE	32
DE PLUS EN PLUS	30
LA MISE EN PLACE	30
DANS LE DOMAINE DE	29
LA MISE EN ŒUVRE	26
UN CERTAIN NOMBRE DE	26
DES DROITS DE LHOMME	21
LE DOMAINE DE LA	20
POUR LA PREMIÈRE FOIS	19
TOUT AU LONG DE	16
À LA FIN DE	15
DANS LE CADRE DU	15
IL Y A UN	15
LE CADRE DE LA	15
LA LUTTE CONTRE LA	12
DANS LE DOMAINE DES	11
DE LA CONSTRUCTION EUROPÉENNE	10
DE LA RECHERCHE ET	10
IL NY A PAS	10
LES DROITS DE LHOMME	10
MISE EN ŒUVRE DE	10
3-word sequences	
DE LA COMMISSION	262
DE LA POLITIQUE	112
DE LUNION EUROPÉENNE	104
LA MISE EN	97
EN MATIÈRE DE	92
ET DE LA	92

124 Sequences with a frequency of occurrence of at least 10

DANS LE CADRE	91
IL Y A	84
MESDAMES ET MESSIEURS	79
MONSIEUR LE PRÉSIDENT	75
DANS LE DOMAINE	60
LE CADRE DE	57
PRÉSIDENT DE LA	50
JE VOUS REMERCIE	49
À LA FOIS	48
DE LA CROISSANCE	47
ET À LA	46
AU COURS DE	45
AU COURS DES	43
MISE EN ŒUVRE	43
DES POLITIQUES ÉCONOMIQUES	42
DANS CE DOMAINE	41
LE #ER JANVIER	41
AU SEIN DE	40
DE LA COMMUNAUTÉ	40
LA FIN DE	40
CEST-À-DIRE	39
EST-À-DIRE	39
ET MESSIEURS LES	37
LA CRÉATION DE	37
NE SONT PAS	37
SUR LE PLAN	37
QUE NOUS AVONS	36
UN CERTAIN NOMBRE	36
EN CE QUI	35
CE QUI CONCERNE	34
LA MONNAIE UNIQUE	34
MISE EN PLACE	34
DROITS DE LHOMME	33
MISE EN ŒUVRE	33
DE LA RECHERCHE	31
PLUS DE #	31
DE PLUS EN	30
LA CROISSANCE ET	30
PLUS EN PLUS	30
DES DROITS DE	29
LA LUTTE CONTRE	29
LE DOMAINE DE	29
EN # ET	28
EN FAVEUR DE	28
LA PLUPART DES	28

À CE QUE	27
UNE PLUS GRANDE	27
CERTAIN NOMBRE DE	26
DE LA POPULATION	26
DE LA SOCIÉTÉ	26
À CET ÉGARD	25
DE TOUS LES	25
LE RESPECT DES	25
DE LA CONSTRUCTION	24
DE LA COOPÉRATION	24
EN PREMIER LIEU	24
DE LA PART	23
DOMAINE DE LA	23
IL NOUS FAUT	23
LA CONSTRUCTION EUROPÉENNE	23
POINT DE VUE	23
AUX ETATS-UNIS	22
CE QUI EST	22
DANS LE MONDE	21
DORES ET DÉJÀ	21
EN MÊME TEMPS	21
IL NY A	21
LA PREMIÈRE FOIS	21
A TOUS LES	20
CE NEST PAS	20
DANS LES DOMAINES	20
DE NE PAS	20
EN TANT QUE	20
ENSEMBLE DE LA	20
LE PASSAGE À	20
NE DOIT PAS	20
ORES ET DÉJÀ	20
À LA FIN	19
AU SEIN DU	19
IL SAGIT DE	19
MIS EN PLACE	19
POUR LA PREMIÈRE	19
À PARTIR DE	18
CELUI DE LA	18
CEST À DIRE	18
DE LA BANQUE	18
EST À DIRE	18
LENSEMBLE DE LA	18
PERMETTEZ-MOI DE	18
TOUT AU LONG	18

IL NE FAUT	17
LA RECHERCHE ET	17
LE CADRE DU	17
LE PROCESSUS DE	17
SUR CE POINT	17
AU LONG DE	16
AU-DELÀ DE	16
DE LA GESTION	16
DE LA VIE	16
DE METTRE EN	16
DE TOUTES LES	16
GRÂCE À LA	16
LA POLITIQUE DE	16
LA QUALITÉ DE	16
LA QUESTION DE	16
LE RESPECT DE	16
VIS-À-VIS	16
À LA MISE	15
CADRE DE LA	15
DANS LE RESPECT	15
DANS LE SECTEUR	15
DE LA NOUVELLE	15
DE LA RÉFORME	15
EN PLACE DE	15
LE # SEPTEMBRE	15
LUTTE CONTRE LA	15
METTRE EN PLACE	15
Y A UN	15
AU SERVICE DE	14
DE # MILLIONS	14
EN CE SENS	14
EN ŒUVRE DE	14
LA POSSIBILITÉ DE	14
LA SOCIÉTÉ CIVILE	14
LUTTE CONTRE LE	14
ÉCONOMIQUE ET SOCIALE	13
IL NEST PAS	13
JE SUIS CONVAINCU	13
LA RESPONSABILITÉ DE	13
LES CONDITIONS DE	13
PRÈS DE #	13
A LOCCASION DE	12
AVANT LA FIN	12
EN ŒUVRE DES	12
IL FAUT QUE	12

JE SOUHAITE QUE	12
LA RÉFORME DE	12
NOUS AVONS BESOIN	12
CE QUE NOUS	11
DE LA NÉGOCIATION	11
JE ME RÉJOUIS	11
JE TIENS À	11
LE DÉVELOPPEMENT DU	11
LE DOMAINE DES	11
LES DROITS DE	11
À METTRE EN	10
ALLER PLUS LOIN	10
AU-DELÀ DES	10
CE QUE LES	10
DE LA RESPONSABILITÉ	10
JE SUIS HEUREUX	10
JE VOUDRAIS VOUS	10
NY A PAS	10
POUR MA PART	10
QUE NOUS DEVONS	10
QUI A ÉTÉ	10
QUI SE SONT	10
QUIL YA	10
RESPECT DE LA	10
Y A PAS	10

Appendix 5: Keywords

FRADCO against Comparator corpus

N	WORD	FRADCO FREQ.[126]	COMP. FREQ.[127]	KEYNESS[125]
1	ARTICLE	7,652	320	8,729.5
2	COMMISSION	6,937	300	7,862.6
3	DES	53,486	32,853	6,119.2
4	MEMBRES	4,060	357	3,823.1
5	CONSEIL	6,455	1,406	3,762.2
6	EUROPÉENNE	3,796	334	3,573.5
7	UNION	3,202	323	2,866.9
8	L	61,785	47,282	2,746.6
9	EUROPÉEN	3,052	333	2,647.8
10	LA	78,257	62,618	2,639.9
11	ÉTATS[128]	2,219	111	2,439.3
12	DISPOSITIONS	2,065	98	2,295.4
13	DE	124,136	107,517	2,223.0
14	DIRECTIVE	1,600	20	2,106.2
15	CADRE	2,416	271	2,071.5
16	SERVICES	2,400	306	1,942.6
17	LES	49,462	39,106	1,786.9

125 A word is said to be 'key' if "its frequency in the text when compared with its frequency in a reference corpus is such that the statistical probability as computed by an appropriate procedure is smaller than or equal to a p value specified by the user" (Scott 1999). The procedure used here is log likelihood, recommended by Scott when comparing long texts or whole genres against a reference corpus.

126 Frequency of keyword in source corpus: here FRADCO.

127 Frequency of keyword in reference corpus: here the Comparator corpus.

128 WordSmith Tools searches for word forms, and counts as distinct forms words which differ only because of the presence or absence of an accent. This allows words which are otherwise homographs to appear separately on keyword lists, but can be misleading in the cases where an initial accented character loses its accent when capitalised, such as in the case of 'état', which is usually capitalised in the European Union sub-corpus (because of its principal use in the collocation 'État membre'). This accounts for the separate entries for État(s) and Etat(s) in the keyword lists. When the two spellings are conflated, it turns out that 'état' is not as key in FREUCO as the lists above suggest.

18	TRAITÉ	1,811	140	1,777.8
19	PARAGRAPHE	1,259	13	1,678.1
20	COOPÉRATION	1,869	196	1,647.5
21	COMMUNAUTÉ	2,139	321	1,592.5
22	MISE	2,326	406	1,583.7
23	RÈGLEMENT	1,424	75	1,547.4
24	MESURES	2,147	365	1,486.2
25	D	40,993	32,422	1,472.1
26	EURO	1,365	75	1,469.0
27	APPLICATION	1,544	132	1,467.1
28	CONCERNANT	1,358	77	1,450.6
29	AUX	9,574	5,374	1,407.0
30	DÉVELOPPEMENT	2,349	504	1,383.8
31	COMMUNAUTAIRE	1,194	47	1,375.5
32	EMPLOI	1,873	296	1,354.3
33	CONFORMÉMENT	1,114	39	1,309.1
34	UE	912	0	1,308.0
35	DÉCISION	1,495	187	1,220.8
36	FORMATION	2,068	457	1,190.2
37	OU	8,444	4,917	1,119.1
38	CONDITIONS	1,983	485	1,047.9
39	PRÉSENT	1,507	257	1,041.0
40	PROCÉDURE	1,032	75	1,031.9
41	DU	29,470	23,432	1,016.7
42	NIVEAU	1,653	335	1,016.4
43	NOTAMMENT	2,219	636	1,006.1
44	ACCÈS	1,061	99	977.7
45	SÉCURITÉ	1,474	277	955.9
46	INFORMATION	1,367	230	952.1
47	ÉTAT	2,024	560	951.7
48	PROGRAMME	1,378	237	946.8
49	MEMBRE	1,627	356	943.7
50	ACCORD	1,705	402	930.1

FREUCO against FRNACO

N	WORD	FREUCO FREQ.	FRNACO FREQ.	KEYNESS
1	COMMISSION	6,010	927	4,129.0
2	ÉTATS	2,158	61	2,501.3
3	MEMBRES	3,533	527	2,472.1
4	EUROPÉEN	2,768	284	2,322.8
5	CONSEIL	4,987	1,468	2,002.2
6	EUROPÉENNE	3,214	582	1,990.2
7	UNION	2,776	426	1,909.9
8	TRAITÉ	1,697	114	1,646.8
9	DIRECTIVE	1,491	109	1,410.9
10	PARAGRAPHE	1,220	39	1,388.0
11	MEMBRE	1,482	145	1,266.9
12	UE	910	2	1,228.3
13	RÈGLEMENT	1,284	140	1,049.5
14	MARCHÉ	1,618	315	950.6
15	COMMUNAUTAIRE	1,060	134	809.1
16	CEE	625	6	801.8
17	COMMUNAUTÉ	1,693	446	765.0
18	EURO	1,166	199	750.5
19	CONSIDÉRANT	639	31	672.6
20	ÉTAT	1,569	455	639.5
21	CONCERNANT	1,124	234	627.1
22	ETATS	1,533	446	622.6
23	DN	425	0	585.6
24	ARTICLE	4,877	2,775	568.8
25	PARLEMENT	1,062	246	541.9
26	CONFORMÉMENT	930	184	539.7
27	BRUXELLES	479	29	478.1
28	COMMUNAUTAIRES	538	55	451.7
29	ACCORD	1,280	425	441.8
30	DÉCISION	1,145	350	438.8
31	EX	436	26	436.9
32	AOP	317	0	436.8
33	AUTORITÉS	684	119	434.6
34	MONÉTAIRE	567	72	431.7
35	ÉCUS	324	2	424.8
36	MESURES	1,537	610	406.1
37	PRÉSENT	1,135	372	398.4
38	PROGRAMME	1,044	334	378.1
39	AFF	271	0	373.4
40	JO	359	24	348.7
41	INSTITUANT	363	27	341.5

42	IP	277	6	331.9
43	STATUANT	301	12	329.6
44	VUE	776	219	325.9
45	VISANT	538	101	324.4
46	STABILITÉ	487	80	321.1
47	EUROPÉENNES	574	120	319.1
48	STRATÉGIE	480	81	311.1
49	PROTOCOLE	400	49	309.9
50	LUXEMBOURG	296	17	299.4

FRNACO against FREUCO

N	WORD	FRNACO FREQ.	FREUCO FREQ.	KEYNESS
1	LOI	1,892	140	1,814.5
2	FRANCE	1,685	358	948.4
3	NATIONALE	1,371	275	806.6
4	MINISTÈRE	863	99	702.9
5	MINISTRE	1,678	500	683.5
6	COLLECTIVITÉS	582	25	638.0
7	CODE	795	112	585.5
8	PERSONNELS	483	12	577.4
9	FORMATION	1,552	516	552.8
10	FRANÇAIS	692	84	549.2
11	DIRECTION	539	33	545.2
12	VOUS	1,338	403	538.2
13	ETAT	1,849	708	538.1
14	DÉCRET	499	25	529.7
15	FEMMES	757	121	518.8
16	ASSEMBLÉE	605	62	516.9
17	GENDARMERIE	353	0	492.5
18	ENSEIGNEMENT	631	80	490.4
19	VILLE	463	24	487.8
20	NOTRE	1,123	319	482.3
21	ART	642	88	479.7
22	FRANÇAISE	614	80	470.8
23	FAMILLES	430	19	468.7
24	ÉTABLISSEMENTS	591	75	459.1
25	MISSION	753	144	458.6
26	EST	9,282	6,673	454.9
27	POLICE	502	45	451.4
28	PARIS	494	49	427.6
29	M	2,092	980	422.1
30	INTERCOMMUNALE	300	0	418.5
31	ON	1,318	483	410.0
32	DÉPARTEMENTS	366	16	399.8
33	JEAN	405	28	396.1
34	RÉDIGÉ	339	10	396.0
35	ENFANT	290	5	360.8
36	PUBLIQUE	886	273	346.9
37	DÉPARTEMENT	279	6	339.3
38	TEMPS	1,190	466	334.1
39	IL	6,137	4,340	327.2
40	TERRITORIALES	299	13	327.0
41	SERVICE	1,098	421	318.7

42	INTERMINISTÉRI+	228	0	318.1
43	PARENTS	299	16	312.7
44	MÊME	1,650	798	310.6
45	HEURES	435	67	304.7
46	SÉNAT	218	0	304.1
47	CONTINUE	460	81	296.5
48	ÉLÈVES	275	13	295.6
49	NOUS	2,137	1,171	295.2
50	TRAVAIL	1,590	780	289.9

Appendix 6: Verbs and verb phrases from R. Catherine (1947) in FRADCO

Environment in Catherine[130]	Instances[129] in FREUCO	/ FRNACO	Typical environment / collocates of verb in FRADCO[131]
aborder:			
une question	23	30	'aborder des questions'
un point particulier	9	4	'aborder la question de...'
aboutir à:			
en vue d'a. à...	2	1	positive prosody e.g. 'à une meilleure cohérence' 'à un accord' 'pour / afin d'aboutir à'
abréger:			
un délai	0	1	only seven instances of verb, especially in 'livre blanc' genre of FREUCO
abroger:			
une loi	0	0	'Article [no.] (abrogé)' 'L'article [no.] est abrogé'
accéder à:			
un poste	0	1	'qualifications pour accéder à...' 'accéder à une formation'
accepter:			
une proposition	9	1	'[member state / La Commission]
une transaction	0	0	accepte...'
une solution	1	1	accepter un amendement 'l'acceptation du présent accord'

---

129 Within a range of five words each side of the node.

130 In the fifth edition (1985), Catherine also includes the verbs: accréditer, affecter, appeler, atteindre, attribuer, automatiser, baser, budgétiser-débudgétiser, commencer, coordonner, déclasser, dégager, émarger, éponger, étatiser, fonctionnariser, fonder, impartir, incorporer, indexer, influer, légaliser, liquider, mandater, manifester, manquer, méconnaître, mensualiser, mériter, mettre, percevoir, perdre, privétiser, radier, rapprocher, reconnaître, reporter, ressortir de, restructurer, revenir, seconder, situer, stipuler, titulariser, viabiliser.

131 Including the verb's nominalised form where appropriate, but not any adjectival forms.

accompagner:			
une remarque de...	0	0	'mesures d'accompagnement' 'modes / moyens / mesures d'accompagnement'
accorder:			
une autorisation	4	4	'l'autorisation / l'aide est accordée' 'la priorité / protection accordée' '... aux travailleurs / personnes / familles'
accuser:			
réception	2	2	'personnes accusées d'avoir (participé au coup d'Etat)' 'mettre en accusation' 'chambre d'accusation'
acquiescer:			
à une demande	0	0	no instances of verb
admettre:			
une façon de voir	0	0	'candidats admis' 'admettre que'
adopter:			
une resolution	26	10	adopter une décision / une approche / un texte / une monnaie unique / un projet de loi / un règlement 'adopter à l'unanimité' 'Discussion et adoption le [date]' 'le Conseil des Ministres / la Commission européenne a adopté les mesures individuelles suivantes'
agir / rétroagir:			
agir rapidement	0	1	one instance of 'rétroagir'
cette disposition	0	0	('faire rétroagir l'application du présent ne rétroagit pas règlement') reflexive verb most common: 's'agissant de' / 'qu'il s'agisse de' / 'il s'agit de' 'Légiférer moins pour agir mieux' '[le comité] agissant conformément à la procédure...'
ajourner:			
une réunion	0	0	'ajourner ou suspendre leurs
l'application de...	0	0	mesures'
allouer:			
une indemnité	0	2	'les fonds / les moyens / les crédits alloués'

aménager:			
un impôt	0	0	'aménagement (et de développement) du territoire (et du l'environnement) / du temps de travail / des rythmes de vie'
amender:			
un projet de texte	2	5	accepter un sous-amendement adopter un amendement du rapporteur 'texte de l'amendement' repousser un amendement
amortir:			
une dépense	0	0	'les coûts de location, de leasing ou d'amortissement' amortir un investissement
annexer:			
un procès-verbal	0	0	'protocoles / dispositions annexés au traité / à la présente loi'
annuler:			
une disposition	1	0	'division d'annulation' 'annulation de la décision de la Commission'
apparaître:			
cette mesure app. inefficace	0	0	faire apparaître, 'il apparaît nécessaire / important / indispensable', '... apparaît comme une nécessité'
appartenir de:			
il a. au Ministre de[132]	1	1	'il appartient au Conseil / au gouvernement / au Parlement' 'sentiment d'appartenance nationale / collective', 'il nous appartient de'
appliquer:			
une règle	16	3	'la bonne application [du loi etc.]'
une sanction	5	2	'[mesure] adoptée en application de [article / droit]' 'champ d'application d'une directive', 'modalités d'a.' 'en a. du présent traité / article' 'en a. de l'article [no.]'

132 Where the indirect object is an individual, but not necessarily 'Ministre'.

apporter:			
du soin à	1	0	apporter des solutions / réponses /
une conclusion	0	0	une contribution / un soutien / les précisions suivantes 'modifications apportées à la loi' 'prêt[e] à apporter une contribution'
apprécier:			
le bien-fondé de...	1	0	porter / apporter une appréciation exprimer son appréciation '[information] pour permettre d'a. le caractère, etc]'
approuver:			
une proposition	8	1	'la Commission / le Conseil a
une disposition	2	0	approuvé [au nom de l'UE] [un
les termes d'une lettre	0	0	projet]' 'la Commission approuve l'acquisition [of one company by another]' 'points approuvés sans débat'
appuyer:			
une requête	0	0	s'appuyer sur 'l'appui au développement / aux réformes'
arguer:			
d'un précédent	0	0	only 3 instances of verb 'arguer' - no patterns
arrêter:			
un compte	0	2	'a arrêté le présent règlement / la
une disposition	28	3	présente décision'
le Préfet a. que...	0	3	'le Conseil, statuant conformément à la procédure visée à l'article [no.] arrête des mesures / des directives' 'la Cour déclare et arrête: [...]'
assigner:			
un but	0	0	'objectifs [qui lui ont été] assignés', 'assigner pour but / objectif'
assujettir:			
à l'impôt	0	4	'assujettis à la taxe / à la TVA' 'le [non-]assujettissement des associations aux impôts commerciaux'
assurer:			
une publicité	1	0	'l'assurance maladie'
la diffusion de...	2	7	assurer la continuité du service / la sécurité / le bon fonctionnement /

			le respect des mesures / l'application du présent article / la cohérence / la coopération
attacher:			
de l'importance à...	22	3	'attacher une grande importance'
du prix à...	0	2	'la Commission s'attache à préparer... / continuer... / à approfondir...'
autoriser:			
l'envoi	0	0	'projet de loi autorisant
l'émission de...	0	1	l'approbation de l'accord'
être autorisé à...	44	33	'la Commission autorise la création / l'acquisition / la fusion' 'autorisation de mise sur le marché' 'loi autorisant la ratification...'
aviser:			
en temps utile	0	0	only 8 instances of vb – no patterns
avoir:			
pour effet de...	32	18	See discussion in Chapter 6 for
une répercussion sur.	14	5	typical uses of 'avoir'
une suite	0	1	
centraliser:			
une gestion	1	2	'procédure / système /
des documents	0	0	informatique centralisé[e]'
certifier:			
conforme	7	2	'animaux de troupeau certifiés indemnes'
charger:			
d'une question	7	1	lots of instances of past participle used adjectivally, e.g. 'membre de la Commission / Ministre chargé [du budget]' 'la Commission est chargée de l'instruction...', etc., 'le Conseil a chargé le Comité de représentants permanents d'examiner / de poursuivre...'
collaborer:			
à la mise en œuvre de..	0	0	'collaboration étroite entre...' collaborer étroitement / pleinement
communiquer:			
une lettre pour information	0	0	'communication' and 'communiqué (de presse)' both frequent as nouns 'ces mesures sont communiquées par la Commission au Conseil',

			'les états membres communiquent à la Commission le texte de...'
comporter:			
une suite	0	1	'l'accord comportera trois volets'
une réponse	0	0	'comporter des mesures / risques'
des observations	0	0	
compromettre:			
une intervention	0	0	'compromettre le (bon)
un résultat	1	0	fonctionnement de... / la sécurité'
concerner:			
un service	15	24	'la Directive [no.] du Conseil de [date] concernant ...' adopter une décision concernant 'en ce qui concerne' 'les ministres / l'état membre / pays / services etc. concernés'
concilier:			
des manières de voir	0	0	'comité de conciliation', 'faciliter la conciliation vie familiale/vie professionnelle', 'mieux concilier vie familiale/vie professionnelle'
concourir:			
à un résultat	0	0	concourir au développment / à l'amélioration
conditionner:			
la bonne marche de...	0	0	conditionner une politique
conférer:			
des droits	25	1	'droits conférés par le brevet'
une dignité	0	1	conférer protection / attributions / compétences
confirmer:			
les termes de...	0	0	volonté / décision / position / accord
consentir:			
à une mesure bienveillante	0	0	'efforts consentis par les états membres / la France etc.', 'avec / sans le consentement de...'
considérer:			
réconsidérer la question	0	0	'considérant que...' used as a recital to a legal document is frequent. 'la Commission considère que...', '... est considéré(e) comme un facteur / un objectif... etc.'
consolider:			
un argument	0	0	'consolidation budgétaire/financière'

			consolider la démocratie / stabilité / version du traité
constater:			
un fait	2	31	'force est de constater que' 'le Conseil constate avec satisfaction que...'
contester:			
une affirmation	0	0	'[Etat Membre] ne conteste pas que le directive n'a pas été transposé dans le délai imparti'
un droit	1	0	
contraindre:			
à prendre une sanction	0	0	noun 'contraintes' is frequent adj. 'contraignant' also frequent, 'juridiquement contraignant' verb is rare and displays no clear patterns
contribuer:			
à la bonne marche du service	0	0	'contribuer au développement / au maintien / à améliorer / à assurer / à l'amélioration / à la réalisation' 'la contribution communautaire / de l'UE / financière' 'apporter une contribution'
contrôler:			
les prix	7	1	'appellation d'origine contrôlée'
les instruments de mesure	0	0	'institutions de contrôle nationales', 'mécanismes / services / processus / système de contrôle'
convenir:			
avec	9	33	'convention' frequent as a noun as part of a recital: 'considérant qu'il convient de...' 'il convient d'accélérer / assurer / effectuer / examiner / constater / notes / préciser / rappeler /souligner'
convoquer:			
à une réunion[133]	0	1	convocation d'une conférence / d'un comité, 'le président / la présidence convoque...'
créditer:			
un compte	0	0	only two instances of verb 'créditer' - no patterns
un chapitre	0	0	

133 Also five instances of 'convoquer une réunion'.

créer:			
un organisme	2	3	'la création d'emplois / d'entreprises / de l'euro'
un service	4	15	'créer les conditions nécessaires' '[article / règlement de [date]] portant création de...'
débiter:			
un compte	1	0	noun: 'à haut débit' only two instances of verb
décider:			
de	343	148	'la Commission [européenne] a décidé de [saisir la Cour de Justice / envoyer un avis motivé]'
que	43	11	'le Conseil, statuant à la majorité qualifiée peut décider de...'
décréter:			
le Ministre d. que...	0	0	noun 'décret' particularly common in FRNACO only two instances of verb in FREUCO 'le Conseil d'Etat [...] Décrète: Art 1.' etc., in FRNACO
défendre:			
de	0	0	'défendre une position commune'
que	0	0	'défendre les intérêts de...'
déférer:			
en Conseil d'État	0	0	'questions déférées' déférer une loi / une affaire
définir:			
le caractère	0	0	'définir les grandes lignes / lignes directrices'
les grandes lignes	1	4	'définition de la politique + adj.'
déléguer:			
des pouvoirs	0	3	many instances of nouns 'délégations' and 'délégué' 'juge / maire délégué'
délivrer:			
une ampliation	0	0	certificats / brevet / diplômes / visas 'autorisation délivrée'
démettre:			
d'une fonction	0	0	no instances of verb
se démettre	0	0	noun: 'en cas de décès / de vacance ou de démission d'office', 'démission collective', 'démission volontaire'

démissionner:			
d'un poste	0	0	'démission d'office'
dénoncer:			
une convention	1	3	'dénoncer la présente Convention' 'dénonciation d'un accord bilatéral'
départager:			
des intérêts	0	0	no instances of verb
des points de vue différents	0	0	
dépendre de:			
l'autorité de	0	0	'zones dépendant de la pêche'
l'appréciation de	0	0	
déposer:			
une demande	3	2	'par requête déposée au greffe de la Cour [de Justice] le [date]...' 'les instruments de ratification seront déposés auprès du...'(both corpora) 'déposer une demande / une proposition de loi'
désavouer:			
une mesure	0	0	only 4 instances of verb avoir le pouvoir de désavouer...
désigner:			
les bénéficiaires de	0	0	'les gouvernements des Etats membres désignent d'un commun accord la personnalité qu'ils envisagent de nommer [président]'
dessaisir:			
d'une question	0	0	all examples in FRNACO
se d. d'un dossier	0	0	'se dessaisir au profit de...'
détacher:			
auprès de	0	1	'pièces détachées pour automobiles', 'travailleurs détachés'
déterminer:			
les cas d'application de	0	0	'un décret en Conseil d'Etat détermine les conditions d'application/les modalités' (FRNACO) "pour une durée déterminé' 'les conditions déterminées par la loi'
devoir:			
rendre compte	1	1	devoir permettre de préciser / favoriser
exécuter	0	1	'les pays candidats doivent....'

			'la Commission doit / devra ...' 'cette décision doit être prise' 'nous devons trouver des solutions / défendre ... / encourager / respecter etc'
différer:			
la mise en application de	0	0	'La Commission diffère une application'
diriger:			
un service	0	0	'l'habilitation à diriger des recherches' '[organisation or group] dirigé par [name]'
une enquête	0	0	
disjoindre:			
une demande	0	0	2 instances of verb in FRNACO
dispenser:			
de	11	22	'dispenser une formation' dispensation d'un médicament
disposer que:			
le texte d. que...	5	8	'les dispositions du présent article / traité / règlement' dispositions communautaires
dissoudre:			
un organisme	0	0	especially in FRNACO 'le Conseil des Ministres a prononcé la dissolution [du Conseil]'
donner:			
une directive	0	1	donner la priorité
son accord	10	10	donner les moyens
son agrément	0	0	donner la possibilité
son avis	8	22	donner son accord
son consentement	0	1	donner feu vert à
lieu à	43	87	
naissance à	5	6	
motif à	1	0	
prétexte à	1	0	
effet	5	1	
édicter:			
une disposition	0	0	édicter un règle / un règlement
émaner de:			
l'ordre é. du Ministre	0	0	'une demande / des demandes émanent de [un individu]'
émettre:			
un avis	45	11	'le comité émet son avis sur ce projet', 'l'avis est émis à la

			majorité prévue à l'article [no.]' (FREUCO - ojlfr)
			'limitation des émissions [de polluants]', 'réduction des émissions de CO2'
			'émissions de gaz à effet de serre'
			'la Commission émet un avis positif / motivé / détaillé'
emporter:			
l'agrément de...	0	0	l'emporter
décision	0	0	
en appeler à:			
l'autorité	0	0	7 occurrences - no repetition
la compétence de	0	0	
encourir:			
des difficultés	0	0	'les risques encourus'
une sanction	0	0	'les peines encourues'
enfreindre:			
une prescription	0	0	enfreindre un article d'un traité / une interdiction
engager:			
des crédits	6	1	'prendre des engagements'
sa responsabilité	1	3	'les Parties s'engagent'
			'concertation engagée'
entamer:			
des pourparlers	0	0	'entamer des négotiations / un processus'
entendre :			
il est entendu que	4	2	'on entend par «[...]»
j'entends que	0	2	[+ explanation]', (FRNACO) 'le gouvernement entend poursuivre / mener / conduire'
entrer:			
en contact	3	0	'[le présent règlement / traité /
en relation avec	0	2	décision etc.] entre en vigueur'
			'date d'entrée en vigueur de...'
entretenir:			
d'une question	0	0	'la construction, [aménagement] et l'entretien [et gestion] de...'
			'je me suis entretenu avec le Premier Ministre / le Président'
			'entretien avec le PM / le Président'

envisager:			
une solution[134]	1	3	'l'action / les actions envisagées' 'les mesures envisagées' 'envisager + vb: prendre / nommer / proposer / présenter'
établir:			
une distinction	8	3	'établir des mesures de protection', l'établissement d'un espace de liberté / d'un plan / d'un programme / de contacts / de relations', 'établissement public de cooperation intercommunale'
une attestation	0	1	
être:			
d'accord sur...	2	2	See discussion in Chapter 6 for typical uses of 'être'
pour...	18	5	
conforme à	52	16	
de nature à	33	30	
donné de	0	2	
en état de[135]	1	2	
en mesure de	105	34	
en règle	0	3	
question de	7	14	
susceptible de	62	54	
étudier:			
un dossier	0	0	'la Commission étudie les moyens de... / étudiera diverses options...', 'étudier la possibilité de...', 'étudier attentivement'
évoquer:			
un cas d'espèce	0	0	'questions évoquées dans le rapport', 'évoquer [...] tout à l'heure / précédemment / plus haut', 'avoir l'occasion d'évoquer' predominantly in spoken genres and very informal written genres
exciper:			
d'un certificat	0	0	no examples of verb 'exciper'
d'une attestation	0	0	

---

134 'Solutions envisageables' is also a recurring pairing in FREUCO.

135 There are also instances of 'en état' with other verbs, especially maintenir, remettre.

exécuter:			
une prescription	0	0	mettre à exécution, 'chargés de l'exécution du présent arrêté', prendre en exécution, exécution d'un programme, du budget, 'la présente loi sera exécutée comme loi de l'Etat'
exercer:			
une fonction	35	69	exercer une mission / une fonction / une activité [professionnelle] /des responsabilités 'avocats exerçant sous leur titre professionnel d'origine'
exonérer:			
d'une redevance	0	0	fiscale / de l'impôt / de taxes / de la TVA
exposer:			
une affaire	0	0	exposer des motifs
exposer que...	0	4	exposer clairement
faire:			
connaître	30	36	See discussion in Chapter 6 for typical uses of 'faire'
savoir que	11	3	
part de	18	20	
droit	3	1	
en sorte	49	34	
état	15	21	
jouer une disposition	1	0	
office	3	0	
le nécessaire pour	2	2	
des réserves	0	0	
parvenir	0	6	
retour	0	1	
suivre	1	0	
valoir	24	27	
fixer:			
la composition de	1	13	'les conditions / critères / règles sont fixé[e]s par...' 'conformément à la procédure fixée à l'article [no.]' (FREUCO - ojlfr) 'un délai que le Président peut fixer en fonction de l'urgence de la question en cause' (ojlfr) 'dans de conditions fixées par décret en Conseil d'Etat'(FRNACO)

			'arrêté du [date] fixant [les dispositions]'
formuler:			
des observations	5	2	'formuler des propositions / recommandations'
habiliter:			
un contrôleur	0	0	[institution] est habilité[e] à
être habilité à	23	11	effectuer / exercer / diriger etc. 'loi portant habilitations du Gouvernement à prendre [des mesures]'
homologuer:			
un règlement	0	0	'arrêté portant homologation du
une norme	0	0	prix de vente', 'homologation des organes spéciaux pour l'alimentation du moteur au gaz'
ignorer:			
ne pas ignorer que	2	3	'[...] ne peut ignorer que...', 'je n'ignore pas que...'
impliquer:			
l'assentiment de	0	0	'avoir des implications dans le domaine de...', 'implications financières/ économiques/ militaires' 'être impliqué dans', 'ceci / cela implique...'
imputer:			
une dépense	3	0	typically occurs with financial information
incomber:			
il vous incombe de[136]	121	25	especially in the Bulletin of the Court of Justice '[état membre] a manqué aux obligations qui lui incombent en vertu de ladite directive'
infirmer:			
la portée d'un argument	0	0	only one instance of verb: 'les formations linguistiques ne suffisent pas à infirmer la diagnostic...'
informer:			
de	172	73	'information' very common as a
que	21	2	noun. tenir informé

136 All uses of the verb 'incomber', both personal and impersonal.

			'le Conseil informe le Parlement / la Commission' etc. 'le président / la présidence a informé...' être informé d'une mesure / une évolution / de discussions / d'opérations
insister:			
sur	49	75	insister sur le fait que / sur
pour que	10	5	l'importance de... / sur la nécessité
instituer:			
une procédure	5	3	'les institutions de contrôle
un contrôle	18	3	nationale' 'traités instituant les Communautés européennes' 'il est institué un comité...'
instruire:			
une réclamation	0	0	'juge d'instruction' noun is frequent, but verb occurs only 20 times in the whole corpus 'instruire un dossier'
interdire:			
l'usage de	0	0	'interdiction des armes biologiques / des exportations' 'article concernant l'interdiction de [nouveaux investissements]' 'il est interdit à [nom d'un pays] de...'
intervenir:			
en vue de	0	0	'champ d'intervention'
en faveur de	7	2	'intervention' frequent: 'intervention de [Mme Edith Cresson]' 'intervention de l'Etat / de la Gendarmerie'
introduire:			
une demande	7	1	especially in the Bulletin of the
un recours	19	2	Court of Justice 'la Commission (...) a introduit un recours visant à faire constater que…' 'l'introduction de l'euro'
justifier:			
une prétention	0	0	'justifier un intérêt / une
une mesure	8	2	importance'

une demande	3	1	'dans un cas dûment justifié' 'cela [ne] se justifie [pas]'
laisser:			
le soin de...	1	4	laisser [à] penser que / apparaître 'laissez-moi revenir / clore etc' (speech genres) predominantly in speeches and informal genres of both sub-corpora
légiférer:			
en matière de	0	0	All instances of 'légiférer' in FREUCO, especially 'légiférer moins pour agir mieux' and 'légiférer mieux' (titles of Commission reports)
libeller:			
correctement	0	0	'billets et pièces libellés en euros'
mander:			
de	0	0	no instances of verb 'mander'
ménager:			
une entrevue	0	0	ne pas ménager aucun effort pour [réduire / atteindre]
modifier:			
un projet	7	25	'la loi du [date] modifie ainsi...' 'vue la loi du [date] modifié [portant droits / dispositions etc.]' 'l'article [description and date] est ainsi modifié / modifé comme suit' 'en cas de modification...' 'proposition de modification' 'organismes génétiquement modifiés' porter modification
négliger:			
ne pas négliger de	0	0	'longtemps négligé[es]' 'sans négliger...'
nommer:			
à un poste	0	0	'membres nommés pour [period of time]' '[individu] est nommé [recteur / directeur / délégué / conseiller d'Etat / préfet de...]'
notifier:			
une décision	11	4	notifier une intention / un avis

observer:			
une prescription	0	0	[individu] fait observer que... 'unité d'observation'
omettre:			
sans omettre de...	0	0	only 18 instances of 'omettre' and 'omission': few clear patterns 'au cas où un Etat Membre omet de'
ordonnancer:			
une dépense	0	0	'article [...] de l'ordonnance no. [...] du [date]' 'l'exécution de la présente ordonnance'
ordonner:			
une enquête	0	0	'selon / vu l'ordonnance [no.] du [date]...' ordonner une politique / l'annulation d'un brevet
organiser:			
un service	7	33	porter organisation 'organisation' very frequent as noun future tense is common: 'un concours / des échanges / des événements sera [seront] organisé[es]' 'la criminalité organisée'
outrepasser:			
des droits	0	0	only one instance of outrepasser
des instructions	0	0	- 'outrepasser la valeur de référence de 3% du PIB'
pallier:			
une difficulté	0	0	usually in the infinitive: 'pallier les conséquences / l'insuffisance / les carences'
paraître:			
il p. souhaitable de..	1	7	'il [me] paraît nécessaire / souhaitable / utile / indispensable etc.', '...peut paraître paradoxal'
parer à:			
toute éventualité	1	0	'parer à un risque'
partager:			
une manière de voir	0	0	'le partage de responsabilités' 'un partage équitable / égal' 'valeurs / volonté / responsabilité partagée[s]' faire partager

			‘en cas de partage égal des voix..’
permuter:			
d’un service à l’autre	0	0	no instances of verb (including nominalised form)
placer:			
en disponibilité	0	0	placer sous la responsabilité / le contrôle / le régime / la tutelle / l’autorité de...
porter:			
atteinte	59	36	‘porter adaptation / adoption /
préjudice	12	1	atteinte / à la connaissance /
intérêt	3	1	création / réforme’
à la connaissance	3	13	‘loi no. [...] portant dispositions
création	9	15	statutaires relatives à’
fixation	0	0	‘portant modification de la loi’
institution	0	0	
organisation	20	11	
rattachement	0	0	
réforme	0	12	
effet	0	0	
préjuger:			
une affaire	0	0	verb is overwhelmingly in the
d’une suite	0	0	negative, ‘ne préjuge en rien’ ‘l’alinéa ne préjuge pas la compétence de Etats membres’
prémunir:			
se p. contre	0	0	no instances of the reflexive only three instances of verb
prendre:			
acte de	106	12	prendre une décision / décisions
l’attache de	0	0	prises par [le gouvernement]
contact	6	0	prendre (toutes) les mesures
effet	16	14	nécessaires / mesures à prendre
en considération	55	24	prendre note de
position sur/	3	0	prendre en compte
à l’égard de	0	0	prendre fin
un texte	0	0	prendre en considération prendre en charge prendre effet prendre acte de / ‘le Conseil a pris acte de’ prendre un engagement prendre une initiative
prescrire:			
une mesure	2	2	‘prescriptions de l’article [no.]’

			'dans le délai prescrit' 'prescriptions qui sont prescrites par la loi'
présenter:			
un intérêt	22	3	'la Commission a présenté une proposition', présenter une communication sur... / un projet de loi 'Monsieur l'avocat général [nom] présente ses conclusions' 'la Commission a présenté [une proposition / un rapport / ses avis'
prêter:			
appui	0	0	prêter assistance, se prêter
son concours	3	0	mutuellement assistance
à l'interprétation	0	0	prêter concours
prévenir:			
une difficulté	0	1	'la prévention et la résolution des conflits', 'actions de prévention' prévention de la criminalité / de la délinquance / des conflits / et de lutte contre le dopage 'prévenir les dysfonctionnements familiaux'
procéder:			
à une étude	3	1	noun 'procédure' is frequent:
à une enquête	3	1	'statuant conformément à la
d'une cause	0	0	procédure visée à l'article [no.]' procéder au vote / à l'examen de / à un débat / à un échange de vues
prohiber:			
l'usage de	0	0	uncommon, but predominantly in FRNACO - no patterns
promouvoir:			
une réforme	2	0	intégration / coopération / coordination / participation / développement / progrès / 'visant à promouvoir'
promulguer:			
une loi	0	50	'la date de promulgation de la présente loi', 'le Président de la République promulgue la loi dont la teneur suit...'
proroger:			
un délai	6	1	'délai / période prorogé(e)'

la validité de	1	2	
proscrire:			
une méthode	0	0	only four instances of verb - no clear patterns
rallier:			
les manières de voir	0	0	'membres de l'Espace Économique Européen se rallient à cette déclaration'
rapporter:			
une mesure	8	1	'rapport final / intérimaire'
un arrêté	0	0	'rapport du Ministre / Conseil / de la Commission' 'rapport de M(adame) [nom] 'rapporteur pour / sur un projet de loi'
ratifier:			
un traité	30	24	'la ratification du Traité d'Amsterdam' 'les instruments de ratification seront déposés auprès du gouvernement' (FRNACO) 'projet de loi autorisant la ratification de l'accord'
rattacher:			
à un service	0	2	predominantly in FRNACO 'les conditions de vote qui s'y rattachent'
reconduire:			
un délai	0	0	'les étrangers reconduits'
reconsidérer:			
une question	0	0	predominantly in infinitive form - no other patterns
recourir:			
à un argument	0	0	noun 'recours' is common: 'la Commission a introduit un recours visant à faire constater que' 'être autorisé à recourir aux institutions, procédures et méchanismes prévus'
recouvrer:			
un impôt	4	1	'le [non-] recouvrement des impôts', 'recouvrement des aides'

recueillir:			
l'agrément	0	0	'pour être adoptées, les décisions doivent recueillir au moins soixante-deux voix' recueillir des données / des indicateurs / des informations '[selon] les informations recueillies'
rédiger:			
un procès-verbal	0	0	overwhelmingly in FRNACO
un rapport	1	6	legal texts 'un article [no]. ainsi rédigé' 'un alinéa / deux alinéas / une phrase ainsi rédigé[s]' in FREUCO: 'rédigé dans la même langue', 'le présent traité, rédigé en un exemplaire unique..'
régler:			
une question	14	8	'régler des problèmes / questions' 'en règle générale' - common
régulariser:			
une situation	0	1	'régularisation des étrangers' 'étrangers (non) régularisés'
rejeter:			
une interprétation	0	0	'projet de loi, rejeté par le Sénat' rejeter une demande / une proposition, rejet de la demande / d'une proposition
relever de:			
la compétence de	22	6	'il convient de relever que...' 'les domaines relevant de la compétence de...', 'une question / une mesure relevant du présent traité / titre', 'relever les défis', 'une question relevant de la politique étrangère'
remanier:			
un projet de texte	0	0	only seven instances of the verb - no clear patterns
rencontrer:			
l'accord	0	0	rencontrer des difficultés / un [vif] succès / un problème
l'assentiment de	0	2	
une difficulté	15	32	

répondre:			
pour répondre à	54	48	'il a proposé à la Cour de répondre [de la manière suivante]' 'pour mieux répondre [aux attentes]' 'pour répondre à des changements de la situation / aux préoccupations / aux exigences'
requérir:			
l'attention	4	0	'les qualifications requises' 'les conditions requises' 'l'autorité requise' 'délibérations qui requièrent une majorité qualifiée'
réserver:			
une suite favorable	0	0	'sous réserve [des dispositions / des exigences / des adaptations' etc.] is frequent '[...] [ne] doit [pas] être réservé à...'
résigner:			
une fonction	0	0	only 8 instances of 'résigner' most common pattern 'nous ne nous résignons pas à [...]' (and paraphrases)
résister:			
à un examen	0	0	'résistance aux antibiotiques' 'résister à la tentation de...'
résoudre:			
une difficulté	4	3	'proposition de résolution'
se r. à	1	3	résoudre un problème / des conflits une résolution du Conseil
ressortir à:			
la compétence de	0	0	one instance of 'ressortir à' 'le chiffre ressort, qui ressort à 10,6%'
révoquer:			
un fonctionnaire	0	0	révoquer une décision pouvoir de révoquer / de révocation
saisir:			
d'une question	8	3	'la Commission a décidé de saisir
une autorité	3	0	la Cour de Justice'
un service	0	0	
une jurisdiction	0	0	
sanctionner:			
par une pénalité	0	0	appliquer une sanction

			'une levée des sanctions [en vigueur]' 'sanctions disciplinaires'
s'arroger:			
le droit de	0	0	no instances of verb
s'attacher à:			
obtenir	0	0	'la Commission s'attachera à...' non reflexive verb also: 'réaffirmer son attachement au maintien de la stabilité...' 'attacher une importance à'
savoir:			
faire s. que	5	1	'il ne saurait être question' 'comme vous le savez' (in speech genres) 'la question [est] de savoir [si]' le savoir-faire
se démettre:			
d'une fonction	0	0	no instances of reflexive verb see also 'démettre'
se départir:			
de ses droits	0	0	few instances of verb - no other
sans se d. de	1	3	patterns
se disposer à:			
à l'intervenir	0	0	reflexive verb is infrequent disposer des compétences nécessaires / statistiques / délai de [time period] also: mettre à la disposition 'conformément aux dispositions de'
se mettre:			
d'accord	17	2	se mettre en place / en cause / d'accord / à l'abri
s'en rapporter à:			
s'en rapporter au jugement de	0	0	three instances of 'se rapporter à' - no clear patterns
s'en remettre à:			
(une personne)	0	0	only one example of the verb in its reflexive form: 'je m'en remets à la Déclaration d'Avignon'
s'en tenir à:			
aux instructions	0	0	s'en tenir aux textes / un objectif
à l'assurance que	0	0	
se permettre de:			
signaler que	0	0	'je me permets [d'insister]'

se prémunir:			
contre	0	2	+ 'contre des ruptures de situation'
se prévaloir de:			
d'un argument	0	0	'se prévaloir des traités / des droits conférés'
se référer à:			
au texte[137]	7	4	no clear patterns with individual collocates - lexical set of text types: e.g. 'se référant à ses conclusions'
se reporter à:			
un précédent	0	0	'se reporter à [un texte]' is the clearest pattern.
se révéler:			
utile	1	0	se révéler essentiel / difficile /
conforme à	1	0	efficace etc.
signer/contresigner:			
un décret	0	3	'accord / convention [etc] signé à [placename]' only four instances of 'contresigner', all in FRNACO
solliciter:			
un entretien	0	0	no clear patterns - lots of one-off
une dérogation	0	0	instances solliciter la protection / l'experience / l'avis de...
soulever:			
une objection	2	2	'problèmes soulevés' 'ces questions ont été soulevées dans le cadre de [...]'
statuer:			
sur une difficulté	0	0	'vu l'avis du Comité [...] statuant conformément à la procédure prévue à l'article [no.]' 'la Conseil, statuant à l'unanimité / à la majorité qualifiée'
substituer:			
une disposition à une autre	0	0	especially in FRNACO Assemblé Nationale texts 'être substitué de plein droit' se substituer à

---

137 'le texte' is interpreted here as a generic term rather than a particular collocate, and therefore includes reference to such texts as 'articles', 'conclusions' and 'règlements'.

surseoir:			
à l'application de	0	0	'ordonner le sursis à exécution'
suspendre:			
un délai	1	2	'les délais prévus sont suspendus' 'les droits de vote sont suspendus' 'le Conseil peut décider de suspendre certains de droits'
tendre à:			
un résultat	0	0	'tendre à la création de / à la sauvegarde de' tendre à favoriser [l'emploi] / à renforcer...
tenir:			
au courant de	2	0	See discussion in Chapter 6 for typical uses of 'tenir'
compte de	605	289	
lieu de	4	7	
pour acquis	0	0	
assuré	0	0	
certain que	0	0	
pour responsable	3	0	
pour valable	0	0	
tirer:			
à conséquence	0	0	'tirer profit / parti de'
argument de	0	0	'tirer des conséquences / leçons de', 'tirer des conclusions de' 'tirer la meilleure parti de'
transmettre:			
pour avis	0	2	'la Commission transmet au Parlement européen et au Conseil...', 'délais de transmission des données' 'les variables doivent être transmises'
valider/invalider:			
l'acte dit loi no. ... du..	0	0	'la validité d'un acte' i. un arrêté préfectoral
viser:			
un document	2	0	'[des efforts] visant / qui visent
à un résultat	0	0	à améliorer [la coopération] / à assurer / développer / faciliter / promouvoir / prévenir / réduire' 'un recours visant à faire constater que [...]' '[le comité] visé à l'article [no.]' 'conformément la procédure visée à l'article [no.]'

Appendix 7: Verbs and verb phrases from R. Georgin (1973) in FRADCO

Verb	Environment in Georgin	Appearance of pair in FREUCO / FRNACO[138]		Typical environment / collocates of verb in FRADCO[139]
accuser	réception	2	2	see App. 6
admettre	une manière de voir	0	0	see App. 6
ajourner	une décision	0	0	see App. 6
	une mesure	5	0	
	une réunion	0	0	
appuyer	une demande	2	0	see App. 6
	une requête	0	0	
comporter	une suite	0	1	see App. 6
	une réponse	0	0	
conférer	des droits	25	1	see App. 6
confirmer	les termes d'une lettre	0	0	see App. 6
	une lettre	0	0	
consolider	une dette	0	0	see App. 6
contracter	un engagement	7	4	'engagements
	un emprunt	0	0	'obligations contractées'
définir	les grandes lignes ...d'un projet	1	4	see App. 6
délivrer	un duplicata	0	0	see App. 6
	une ampliation	0	0	
	une attestation	1	3	

138 Within a range of five words each side of the node verb.

139 Including nominalised forms where appropriate, but not adjectival forms.

dénoncer	une convention	1	3	see App. 6
	un accord	4	1	
	un traité	0	0	
différer	une mesure	0	0	see App. 6
	la mise en application	0	0	
disposer	ce texte dispose que (+ paraphrases)	5	8	see App. 6
donner	(son) avis	8	22	see App. 6
	son accord	10	10	
	son agrément	0	0	
	lieu	43	87	
	prétexte	1	0	
emporter	toute condamnation emporte interdiction de...	0	0	see App. 6
en appeler	à la compétence	0	0	see App. 6
	à l'autorité de	0	0	
encourir	une sanction	1	0	see App. 6
	un blâme	0	0	
engager	des crédits	6	1	see App. 6
	sa responsabilité	1	3	
envisager	une solution[140]	1	3	see App. 6
	une mesure	30[141]	3	
être	en état[142]	1	2	See Chapter 6 for typical uses of 'être'
	en mesure	105	34	
	en règle	0	3	
faire	droit	3	1	See Chapter 6

140 'Solutions envisageables' is also a recurring pairing in FREUCO.

141 This pairing tends to occur in the *Journal Officiel* genre of FREUCO, especially in such environments as 'La Commission arrête les mesures envisagées lorsqu'elles sont conformes à l'avis du comité.'

142 There are also instances of 'en état' with other verbs (esp. maintenir, remettre).

	état de	15	21	for typical uses of 'faire'
	office de	3	0	
	des réserves	0	0	
	retour	0	1	
	faire savoir	11	3	
	faire parvenir	0	6	
	faire valoir	24	27	
financer	un programme	9	4	'financement du budget / du service public / sécurité sociale
formuler	un avis	11	4	see App. 6
	des réserves	3	1	
impartir	un délai	15	8	'dans le délai imparti' 'temps imparti' 'mission qui leur a été impartie'
imputer	une dépense	3	0	see App. 6
incomber	il vous incombe de[143]	121	25	see App. 6
incorporer	une prime dans un salaire	0	0	31 instances of verb - no clear patterns or repetition
instituer	un contrôle	18	3	see App. 6
	une procédure	5	3	
introduire	un recours	19	2	see App. 6
investir	des capitaux	31	2	'entreprises d'investissement' 'banque européenne d'i.' 'projets / programmes d'i.' 'sociétés d'i.'

143 All uses of the verb 'incomber', both personal and impersonal.

mandater	un représentant	1	2	'mandater des salariés' 'agents mandatés'
notifier	une décision	11	4	see App. 6
ordonnancer	une dépense	0	0	see App. 6
outrepasser	des instructions	0	0	see App. 6
	ses droits	0	0	
pallier	un inconvénient	0	0	see App. 6
parer	à une éventualité	1	0	see App. 6
porter	à la connaissance	3	13	see App. 6
	préjudice	12	1	
	effet	0	0	
	création	9	15	
	fixation	0	0	
promouvoir	une réforme	2	0	see App. 6
	un fonctionnaire	0	1	
proroger	la validité d'une carte	1	2	see App. 6
rapporter	une mesure	8	1	see App. 6
	dans un autre sens	0	0	
	un projet de loi	0	9	
reconduire	une loi	0	0	see App. 6
	un budget	0	0	
régler	une question	14	8	see App. 6
régulariser	une situation	0	1	see App. 6
remanier	un projet	0	0	see App. 6
	un texte	0	0	
requérir	l'attention	4	0	see App. 6
résigner	une fonction	0	0	see App. 6

ressortir de	une enquête d'un examen	0 0	0 0	'il ressort [du dossier / présent Livre Blanc etc] que...' 'ressortissant d'un état' - frequent 'en dernier ressort'
ressortir à	une autorité la compétence de	0 0	0 0	see App. 6
saisir	une autorité (d'une ...question)	3	0	see App. 6
s'en rapporter	au jugement de	0	0	see App. 6
s'en remettre	à quelqu'un	0	0	see App. 6
se prémunir	contre un danger	0	1	see App. 6
se prévaloir	d'un argument d'un précédent	0 0	0 0	see App. 6
se référer	à (un texte)[144] à une décision antérieure	7 0	4 0	see App. 6
se reporter	à un précédent à un texte[145]	0 2	0 5	see App. 6
soulever	une question une objection	25 2	12 2	see App. 6
statuer	sur un cas	5	0	see App. 6
stipuler	le règlement stipule que[146]	12	6	'le [texte] stipule que [...]'
tenir	au courant pour responsable	2 3	0 0	See Chapter 6 for typical uses of

144 'Un texte' is interpreted here as a generic term rather than a particular collocate, and includes such texts as 'articles', 'conclusions', 'règlements'.

145 See footnote 7.

146 'Le règlement, traité, texte, directive, etc. stipule que'.

	pour certain	0	0	'tenir'
	compte de	605	289	
	lieu de	4	7	
tirer	argument de	0	0	see App. 6
	à conséquence	0	0	
valider	un acte	8	0	see App. 6
venir	en déduction	0	1	See Chapter 6 for typical uses of 'venir'
viser	un document	2	0	see App. 6
	à un résultat	0	0	

Index